The Paranormal

Edited by Kenneth Partridge

The Reference Shelf
Volume 81 • Number 5
The H.W. Wilson Company
New York • Dublin
2009

The Reference Shelf

The books in this series contain reprints of articles, excerpts from books, addresses on current issues, and studies of social trends in the United States and other countries. There are six separately bound numbers in each volume, all of which are usually published in the same calendar year. Numbers one through five are each devoted to a single subject, providing background information and discussion from various points of view and concluding with a subject index and comprehensive bibliography that lists books, pamphlets, and abstracts of additional articles on the subject. The final number of each volume is a collection of recent speeches, and it contains a cumulative speaker index. Books in the series may be purchased individually or on subscription.

Library of Congress has cataloged this serial title as follows:

The paranormal / edited by Kenneth Partridge.
    p. cm.—(The reference shelf ; v. 81, no. 5)
  Includes bibliographical references and index.
  ISBN 978-0-8242-1092-2 (alk. paper)
  1. Parapsychology. I. Partridge, Kenneth, 1980-
  BF1031.P325 2009
  130—dc22

                                2009035127

Cover: Courtesy of the Library of Congress.

Visit H.W. Wilson's Web site: www.hwwilson.com

Printed in the United States of America

The
Reference Shelf®

Contents

Preface

Late at night, high above the treetops, five reddish-orange lights dot the black sky. They form the outline of a triangle, or maybe a wedge, and as they pass overhead, traveling far more slowly than any known jet plane, they seem to glide through the air, making no sound. Minutes later, they're gone, leaving onlookers scratching their heads.

Elsewhere, a spooked homeowner sits upright in bed, gripping her blanket as strange creaking noises emanate from the hallway. Is it the house settling, as her friends and family members keep assuring her, or is it something else? What about that strange hiss she picked up on her tape recorder? Was that someone whispering "Help me," or was it only the wind?

Such episodes may seem the stuff of campfire tales or science-fiction movies, but to some people, they're quite real. The story of the mysterious lights echoes one told by numerous residents of Phoenix, Arizona—folks who, on the night of March 13, 1997, happened to look up and see what they could only describe as a UFO, or unidentified flying object. The woman who fears her house is haunted, on the other hand, is precisely the type of person who generally enlists the services of the Atlantic Paranormal Society (TAPS), a team of investigators featured on the popular reality television series *Ghost Hunters*.

According to a 2005 Gallup poll, three-quarters of Americans believe in paranormal phenomena—a term used to describe haunted houses, UFOs, mental telepathy, reincarnation, and a host of other things science has yet to explain. The data is curious, considering mankind now finds itself in an age of great scientific breakthroughs. Even as researchers explore the intricacies of atoms and launch shuttles into outer space, all the while gaining new knowledge of the natural world, the majority of the population would agree with the titular character of William Shakespeare's *Hamlet*, who famously told a skeptical friend, "There are more things in heaven and earth, Horatio, than are dreamt of in your philosophy."

This edition of The Reference Shelf series aims to explore Hamlet's claim. The first chapter, "Why We Believe: An Introduction to the Paranormal," considers what goes through the minds of those who visit psychics and scan the skies for flying saucers. While believers in the paranormal are often labeled as gullible kooks—irrational conspiracy theorists with tinfoil hats and too much time on their hands—they may actually be savvier than they seem. According to some scientists, there are certain evolutionary benefits that come with jumping to conclusions and putting stock in ideas that cannot be proved.

The second chapter, "'If You're Here, Please Give Us a Sign': Ghosts and Haunted Houses," considers whether the so-called "dearly departed" are not so departed, after all. Two of the included selections highlight ghost-hunting organizations—one in Cincinnati, Ohio, the other in Washington, D.C.—that use high-tech equipment to determine whether clients' homes are haunted. The third chapter, "Are We Alone? UFOs and Extraterrestrials," examines more than 60 years' worth of UFO evidence. Several of the pieces mention Roswell, New Mexico, the site of what is perhaps history's most famous UFO-related event. In July 1947, something—people can't seem to agree what, exactly—fell from the sky and crashed in the desert. For decades, U.S. Air Force officials claimed it was a weather balloon. Recently, the military changed its tune and said the wreckage was part of a secret Cold War spy project. That story has left many skeptical, and UFO enthusiasts maintain that the official Roswell explanation is part of an elaborate cover-up, the likes of which continue to be perpetrated by governments around the world.

"Parapsychology," the fourth chapter, touches on extra-sensory perception, reincarnation, fortune telling, and other such "psi," or psychic phenomena. While those who claim they can read minds or engage in "remote viewing" are often exposed as frauds, it's worth noting that various police departments and government intelligence agencies have long sought to utilize such mental abilities. The fifth chapter, "Cryptozoology," centers on the study of "cryptids": Bigfoot, Yeti, the Loch Ness Monster, and other critters whose existence has not been verified. The sixth and final chapter, "Ghosts Go Primetime: The Paranormal in Pop Culture," charts the rising popularity of ghost- and vampire-related books and TV programs.

Compiling the articles in this volume has given me cause to reflect on my own beliefs, and though I tend to prefer science to superstition, I consider myself fairly open-minded—more Hamlet than Horatio. In fact, reading through the UFO material made me think back to one morning in the late '80s. I was on my way to school, same as any other day, when something on the horizon caught my eye. It appeared to be some kind of silver disc, and though it moved pretty fast, I swore I saw flames shooting out of the back. Could this have been an alien spaceship, or had I simply spent too much time reading comic books and watching *In Search Of?* I'll probably never know.

In conclusion, I would like to thank the authors and publishers who allowed their material to be reprinted in this book, as well as Paul McCaffrey and Richard Stein, colleagues who helped get the volume to press. I would also like to extend my heartfelt gratitude to Geoff Bickford and Tim Hight, childhood friends who often joined me in investigating UFOs, ghosts, and "Goatman," a hammer-wielding creature we were certain lurked in the woods of our neighborhood.

Kenneth Partridge
October 2009

1

Why We Believe:
An Introduction to the Paranormal

Editor's Introduction

On the popular 1990s TV series *The X-Files*, the character of FBI agent Fox Mulder, portrayed by David Duchovny, had hanging above his desk a photograph of a UFO. Below the image was a slogan that, years after the show's run, remains part of the cultural lexicon: "I Want to Believe." Whether referring to UFOs or ghosts, ape-men or Loch Ness Monsters, those words speak to a fundamental part of people's tendency to believe in paranormal phenomena: desire. Simply put, people want—perhaps even need—to make sense of the world, explain the unexplainable. In the absence of concrete answers, that sometimes means putting faith in things that cannot be seen.

This quest for meaning is nothing new. Consider the earliest humans: hunter-gatherers with little or no knowledge of the laws governing the natural world. What must they have thought when thunder cracked or blizzards raged? Thousands of years before Doppler radar, our ancient ancestors may have reasoned that such extreme conditions were caused by sky-dwelling weather deities. Today, such views might be considered primitive and farfetched, even as followers of the world's major religions espouse supernatural beliefs that, at least on some level, share certain similarities.

According to several of the articles in this chapter, it makes sense for people to assign agency—the notion that actions and events are being driven by conscious, unseen beings—to natural phenomena. In "Glad to be Gullible," the first selection, Clare Wilson interviews Peter Brugger, a neuroscientist who invites readers to imagine being outside and hearing a rustling in the grass. While the sound could be the result of something harmless, like the wind, it could also signal the presence of a tiger. "If you miss the tiger hidden in the grass, then you are dead," he tells Wilson, explaining why, from an evolutionary standpoint, the smart play is to assume the worst and run like mad. "If you always see tigers, you are always running away but you're not dead."

In "Why We Believe," the second piece, Sharon Begley discusses how people's emotions can influence their perceptions and promote illogical beliefs. "The universal human need to find meaning and purpose in life is stronger and more basic than any attachment to empiricism, logic, or objective reality," Begley writes. It's for this reason, Fordham University professor Stewart Guthrie tells Begley, that people see faces in clouds and images of the Virgin Mary in potato chips. "Perceptually, the world is chronically ambiguous and requires an interpretation," Guthrie says.

The next entry in this chapter, Walt Williams's "Science vs. ESP: Skeptics Ponder UFOs, Mothman," takes a closer look at why people put stock in ideas that science can't prove. Williams concludes that humans are "hardwired to assume there is an agent controlling the forces around them." In "Personality and Motivations to Believe, Misbelieve, and Disbelieve in Paranormal Phenomena," the fourth article, J. E. Kennedy summarizes numerous studies that have been conducted on paranormal belief. He insists that believers and skeptics alike seek to assert their superiority over those in the opposing camp. Examining the concept of psi, or psychic phenomena, such as mind reading and extra-sensory perception (ESP), Kennedy touches on one of the major reasons skeptics refuse to believe: No one has yet figured out a way to harness such mental powers and, say, bankrupt a casino or make a killing in the stock market. Even so, Kennedy argues, believers aren't necessarily wrong. "The evidence for psi and its association with transcendent experiences may hint that there is a spiritual realm that tentatively encourages development in a transcendent, humble, non-self-serving, nonmaterialistic direction," he writes.

In the final selection, "Not All Beliefs Treated Equally," Kristen Campbell considers whether individuals with strong religious convictions are more or less likely to believe in Bigfoot, UFOs, and other such paranormal phenomena.

Glad to Be Gullible[*]

By Clare Wilson
New Scientist, January 28, 2006

It is five minutes past midnight and I am alone in my house. I am working late, and the only illumination is the blue-white glow from my laptop computer. I live in a quiet London suburb, and at this time of night distractions are confined to the occasional eerie screeches and hisses from marauding urban foxes.

I pick up the phone to call Michael Thalbourne, a psychologist at the University of Adelaide in Australia. I want to talk to him about his research on chance, coincidence and the paranormal. Although the interview time has not been pre-arranged, we have been in contact by email, so it is disconcerting to hear a long pause when I introduce myself. When Thalbourne eventually speaks he sounds taken aback. "I was right in the middle of typing out an email to you," he says.

Thalbourne's instinct is to suspect some paranormal explanation for our synchronicity. My gut reaction is to suggest a more mundane alternative. It looks as if he is what some psychologists would call a sheep, while I am a goat.

The animal terminology stems from a passage in the Bible about a shepherd sorting through his flock to separate the sheep—representing the nations that believe in God—from the goats, or those that do not. Thalbourne and his ilk, however, are interested in belief in the paranormal and supernatural. And such beliefs turn out to be surprisingly common. For example, a 1998 survey of 1000 adults in the UK showed that one-third believed in fortune telling, half believed in telepathy, and a whopping two-thirds agreed with the statement that some people have powers that science cannot explain.

Decades of scientific research into parapsychology have produced no convincing demonstration of the paranormal that can be reliably reproduced—the acid test of scientific inquiry. So why should scientists be so interested in whether or not people believe in it? Research into the differences between sheep and goats has over the years produced some intriguing findings about how the brain works.

Until recently, sheep might have been forgiven for being cheesed off by all this research—most of the findings were less than complimentary about them. Study after study suggested that sheep saw paranormal events where there were none, simply because they were worse at judging probabilities and randomness, and even at using logical reasoning. But newer research might restore some sheepish pride. It turns out that the kind of thinking involved in belief in the paranormal helps us carry out a range of important cognitive tasks, from spotting predators to recognising familiar faces. Sheep also tend to be more imaginative and more creative. Some psychologists even think that people who believe they have paranormal powers such as telepathy, dreams that foretell the future, or other forms of extrasensory perception (ESP) might actually be accessing information stored in their subconscious without realising it.

Imagine, for example, that you are walking along the street with your old friend Bob, when you start thinking about a mutual college chum, Joe. "I wonder what Joe Smith is getting up to these days," you say. "That's amazing!" says Bob. "I was just thinking of Joe myself." You believe it is simply a coincidence. Bob suspects some form of telepathy. But there is a third explanation: without being consciously aware of it, both you and Bob noticed something that reminded you of Joe. Maybe you passed someone who looked just a little bit like him, or maybe it was something in a shop window that reminded you of him.

It was Thalbourne who first suggested that people who regularly have subconscious information such as this surfacing in their conscious mind would often seem to require the paranormal to explain their experiences. He coined the term "transliminality" for this tendency for information to pass between our subconscious and our conscious mind. He has also designed a questionnaire to measure transliminality. It asks questions such as how good people are at using their imagination, whether they have a heightened awareness of sights and sound and whether they have ever felt they have received "special wisdom". Thalbourne and others have shown in several studies that transliminality corresponds to where people fall on a sheep-goat scale. In other words, the better you are at tuning in to your subconscious, the more likely you are to believe in the paranormal.

This correlation alone suggests Thalbourne may be onto something. And in 2002, a group at Goldsmiths College in London reported an intriguing practical demonstration of transliminality (*Perception*, vol 31, p 887). They asked people to take part in an apparent test of ESP with Zener cards, which display one of five symbols: a circle, a cross, a square, a star or three wavy lines. The subjects sat in front of a computer monitor displaying the back of a card. They pressed a key to choose which symbol they thought it was. Then they got to see the card's face.

SUBLIMINAL CLUES

What they did not know was that they were being given subliminal clues as to which symbol was about to appear. Before a card's back was shown, they saw a flash of its face lasting for just 14.3 milliseconds, too fast for most people to register. Some participants, however, were able to subconsciously pick up on the clue, and as a result they scored better than chance at predicting which symbol would appear. "To those participants it would appear that they had ESP abilities," says psychologist Chris French, who led the research. And people who were best at picking up the subliminal image also turned out to be the most transliminal as measured by Thalbourne's questionnaire. It was a neat demonstration of how access to subconscious information can give the appearance of psychic abilities.

The talents of people who believe in the paranormal don't end there. It seems that they are also better than non-believers at perceiving meaningful patterns in apparently random noise. The classic example of this trait, which is known as pareidolia, is when people claim to see images of the Virgin Mary, say, on the wall of a building or a tortilla. Pareidolia can be auditory as well as visual, as shown by the current craze for detecting electronic voice phenomena (EVP), supposed messages from the dead buried in the random noise of audio recordings.

Psychologists have traditionally viewed this quality as a shortcoming on the part of sheep. But Peter Brugger, a neuroscientist at the University Hospital Zurich in Switzerland, does not think it is a black-and-white issue. He explains that people commit what statisticians call a type 1 error when they perceive a pattern where none exists—when they are overly gullible, in other words. A type 2 error is when they fail to recognise a pattern that does exist—when they are too sceptical. Brugger points out that pattern recognition is an important aspect of human cognition, allowing us to recognise familiar faces or camouflaged predators. "From an evolutionary perspective, the price for protection against type 2 errors is a susceptibility to type 1 errors," Brugger says. He theorises that it may be safest to err on the side of gullibility. "If you miss the tiger hidden in the grass, then you are dead. If you always see tigers, you are always running away but you're not dead."

What determines our tendency to spot patterns and form associations? It turns out that a key factor is the relative dominance of the right and left hemispheres of the brain. There has been much dubious pop psychology written about the differences between "right-brain people" and "left-brain people". But most neuroscientists would accept that the left side of the brain is primarily responsible for language and logical analysis, while the right side is more involved in creativity and what might be called lateral thinking—making connections between disparate concepts.

Several recent studies using various techniques suggest that people who believe in the paranormal have greater right-brain dominance. In 2000 Brugger's group showed, for example, that believers have greater electrical activity in the right hemisphere than non-believers as measured by electroencephalogram (EEG) recordings (*Psychiatry Research: Neuroimaging*, vol 100, p 139). In a different approach, in 2001 they asked people to carry out word-association tasks using different sides of their brain by looking at the words with just one eye at a time. When using their right brains, the sheep among them were faster than the goats at finding connections between distantly related words such as "lion" and "stripe" (the connection is "tiger") (*Psychopathology*, vol 34, p 75). In some cases, says Brugger, "the disbelievers didn't even note that there was a relationship".

But when taken to extremes, there can be a less welcome side to right-brain thinking. Brugger and others have shown that there is also relatively more right-brain activity in people with schizophrenia, particularly in those whose symptoms involve delusional beliefs. Brugger says this aspect of his research has not gone down well with the paranormal community. "I'm a very disliked person," he admits.

Of course neither Brugger nor anyone else is saying that people who believe in the paranormal are schizophrenic. But while an enhanced ability to spot real patterns and form connections is desirable, it could be argued that believers in the paranormal have taken this tendency too far. Then again, that depends on whether you are a sheep or a goat.

As a goat myself, I tend to opt for down-to-earth explanations. Here, for example, is how I account for the fact that Thalbourne was emailing me just as I phoned for that interview. Earlier that day, while it was already night-time in Adelaide, I had sent him an email asking if we could arrange a time to talk. Later I decided to chance a phone call anyway, and not wanting to stay up working any longer than necessary, I called at midnight my time, or 8.30 AM in Adelaide, which I figured was probably the earliest he would arrive at his office. He had actually got to work shortly before, and started his day as many of us do by turning on his computer and was responding to the emails he received overnight—which happened to include one from me. QED.

Thalbourne, however, persists in viewing the event as one of life's intriguing little coincidences. But then he does happily admit to being a sheep. "My life is full of many small and occasionally large coincidences that suggest some unusual form of cause and effect," he says. "I believe that I can't disbelieve in it."

Why We Believe[*]

By Sharon Begley
Newsweek, November 3, 2008

It wasn't immediately obvious to Walter Semkiw that he was the reincarnation of John Adams. Adams was a lawyer and rabble-rouser who helped overthrow a government; Semkiw is a doctor who has never so much as challenged a parking ticket. The second president was balding and wore a powdered wig; Semkiw has a full head of hair. But in 1984, a psychic told the then medical resident and psychiatrist-in-training that he is the reincarnation of a major figure of the Revolution, possibly Adams. Once Semkiw got over his skepticism—as a student of the human mind, he was of course familiar with "how people get misled and believe something that might not be true," he recalls—he wasn't going to let superficial dissimilarities dissuade him so easily. As he researched Adams's life, Semkiw began finding many tantalizing details. For instance, Adams described his handwriting as "tight-fisted and concise"—"just like mine," Semkiw realized. He also saw an echo of himself in Adams's dedication to the cause of independence from England. "I can be very passionate," Semkiw says. The details accumulated and, after much deliberation, Semkiw went with his scientific side, dismissing the reincarnation idea.

But one day in 1995, when Semkiw was the medical director for Unocal 76, the oil company, he heard a voice in his head intoning, "Study the life of Adams!" Now he found details much more telling than those silly coincidences he had learned a dozen years earlier. He looked quite a bit like the second president, Semkiw realized. Adams's description of parishioners in church pews as resembling rows of cabbages was "something *I* would have said," Semkiw realized. "We are both very visual." And surely it was telling that Unocal's slogan was "the spirit of '76." It was all so persuasive, thought Semkiw, who is now a doctor at the Kaiser Permanente Medical Group in California, that as a man of science and reason whose work requires him to critically evaluate empirical evidence, he had to accept that he was Adams reincarnated.

Perhaps you don't believe that Semkiw is the reincarnation of John Adams. Or that playwright August Wilson is the reincarnation of Shakespeare, or George W. Bush the reincarnation of Daniel Morgan, a colonel in the American Revolution who was known for his "awkward speech" and "coarse manners," as Semkiw chronicles on his Web site johnadams.net. But if you don't believe in reincarnation, then the odds are that you have at least felt a ghostly presence behind you in an "empty" house. Or that you have heard loved ones speak to you after they passed away. Or that you have a lucky shirt. Or that you can tell when a certain person is about to text you, or when someone unseen is looking at you. For if you have never had a paranormal experience such as these, and believe in none of the things that science says do not exist except as tricks played on the gullible or—as neuroscientists are now beginning to see—by the normal workings of the mind carried to an extreme, well, then you are in a lonely minority. According to periodic surveys by Gallup and other pollsters, fully 90 percent of Americans say they have experienced such things or believe they exist.

If you take the word "normal" as characteristic of the norm or majority, then it is the superstitious and those who believe in ESP, ghosts and psychic phenomena who are normal. Most scientists and skeptics roll their eyes at such sleight of word, asserting that belief in anything for which there is no empirical evidence is a sign of mental pathology and not normalcy. But a growing number of researchers, in fields such as evolutionary psychology and neurobiology, are taking such beliefs seriously in one important sense: as a window into the workings of the human mind. The studies are an outgrowth of research on religious faith, a (nearly) human universal, and are turning out to be useful for explaining fringe beliefs, too. The emerging consensus is that belief in the supernatural seems to arise from the same mental processes that underlie everyday reasoning and perception. But while the belief in ghosts, past lives, the ability of the mind to move matter and the like originate in normal mental processes, those processes become hijacked and exaggerated, so that the result is, well, Walter Semkiw.

Raised as a Roman Catholic, Semkiw is driven by a what-if optimism. If only people could accept reincarnation, he believes, Iraq's Sunnis and Shiites might stop fighting (since they might be killing someone who was once one of them). He is dismissive of the idea that reincarnation has not been empirically proved. That was the status of everything science has since proved, be it the ability of atoms to vibrate in synchrony (the basis of the laser) or of mold to cure once-lethal infections (penicillin). Dedicated to the empirical method, Semkiw believes the world is on the brink of "a science of spirituality," he says. "I don't know how you can't believe in reincarnation. All it takes is an open mind."

On that, he is in agreement with researchers who study the processes of mind and brain that underlie belief. As scientists began studying belief in the paranormal, it quickly became clear that belief requires an open mind—one not bound by the evidence of the senses, but in which emotions such as hope and despair can trump that evidence. Consider the Tichborne affair. In 1854, Sir Roger Tichborne, age 25, was reported lost at sea off the coast of Brazil. His inconsolable mother refused to accept that her son was dead. Twelve years later a man from Wagga Wagga, in New South Wales, Australia, got in touch with her. He claimed to be Sir Roger, so Lady Tichborne immediately sent him money to sail to England. When the claimant arrived, he turned out to be grossly obese, E.J. Wagner recounts in her 2006 book "The Science of Sherlock Holmes." Sir Roger had been very thin. Sir Roger had had tattoos on his arm. The claimant had none. He did, however, have a birthmark on his torso; Sir Roger had not. Although Sir Roger's eyes had been blue, the claimant's were brown. Lady Tichborne nevertheless joyfully proclaimed the claimant her son and granted him £1,000 per annum. Lawsuits eventually established that the claimant was an impostor.

Letting hope run roughshod over the evidence of your eyes, as Lady Tichborne did, is surprisingly easy to do: the idea that the brain constructs reality from the bottom up, starting with perceptions, is woefully wrong, new research shows. The reason the grieving mother did not "see" the claimant as others did is that the brain's sensory regions, including vision, are at the mercy of higher-order systems, such as those that run attention and emotions. If attention is not engaged, images that land on the retina and zip back to the visual cortex never make it to the next stop in the brain, where they would be processed and identified and examined critically. If Lady Tichborne chose not to focus too much on the claimant's appearance, she effectively blinded herself. Also, there is a constant back-and-forth between cognitive and emotion regions of the brain, neuroimaging studies have shown. That can heighten perception, as when fear sharpens hearing. But it can also override the senses. No wonder the poor woman didn't notice those missing tattoos on the man from Wagga Wagga.

The pervasiveness of belief in the supernatural and paranormal may seem odd in an age of science. But ours is also an age of anxiety, a time of economic distress and social anomie, as denizens of a mobile society are repeatedly uprooted from family and friends. Historically, such times have been marked by a surge in belief in astrology, ESP and other paranormal phenomena, spurred in part by a desperate yearning to feel a sense of control in a world spinning out of control. A study reported a few weeks ago in the journal Science found that people asked to recall a time when they felt a loss of control saw more patterns in random noise, perceived more conspiracies in stories they read and imagined illusory correlations in financial markets than people who were not reminded that events are sometimes beyond their control. "In the absence of perceived control, people become susceptible to detecting patterns in an effort to regain some sense of organization," says psychology researcher Bruce Hood of the University of Bristol, whose upcoming book "Supersense: Why We Believe in the Unbelievable" explores the mental processes behind belief in the paranormal. "No wonder those stock market traders are clutching their rabbit's feet"—or that psychics and the paranormal seem to be rivaling reality stars for TV hegemony ("Medium," "Psychic Kids," "Lost" and the new "Fringe" and "Eleventh Hour"). Just as great religious awakenings have coincided with tumultuous eras, so belief in the paranormal also becomes much more prevalent during social and political turmoil. Such events "lead the mind to look for explanations," says Michael Shermer, president of the Skeptics Society and author of the 1997 book "Why People Believe Weird Things." "The mind often takes a turn toward the supernatural and paranormal," which offer the comfort that benign beings are watching over you (angels), or that you will always be connected to a larger reality beyond the woes of this world (ghosts).

As science replaces the supernatural with the natural, explaining everything from thunder and lightning to the formation of planets, many people seek another source of mystery and wonder in the world. People can get that from belief in several paranormal phenomena, but none more so than thinking they were abducted by aliens. When Susan Clancy was a graduate student in psychology at Harvard University, she was struck by how ordinary the "abductees" she was studying seemed. They were respectable, job-holding, functioning members of society, normal except for their belief that short beings with big eyes once scooped them up and took them to a spaceship. They are men like Will, a massage therapist, who was abducted repeatedly by aliens, he told Clancy, and became so close to one that their union produced twin boys whom, sadly, he never sees. Numerous studies have found that abductees are not suffering from any known mental illness. They are unusually prone to false memories, and tend to be creative, fantasy-prone and imaginative. But so are lots of people who have never met a little green man.

Some 40 percent of Americans believe it's possible that aliens have grabbed some of us, polls show, compared with 25 percent in the 1980s. What makes abductees stand out is something so common, it's a wonder there aren't more of them: an inability to think scientifically. Clancy asked abductees if they understand that sleep paralysis, in which waking up during a dream causes the dream to leak into consciousness even while you remain immobilized, can produce the weird visions and helplessness that abductees describe. Of course, they say, but that doesn't apply to them. And do they understand that the most likely explanation of bad dreams, impotence, nosebleeds, loneliness, bruises or just waking up to find their pajamas on the floor does not involve aliens? Yes, they told her, but abduction feels like the best explanation. Larry, for instance, woke from a dream, saw shadowy figures around his bed and felt a stabbing pain in his groin. He ran through the possibilities—a biotech firm's stealing his sperm, angels, repressed memory of childhood sexual abuse—and only then settled on alien abduction as the most plausible. The scientific principle that the simplest explanation is most likely to be right is, well, alien to abductees. But again, an inability to think scientifically is exceedingly common. We are more irrational than we are rational; emotions drive voting behavior more strongly than analysis of candidates' records and positions does. The universal human need to find meaning and purpose in life is stronger and more basic than any attachment to empiricism, logic or objective reality.

Something as common as loneliness can draw us to the paranormal. In a study published in February, scientists induced feelings of loneliness in people by telling them that a personality questionnaire they filled out revealed that, by middle age, they would have few friends and be socially isolated. After this ruse, participants were more likely to say they believed in ghosts, angels, the Devil, miracles, curses and God than were participants who were told their future held many friendships, found Nicholas Epley, of the University of Chicago, and colleagues.

That we are suckers for weird beliefs reflects the fact that the brain systems that allow and even encourage them "evolved for other things," says James Griffith, a psychiatrist and neurologist at George Washington University. A bundle of neurons in the superior parietal lobe, a region toward the top and rear of the brain, for instance, distinguishes where your body ends and the material world begins. Without it, you couldn't navigate through a door frame. But other areas of the brain, including the thinking regions in the frontal lobes, sometimes send "turn off!" signals to this structure, such as when we are falling asleep or when we feel physical communion with another person (that's a euphemism for sex). During intense prayer or meditation, brain-imaging studies show, the structure is also especially quiet. Unable to find the dividing line between self and world, the brain adapts by experiencing a sense of holism and connectedness. You feel a part of something larger than yourself. This ability to shut off the sense of where you end and the world begins, then, may promote other beliefs that bring a sense of connection, even if they involve alien kidnappers.

Other normal brain functions can be hijacked for spooky purposes, too. Neither the eyes nor the ears can take in every aspect of an object. The brain, therefore, fills in the blanks. Consider the optical illusion known as the Kanizsa triangle, in which three black Pac-Man shapes sit at what could be the corners of a triangle, their open mouths pointed inward. Almost everyone "sees" three white lines forming that triangle, but there are in fact no lines. What does the "seeing" is not the eyes but the brain, which habitually takes messy, incomplete input and turns it into a meaningful, complete picture. This drive to see even what is not objectively there is easily hijacked. "Perceptually, the world is chronically ambiguous and requires an interpretation," says Stewart Guthrie, professor emeritus of anthropology at Fordham University and author of "Faces in the Clouds." And suddenly you see Satan in the smoke from the World Trade Center. "We see the Virgin Mary in a potato chip or Jesus on an underpass wall because we're using our existing cognitive structures to make sense of an ambiguous or amorphous stimuli," says psychologist Mark Reinecke, professor of psychiatry and behavioral sciences at Northwestern University.

Scientists mean "see" literally. Brain imaging shows that the regions that become active when people imagine seeing or hearing something are identical to those that become active when they really do see or hear something in the outside world. This holds true for schizophrenics (their visual cortex becomes active when they hallucinate people, and their auditory cortex when they hear voices, in ways that are indistinguishable from when they perceive real people and voices) and for healthy people engaging in mental imagery (think of a pink elephant). It is not too far a step for mentally healthy people to see or hear what they are thinking intensely about. Christina Puchalski, director of the George Washington Institute for Spirituality and Health, felt her dead mother's presence "with me in a very deep and profound way, emanating from a certain direction," she says. "Maybe if you're thinking very strongly about that person, your mind is creating the sense that he is there."

A more common experience is to see patterns in coincidences, something that also represents a hijacking of normal and useful brain function. You think about the girl at the party last Saturday and—bam!—she calls you. You think about the girl who chatted you up in class—and never hear from her. Guess which experience you remember? Thanks to the psychological glitch called confirmatory bias, the mind better recalls events and experiences that validate what we believe than those that refute those beliefs.

But why? Why do we remember the times we thought of someone just before she texted us and forget all the times we had no such premonition? When the mind was evolving, failing to make an association (snakes with rattles are to be avoided) could get you killed, while making a false association (dancing will make it rain) mostly just wasted time, Michael Shermer points out. "We are left with a legacy of false positives," he says. "Hallucinations become ghosts or aliens; knocking noises in an empty house indicate spirits and poltergeists; shadows and lights in a tree become the Virgin Mary."

The brain also evolved to recoil from danger, and the most frequent sources of danger back in the Stone Age were not guns and cars but saber-toothed tigers and other living things. As a result, we are programmed to impute vitality to even inanimate threats, as Bristol's Hood has demonstrated. When he gives a speech about irrational beliefs, he holds up an old cardigan and asks who would be willing to wear it in exchange for about $40. Usually, every hand in the audience shoots up. But when Hood adds that the sweater was once worn by a notorious murderer, almost every hand disappears. "People view evil as something physical, even tangible, and able to infect the sweater" as easily as lice, Hood says. "The idea of spirits and souls appearing in this world becomes more plausible if we believe in general that the nonphysical can transfer over to the physical world. From there it's only a small step to believing that a thunk in an empty house is a footstep."

There is a clear survival advantage to imputing aliveness and asking questions later. That's why, during human evolution, our ancestors developed what is called a hypersensitive agency-detection device, says Benson Saler, professor emeritus of anthropology at Brandeis University. This is an acute sensitivity to the presence of living beings, something we default to when what we perceive could be alive or inanimate. "Whether it's a rock formation or a hungry bear, it's better to assume it's a hungry bear," says Saler. "If you suppose it's a rock formation, and it turns out to be a hungry bear, you're not in business much longer." Defaulting to the "it's alive!" assumption was "of such considerable value that evolution provided us with greater sensitivity to the presence of living agents than we needed," says Saler. "We respond to the slightest hint or indication of agency by assuming there are living things present. Developing ideas about ghosts and spirits is simply a derivative of this hypersensitivity to the possibility" that a living being is present, and too bad if it also produces the occasional (or even frequent) false positives.

The belief that minds are not bound to bodies, and therefore that ghosts and other spirits exist here in the physical world, reflects a deep dualism in the human psyche. No matter how many times neuroscientists assert that the mind has no existence independent of the brain, "we still think of our essence as mental, and of our mind as being independent of body," says Fordham's Guthrie. "Once you've signed on to that, existence after death is really quite natural." This dualism shows up in children as young as 2, says psychologist Paul Bloom of Yale University: kids readily believe that people can exchange bodies, for instance, and since ghosts lack material bodies but have minds and memories, belief in dualism makes them perfectly plausible. At the even more basic level of perception, the brain is wired for faces, says Northwestern's Reinecke. "Even in the first weeks of life, infants tend to perceive angles, contours and shapes that are consistent with faces," he says. There's Mary on the potato chip again.

All of which raises a question. If the brain is wired so as to make belief in the paranormal seemingly inevitable, why are there any skeptics? And not just "any," but more assertive, activist ones. Groups such as the Committee for Skeptical Inquiry, the Skeptics Society and the James Randi Educational Foundation all work to debunk claims of the paranormal. A growing number of scientists and others now proudly wear the badge of "skeptic," just as more scholars are coming out as atheists, like Richard Dawkins did in his 2006 book "The God Delusion" and as Christopher Hitchens did in his 2007 tome "God Is Not Great." The growing numbers and assertiveness of skeptics (and public atheists) reflects the fact that they "have long felt like we belong to a beleaguered minority," says Shermer, who was once a born-again Christian. Their more aggressive attitude provides a sense of mission and community that skeptics, no less than believers, crave. It takes effort to resist the allure of belief, with its promise of fellowship, community and comfort in the face of mortality and a pointless, uncaring universe. There must be compensating rewards.

One such compensation, it is fair to say, is a feeling of intellectual superiority. It is rewarding to look at the vast hordes of believers, conclude that they are idiots and delight in the fact that you aren't. Another is that skeptics believe, or at least hope, that they can achieve at least one thing that believers seek, but without abandoning their principles. Skeptics, no less than believers, think it would be wonderful if we could speak to dead loved ones, or if we ourselves never died. But skeptics instead "seek immortality through our . . . lasting achievements," Shermer explains. "We, too, hope that our wishes for eternity might be fulfilled." Too bad that as they fight the good fight for rationality, their most powerful opponent is nothing less than the human brain.

Science vs. ESP[*]

Skeptics Ponder UFOs, Mothman

By Walt Williams
The State Journal (Charleston, W.V.), April 17, 2009

Where did the guy in the monkey suit come from?

That was the question on many people's minds at the 2009 Science, Technology and Research Symposium at the Charleston [West, Virginia] Marriott Town Center after they participated in a devious experiment by economist and professional debunker of the paranormal Michael Shermer.

The setup was simple enough: Shermer played a video of six young people passing basketballs, three of them in white shirts and three in black shirts. He asked the crowd to count how many times the three in white shirts passed the basketball to each other.

Afterward, Shermer had the crowd call out answers. Then he played the video again, telling everyone just to relax and not worry about counting passes this time. And to the amazement of many, about halfway through a person in a monkey suit walked from out-of-frame into the middle of the scene, paused, gave a friendly wave and then promptly walked off screen.

It was the same video. The crowd had been so focused on counting passes that many of them missed the scene playing out before their eyes.

Shermer's trick illustrated how easily the senses could be fooled. And he said that is a large reason why belief in the paranormal, from alien abductions to spoon-bending psychics, is so common.

"We already know that people lie; that happens all the time. . . . The more interesting question is why do people fall for it," he said.

Shermer, a resident of California, is a best-selling author and the founding publisher of *Skeptic* magazine. He is the author of *Why People Believe Weird Things,*

Why Darwin Matters and *The Mind of the Market*, the latter a look at why irrational behavior drives so many economic decisions.

His focus at the StaR symposium was why people are gullible and believe in things such as UFOs, ghosts, ESP, alternative medicine and psychic powers even though no evidence exists proving they are real, he said.

At first glance, Shermer might have appeared to be preaching to the choir given that the StaR symposium brings together scientists and science students from across the state, but the skeptic said he has found scientists particularly susceptible to deception when testing paranormal claims. They are not trained in the art of the deception and are so meticulous in setting up controlled conditions for experiments that they have a hard time seeing how others can find flaws in those conditions and exploit them.

That's not saying that science hasn't found rational explanations to many paranormal claims. He noted research into sleep paralysis and the vivid dreams it produces has explained why many people report alien abductions. So-called "near-death experiences" have been linked to hallucinations caused by oxygen starvation of the brain.

Shermer said he once had an out-of-body experience successfully recreated under laboratory conditions. It had nothing to do with his consciousness actually leaving his body.

The skeptic isn't familiar with West Virginia's most famous paranormal resident, Mothman, but he is with Bigfoot. He noted that no trained biologist can name a new species without producing a body. So far no Bigfoot hunters have turned up a scrap of evidence the creature exists.

As for the reason people believe strange things, Shermer said it is rooted in humanity's evolutionary history and its psychological drive to connect invisible causes to the events around them. That movement in the grass may be the wind or it could be a predator.

In evolutionary terms, it makes more sense to assume it's a predator. In other words, it's better to be safe than sorry, and therefore people are hardwired to assume there is an agent controlling the forces around them.

Personality and Motivations to Believe, Misbelieve, and Disbelieve in Paranormal Phenomena*

By J. E. Kennedy
Journal of Parapsychology, Fall 2005

ABSTRACT

Paranormal beliefs and experiences are associated with certain personality factors, including absorption, fantasy proneness, and the Myers-Briggs intuition and feeling personality dimensions. Skepticism appears to be associated with materialistic, rational, pragmatic personality types. Attitude toward psi may also be influenced by motivations to have control and efficacy, to have a sense of meaning and purpose in life, to be connected with others, to have transcendent experiences, to have self-worth, to feel superior to others, and to be healed. The efforts to obtain reliable control of psi in experimental parapsychology have not been successful. Given the lack of control and lack of practical application of psi, it is not surprising that those who are by disposition materialistic and pragmatic find the evidence for psi to be unconvincing. When psi experiences have been examined without a bias for control, the primary effect has been found to be enhanced meaning in life and spirituality, similar to mystical experiences. Tensions among those with mystical, authoritarian, and scientific dispositions have been common in the history of paranormal and religious beliefs. Scientific research can do much to create better understanding among people with different dispositions. Understanding the motivations related to paranormal beliefs is a prerequisite for addressing questions about when and if psi actually occurs.

The striking diversity of beliefs about paranormal phenomena is a noteworthy and poorly understood characteristic of humanity. On the extremes, some people are almost violently opposed to the very concept of paranormal phenomena and others are equally adamant that such phenomena are real. Neither side has prevailed and there is no indication that either is getting the upper hand (Mathews, 2004; Musella, 2005). Even those who claim tempered scientific perspectives sometimes appear to be living in different worlds. For example, Schumaker (1990),

* Article from the *Journal of Parapsychology*, (Fall 2005). Copyright © The Rhine Research Center, 2741 Campus Walk Avenue, Building 500, Durham, NC 27705. Reprinted with permission. All rights reserved.

a skeptic, described belief in paranormal phenomena as one of the strongest human motivations and as resulting from the "terror" of facing reality without irrational illusions. On the other hand, Tart (1984), a proponent of psi, described the fear of psi as a powerful, pervasive, instinctive human motivation that prevents the acceptance and occurrence of psi.

As might be expected, the proposed explanations for paranormal beliefs tend to reflect the attitudes of the person proposing the explanation. In his extensive review, Irwin (1993) noted that "much of the skeptical research on the topic seems to have the implicit objective of demonstrating that believers in the paranormal are grossly deficient in intelligence, personality, education, and social standing" (p. 6). These skeptical efforts have also carefully ignored the obvious fact that the deep hostility of some extreme skeptics indicates an irrational prejudice that needs explanation.

At the same time, proponents have done little to offer alternative models or to explain the prevalence of misbeliefs about psi. Many people apparently misinterpret normal experiences as paranormal. Broughton (1991, p. 10) noted that surveys typically find that over half of the population report having had a psi experience, but closer examination of the cases suggests that only about 10% to 15% of the population have had experiences that appear to be possible psi. This estimate is consistent with early surveys (Rhine, 1934/1973, p. 17) and with later studies (Haight, 1979; Schmiedler, 1964). At least 70% to 80% of the people reporting psychic experiences appear to be misinterpreting the experiences.

The motivations for such extensive misinterpretations need to be explored. In fact, understanding the motivations related to attitude toward psi would seem to be a prerequisite for understanding whether, when, and how psi occurs.

The purpose of this article is to summarize and discuss some of the key personality factors and motivations that appear to be relevant for understanding why people believe, misbelieve, and disbelieve in the paranormal. Of course, innumerable personal, social, and cultural factors may have a role in attitude toward the paranormal. The present discussion is intended as a starting point focusing on selected prominent factors. These factors are diverse, and the possibility of conflicting motivations should be recognized.

BACKGROUND

TERMINOLOGY AND CONCEPTS

Certain distinctions in the terminology and concepts related to paranormal phenomena are useful for this discussion. According to the definitions in the *American Heritage Dictionary* (3rd Edition), "paranormal" is a broad term that means beyond scientific explanation. The term "psychic" is more narrow and refers to extraordinary mental powers such as ESP. This definition of psychic implies that a person is the causal factor for the phenomena, although it can include communication with the spirit of a deceased person. The term "supernatural" means outside the natural world or attributed to divine power. Supernatural typically implies paranormal phenomena caused by a nonphysical being or power that has motivations and intentions separate from those of living persons. Such beings are often considered as God or gods if the motivations are beneficial for people, or as the devil or demons if the motivations are detrimental or evil. The term "miracle" means an event with a supernatural origin. According to the glossary in the *Journal of Parapsychology*, the term "psi" refers to ESP and PK, which also implies that the phenomena are produced by the mind of a person. Also in that glossary, the term "parapsychology" primarily refers to the study of ESP and PR. Supernatural interpretations tend to be excluded from parapsychological writings and are often assumed to be misinterpretations of psi phenomena produced by living persons. The extent to which psychic and supernatural are different interpretations for the same basic phenomena is an interesting empirical question that remains to be investigated.

The most widely used measures for paranormal beliefs are sheep-goat scales based on psychic phenomena (Palmer, 1971; Thalbourne & Delin, 1993) and the much broader paranormal beliefs scales that also include things like the Loch Ness monster, that black cats bring bad luck, and heaven and hell (Tobacyk & Milford, 1983). The sheep-goat scales were developed by parapsychologists and the broader paranormal belief scales were generally developed by researchers who were more skeptical. The number, validity, and orthogonality of factors in paranormal beliefs have been persistent, unresolved topics of debate (Hartman, 1999; Lange, Irwin, & Houran, 2000; Lawrence, Roe, & Williams, 1997; Tobacyk & Thomas, 1997).

The most widely held beliefs about paranormal phenomena involve supernatural religious interpretations and are not included in these scales. In U.S. national surveys, 89% of respondents strongly or somewhat agreed that "there is a God who watches over you and answers your prayers" (Barna, 1991) and 82% agreed that "even today, miracles are performed by the power of God" (Gallup & Castelli, 1989). Measures that do not capture the most widely held beliefs may be of limited value in understanding the characteristics of paranormal beliefs.

PERSONALITY AND GENETICS

Behavioral genetic and related research indicates that personality has significant genetic components and is also influenced by experiences, particularly during childhood (Cary, 2003; Collins, Maccoby, Steinberg, Hetherington, & Bornstein, 2000; Heath, Cloninger, & Martin, 1994; Rutter, Pickles, Murray, & Eaves, 2001; Stallings, Hewitt, Cloninger, Heath, & Eaves, 1996; Tellegen et al., 1988). Attempts to isolate genetic from environmental effects are difficult because of methodological factors, such as the possibility that genes can influence which environments a person chooses to experience (Rutter et al., 2001). However, for purposes of the present article, the basic concept that personality depends on both genetic dispositions and environmental experiences is sufficient.

The discussions of personality types here are primarily intended to show that these factors appear to have a significant role in attitude toward the paranormal. These discussions are not intended to limit the recognition of the variability among people or the likelihood that an individual may have motivations associated with various personality factors. The research studies discussed here have often employed the Myers-Briggs personality model. A summary of that model is described in the Appendix for those who may not be familiar with it. Other personality models could probably be developed that would be more useful for research on paranormal beliefs.

CAPRICIOUS, EVASIVE PSI

Discussions of belief in psi must recognize the problematic properties of psi experiments that make scientific conclusions controversial. The inability to develop reliable practical applications of psi after a century of research indicates a fundamental lack of scientific progress (Kennedy, 2003a). The research efforts have not been able to overcome the capricious, evasive properties of psi that include unintended and undesired psi-missing and loss of effects. If the basic assumptions of experimental parapsychology were true, gambling industries such as casinos, lotteries, and commodity markets would not be expected to be viable. The fact that these industries remain in business and appear to make profits consistent with the laws of probability places significant restrictions on the scientific expectations about psi. Parapsychological writings generally have not addressed this central dilemma. Greater acceptance of and attention to the capricious, evasive nature of psi may be a prerequisite for scientific progress in parapsychology (Kennedy 2003a).

One of the most revealing properties of psi research is that meta-analyses consistently find that experimental results do not become more reliably significant with larger sample sizes as assumed by statistical theory (Kennedy, 2003b; 2004). This means that the methods of statistical power analysis for experimental design do not apply, which implies a fundamental lack of replicability.

This property also manifests as a negative correlation between sample size and effect size. Meta-analysis assumes that effect size is independent of sample size. In medical research, a negative correlation between effect size and sample size is interpreted as evidence for methodological bias (Egger, Smith, Schneider, & Minder, 1997).

The normal factors that can produce a negative correlation between effect size and sample size include publication bias, study selection bias, and the possibility that the smaller studies have lower methodological quality, selected subjects, or different experimenter influences. All of these factors reduce confidence in a meta-analysis. However, for psi experiments, the failure to obtain more reliable results with larger sample sizes could be a manifestation of goal-oriented psi experimenter effects or decline effects (Kennedy, 1995; 2003a). Even if these effects are properties of psi, parapsychologists cannot expect that other scientists will find the experimental results convincing if methods such as power analysis cannot be meaningfully applied. Further, for the past two decades, the debates about the reality of psi have focused on meta-analysis. The evidence that psi experiments typically do not have properties consistent with the assumptions for meta-analysis adds substantial doubts to the already controversial (Kennedy, 2004) claims about meta-analysis findings in parapsychology.

THE TRANSCENDENCE FACTOR

Paranormal and mystical beliefs are closely related. The personality factors most consistently associated with paranormal beliefs and experiences are the interrelated cluster of absorption, fantasy-proneness, and temporal lobe symptoms. All three of these personality constructs involve a high degree of imagination and fantasy. These factors generally correlate in the .5 to .6 range with each other and with mystical and paranormal experiences (summarized in Kennedy, Kanthamani, & Palmer, 1994).

Thalbourne (1998; Lange, Thalbourne, Houran, & Storm, 2000) found that mystical experience, belief in paranormal phenomena, absorption, and fantasy proneness actually constitute a single factor. He proposed that it reflects a tendency for unconscious processes to emerge into consciousness and called the factor transliminality. Hartmann's (1991) earlier concept of thin boundaries of the mind is the same idea and has been associated with paranormal experiences (Palmer & Braud, 2002; Richards, 1996) and with the transliminality scale (r= .66) (Houran, Thalbourne, & Hartmann, 2003).

Based on his work with the Myers-Briggs personality model, Keirsey (1998) stated that people having intuitive, feeling (NF) personality types are mystical in outlook and often explore occultism, parapsychology, and esoteric metaphysical systems. Those with NF dispositions aspire

> to transcend the material world (and thus gain insight into the essence of things), to transcend the senses (and thus gain knowledge of the soul), to transcend the ego (and thus feel united with all creation), [and] to transcend even time (and thus feel the force of past lives and prophecies) (p. 145).

Research studies have found that belief in paranormal phenomena is associated with the N and F personality factors (Gow, et. al., 2001; Lester, Thinschmidt, & Trautman, 1987; Murphy & Lester, 1976). In a study of a technique attempting to induce a sense of contact with someone who had died, 96% of the participants with NF personality types reported after-death contact experiences, whereas 100% of the participants with ST (sensing, thinking) personality types did not have these experiences (Arcangel, 1997). In a survey of parapsychological researchers, Smith (2003) found that the F factor was associated with experimenters who were rated as psi-conducive. Temporal lobe symptoms have been found to be associated with the N and P Myers-Briggs personality factors, and to a weaker extent with F (Makarec & Persinger, 1989). Thin boundaries have been found to be associated with NF personality dispositions (Barbuto & Plummer, 1998).

Taken together, these findings indicate that certain people have innate interests in and motivations for mystical and paranormal experiences. Behavioral genetic research indicates that absorption, the Myers-Briggs personality types, and interest in spirituality all have significant genetic components similar to other personality factors (Bouchard & Hur, 1998; Cary, 2003; Hammer, 2004; Tellegen et al., 1988).

COMMON SOURCE FOR PSI AND MYSTICISM

Psychical and mystical experiences have several characteristics in common that suggest that they derive from the same or very similar processes.

Personality. As discussed above, paranormal and mystical experiences are associated with the same personality characteristics and appear to be components of one personality factor.

Unconscious. Psychical and mystical experiences are both thought to arise from an unconscious or higher part of the mind and to be facilitated by efforts to still the conscious mind and to reduce superficial unconscious activity. Both types of experience are viewed as a link or doorway to a higher realm of interconnectedness. In fact, the primary difference is that psychical experiences provide information about the material world whereas mystical experiences provide information about the higher realm of interconnectedness itself. William James (1902/1982) noted that the knowledge revealed in mystical experiences may pertain to sensory events (e.g., precognition or clairvoyance) or to metaphysics.

Lack of control. Both psychical and mystical experiences are spontaneous and normally outside of direct conscious control. At best, one can create conditions that set the stage for the experiences. Claims for direct, sustained, consistent control of mystical experiences or psi are very controversial (Kennedy, 2003a; Kornfield, 2000). Such claims for sustained control appear to be illusions in virtually all cases.

After-effects. As discussed in a later section, the primary effects of both mystical and paranormal experiences are increased sense of meaning in life, interconnectedness, and spirituality. Mystical experiences and paranormal miracles have both had major roles in most spiritual traditions (Woodward, 2000).

Lack of evident evolutionary advantage. According to the prevailing scientific perspective, humans have emerged through biological evolution, which is driven by self-serving enhancement of reproductive and associated material success. However, mystical and psychical experiences both have characteristics that do not appear to be driven by the self-serving materialism associated with biological evolution. The pursuit of mystical transcendence in the form of monastery traditions inhibits reproductive success and has the goal of reducing the motivations for material self-interest and status. These conditions are in direct opposition to the assumed driving forces of biological evolution. Similarly, the inability to develop or demonstrate practical applications of psi prevents its use for material self-interest (Kennedy, 2003a; in press). The personality constructs of thin boundaries and transliminality are both reported to be associated with susceptibility to mental illness (Hartmann, 1991; Thalbourne & Delin, 1994), which further detracts from any evolutionary advantage.

On the other hand, speculations about the benefits of these personality types that may keep them in the gene pool include: (a) enhanced imagination and creativity (Hartmann, 1991; Thalbourne & Delin, 1994), (b) enhanced flexibility and adaptability (Hartmann, 1991), (c) reduced tendency to create stress and conflict (Hartmann, 1991), (d) enhanced tendency to develop a strong sense of meaning and purpose in life and to inspire a sense of purpose in others (Keirsey, 1998; McClenon, 1994; White, 1997b), (e) highly cooperative, compassionate, altruistic, and motivated by ideals (Keirsey, 1998), and (f) enhanced self-healing through placebo and hypnotic effects (McClenon, 2002). The evolutionary implications of mystical and paranormal experiences remain an open and fascinating topic of inquiry.

THE MOTIVATION FOR CONTROL

The need for control has been investigated in numerous studies and is a basic human motivation that influences many activities, including religion and science (Baumeister, 1991; Schumaker, 2001; Spilka, Hood, Hunsberger, & Gorsuch, 2003). Spilka and colleagues (2003, pp. 46–47, 58, 484–485) note that need for control has many aspects and has a genetic component that varies among people. Control can be direct, interpretive, predictive or vicarious and may involve self, powerful others, God, or supernatural powers in a self-directive, collaborative, or deferring mode.

Baumeister (1991) considered control as part of a need for efficacy, which includes having an impact on the world and changing the world. He considered this need to be an aspect of obtaining a sense of meaning in life.

From the perspective of daily life, the drive to impress one's self on the world manifests in various forms, including creating technology, building construction projects, climbing or conquering mountains "because they are there," making scientific discoveries, writing books, and creating various forms of entertainment. Conflicts with other people are another way of impressing one's self on the world. This includes various forms of competition in sports, business, and politics. The development of computer viruses may be some of the clearest evidence for this motivation. Most computer viruses have no apparent purpose other than for the developers to impress themselves on the world just because they can. As indicated by the fact that computer viruses are developed almost entirely by males, this motivation appears to be more prominent in males but certainly can also be present in females.

THE RATIONAL SCIENTIFIC PERSONALITY

Keirsey (1998) described the development of rational scientific understanding and pragmatic application of science as the central motivations for people with intuitive, thinking (NT) personality types. People with these dispositions are naturally attracted to the process and results of the scientific method. Of course, experiencing scientific culture presumably enhances rationality and empiricism. The tendency to elevate a rational, scientific, mathematical style of thinking to an almost religious-like level of commitment and faith is widely apparent in scientific writings.

The inability to reliably control, predict, or understand psi may exclude paranormal phenomena from the interests of many who have pragmatic, scientific orientations. From this perspective, it is not surprising that scientists tend to be skeptical of psi (McClenon, 1982; McConnell & Clark, 1991). Prediction is the foundation of science, and control and application provide the most compelling evidence and value. For example, the concepts of quantum physics are as radical as the ideas of parapsychology; however, quantum physics has provided numerous successful applications, including lasers and transistors. If psi experiments produced reliable results, and particularly if they produced useful applications, scientists would likely accept the phenomena and begin developing theories for further control and application.

Skeptical scientists tend to explain belief in psi as due to a failure of rational, empirical analysis (e.g., Alcock & Otis, 1980; Blackmore & Troscianko, 1985; Gray & Mill, 1990). These explanations often imply that all people should share the scientist's devotion to rational, empirical analysis. The possibility that alternative values, personalities, and ways of processing information may also have value is rarely acknowledged in these writings.

Skeptics also tend to have a greater internal locus of control (belief that they control the events in their lives) than those who believe in psi (summarized in Irwin, 1993). This is consistent with a stronger motivation for control by skeptics or possibly with less belief in supernatural influences.

I suspect that there is a closely related motivation for rational explanations but with less emphasis on pragmatic application and empiricism. This motivation would underlie the pursuit of philosophy and the more abstract, intellectual approaches to religion. However, I have not found a specific personality description that aligns with such a motivation.

EXPERIMENTAL PARAPSYCHOLOGY

Belief in instrumental control of psi occurs in spite of the persistent failure to develop reliable applications of psi. The assumption of instrumental control of psi is the foundation for experimental parapsychology as well as for occultism, new age beliefs, and commercial psychics and fortune tellers. These belief systems basically view psi as a magical power that can fulfill a person's wants or provide information about the future.

Numerous authors have speculated that belief in psi results from an illusion of control or mastery over uncertain events motivated by the need for control (e.g., Blackmore & Troscianko, 1985; Irwin, 2000; Schumaker, 1990; Vyse, 1997). Motivations for control probably have a significant role in the pursuit of experimental parapsychology. Carrying out a psi experiment with an expectation of success requires the assumption and belief that people can control psi, even if only to a weak, statistical degree. However, other factors besides control also appear to be involved in the pursuit of experimental parapsychology. These factors may include an intense fascination with the subject matter and a tendency to overlook the problematic properties of the results or to optimistically assume that these properties will soon be overcome.

THE PROPENSITY TO EXPLAIN

The motivation for control is closely linked to motivations to learn and to understand causes (Baumeister, 2005). The evolution in humans of imagination, symbolic thought, memory, symbolic communication, planning based on hypothetical futures, and creativity greatly enhanced the abilities to learn, to control, and to adapt (Baumeister, 2005; Donald, 2001).

However, the propensity to explain may go beyond achieving control. Donald (2001) argued that the human mind and human culture co-evolved, with the mind becoming extremely plastic in order to adapt to the diversity of culture. He argued that culture and particularly myths provide a needed framework for experiencing life and are actively sought. The cultural framework for experiencing and explaining life can include myths, religion, and science.

Science in theory focuses on empirically verifiable explanations but in practice often seems to be a constant struggle to control the propensity to imagine extensive myths. In the social sciences in particular, a few selected observations tend to be extrapolated way beyond scientific confidence to develop all-inclusive theories that, like myths, are abstract explanations with little empirical support. One can make a strong argument that the writings and associated subcultures of psychoanalysis and behaviorism were more similar to religions than to science. Even for the most well established physical forces such as gravity, the diversity of conceptual explanations over the years (general relativity, quantum physics, string theory, etc.) indicates that scientific concepts are products of imagination that are at least as much cultural fads as enduring truths.

The propensity for mythology, including within science, makes it likely that the diversity of attitudes toward the paranormal will remain for the foreseeable future. In modern pluralistic societies, people are exposed to and can select from a diversity of alternative world views and mythologies.

SUMMARY

The motivation for control may contribute to both skepticism and belief in psi. Research on various aspects of the motivation for control and its interaction with other psychological factors is needed to understand its role in attitude toward the paranormal. The initial evidence suggests that skeptics may tend to have a greater need for control. In fact, the speculations that an illusion of control is a significant factor in psi beliefs have primarily been proposed by skeptics and may be projections of their own needs for control.

THE MOTIVATION FOR MEANING AND PURPOSE

If one moves beyond the motivation for control and looks at psi on its own terms, a different motivation emerges as prominent. Many people report experiences of ostensible spontaneous paranormal phenomena that occur without attempting to elicit or control the phenomena (Rhine, 1981; Stokes, 1997). Even a casual review of these reports indicates that the experiences do not seem to be guided by self-serving, materialistic motivations or needs for control.

Research indicates the primary effect of psi experiences is an altered worldview and an increased sense of meaning and purpose in life and spirituality (Kennedy & Kanthamani, 1995; McClenon, 1994, 2002; Palmer, 1979; Palmer & Braud, 2002; White, 1997a, 1997c). For example, Dossey (1999, p. 3) describes how a series of unexpected paranormal experiences changed the direction of his professional career. Similarly, a survey of people who were interested in parapsychology and reported having paranormal or transcendent experiences found that (a) 72% agreed with the statement "As a result of my paranormal or transcendent experience, I believe my life is guided or watched over by a higher force or being," (b) 45% agreed with the statement "I feel like I have a purpose or mission in life as a result of my paranormal or transcendent experience(s)," (c) 25% agreed with "One or more paranormal or transcendent experiences motivated me to make a major life change that I was not previously thinking about making," and (d) 38% agreed with "One or more paranormal or transcendent experiences seemed to confirm or reinforce that I was doing what I should be doing" (Kennedy & Kanthamani, 1995). White (1997a, 1997c) has collected and evaluated cases of exceptional experiences and found that transformative aftermaths that redirected a person's worldview and focus in life were common. Ostensible paranormal miracles have been a decisive factor in persuading people to join particular religious groups (McClenon, 1994).

The transformative psi experiences appear to guide a person rather than the person guiding psi. This is a significantly different world view than the assumptions of experimental parapsychology. These types of cases may induce an attitude of a humble seeker rather than a sense of control. Dossey (1999, p. 3) characterized his series of psi experiences as: "It was as if the universe, having delivered the message, hung up the phone. It was now up to me to make sense of it."

The source of the experience is viewed as external to the person. Without a bias for efficacy and control, the spiritual implications and supernatural aspects of paranormal phenomena predominate. The relatively few spontaneous psi cases that appear to have direct benefits related to motivation may actually serve as vehicles for this transformative aspect of psi (Kennedy, 2000).

White (1993) suggested that the best research strategy for parapsychology may be to let psi lead us rather than to try to control or apply psi. One could argue that the persistent failure to control psi leaves no choice but to pursue a more humble, learning approach.

THE NEED FOR MEANING

Baumeister (1991) integrated a wide diversity of information and ideas about the human need for a sense of meaning in life. He concluded that there are at least four aspects to the sense of meaning in life. These are:

Purpose: The need to be able to interpret current events in relation to expectations about the future, and to have and achieve goals.

Value: The need to know right and wrong behavior and to regard one's actions as right and good.

Efficacy: The need to be able to control the environment and to have an impact on the world.

Self-worth: The need to have self-respect and the respect of others, which is typically based on feeling superior to others.

Baumeister (1991) described religion as the central source of meaning in life historically. The need for meaning is also reflected in the propensity for myths described by Donald (2001). Religion can fulfill all four aspects of meaning. Baumeister and Donald both noted that science has an increasing role in the cultural explanatory framework.

Baumeister also commented that science is highly successful at providing control and efficacy but does not provide a sense of purpose, values, and self-worth. He noted that this makes it more difficult to obtain a sense of meaning and to handle stresses and traumas. Schumaker (1995, 2001) similarly argued that religion and transcendence have important roles in human mental health that are not being fulfilled by the secular rationality and materialism of modern society. Schumaker (2001) argued that the declining meaning, purpose, values, and spirituality are contrary to human nature and are causing mental health and ecological crises.

Paranormal beliefs and experiences can be directly related to purpose, efficacy, and self-worth. The extent to which paranormal beliefs provide a sense of meaning and purpose only for persons who are by disposition attracted to transcendence and spirituality is an important topic that merits empirical investigation.

THE MOTIVATION FOR SELF-WORTH/SUPERIORITY

Baumeister (1991) noted that the motivation for self-worth often manifests as a need to feel superior. Judging oneself as better off than others is a significant factor in human happiness, and comparing oneself to less fortunate persons is a standard technique for coping with unfortunate events (Baumeister, 1991; Myers, 1992). Exaggerated positive self-evaluations and illusions have long been recognized as a characteristic of people (Hornsey, 2003; Taylor & Brown, 1988). Human males in particular tend to have an innate drive to compete for power and status and to feel superior to most other persons (e.g., Campbell, 2002; Geary, 1998).

The motivations for superiority and efficacy (including control) are closely related, particularly when competition is involved. The tendency to divide into polarized groups and attempt to prevail over opponents provides both efficacy and superiority. The motivation of some individuals to persuade others to accept their views, beliefs, and values may be related more to these drives, similar to sports competitions, than to the specific content of the beliefs. This could be a motivating factor for both belief and skepticism about the paranormal.

SUPERIORITY THROUGH AUTHORITY AND DOMINANCE

Keirsey (1998) described the sensing, judging (SJ) personality types as materialistic, distrusting of fantasy and abstract ideas, and tending to feel a duty to maintain traditional rules of right and wrong. These personality types focus on external authority and tradition rather than internal experience.

People with STJ personality types tend to rise to positions of leadership and authority in hierarchical organizations (Keirsey, 1998; Kroeger, Thuesen, & Rutledge, 2002). Fudjack and Dinkelaker (1994) noted that the masculine "extraverted/rational-empirical/pragmatic/materialist" ESTJ personality is prominent in western culture and tends to prefer hierarchical organizations that emphasize power and control rather than creativity and flexibility. Kroeger, Thuesen, and Rutledge (2002) administered the Myers-Briggs personality test to over 20,000 people in all levels of a wide variety of corporate, government, and military organizations. Across these diverse groups, they found that 60% of 2,245 people in top executive positions had STJ personalities (ESTJ or ISTJ). The proportion of STJ types increased as the level on the management hierarchy increased.

On the other hand, only about 1% of top executives had NFP personalities, which would be more interested in psi and mysticism. For comparison, general population samples have found STJ for 26%–43% of males and 18%–29% of females, and NFP for 6%–12% of males and 9%–18% of females (Macdaid, McCaulley, & Kainz, 1986). Kroeger, Thuesen, and Rutledge also commented that 95% of top executives were T (thinking) types rather than F (feeling) types.

This rational, pragmatic, materialist personality bias in the upper echelons of power and status may be a major factor in the institutional skepticism and resistance to psi described by Hansen (2001). This value system may also be associated with the "hypercompetition" and "hypermaterialism" that Schumaker (2001) believes prevail in modern society and contribute to depression and anxiety. Somit and Peterson (1997) discuss the evolutionary and social aspects of the biological basis for dominance and hierarchy.

Baumeister (1991) observed that religion often provides a sense of superiority. He also noted that this sense of superiority unfortunately has a long history of hostility and violence toward those who are viewed as being inferior. The sense of superiority is particularly prominent in fundamentalist groups, which are found among most of the world's major religions and believe that their particular set of beliefs and values, and only theirs, has been chosen for a special relationship with God (Hunsberger, 1996). Fundamentalists also emphasize authority and tradition. Religious terrorists are characterized by extreme fundamentalism, including superiority, adherence to the authority of a particular tradition and its leader (s), and lack of respect for, dehumanization of, feelings of threat by, and hostility toward people with different beliefs and values (Stern, 2003).

Research indicates that the S personality types are associated with conservative religions that emphasize institutional religious authority and tradition whereas the intuitive (N) types are associated with more liberal, subjective, experiential approaches to religion and tolerance for religious uncertainty (Francis and Ross, 1997; Francis and Jones, 1998, 1999; Macdaid, McCaulley, & Kainz, 1986). Similarly, greater dogmatism was associated with the S and J personality types (Ross, Francis, & Craig, 2005).

Other personality models describe related factors like authoritarianism, traditionalism, or right-wing authoritarianism (Altemeyer, 1996; Carey, 2003, pp. 395–398; Spilka et al., 2003, pp. 467–468). Altemeyer (1996) argued that fundamentalism is a religious manifestation of the authoritarian personality. Monaghan (1967) described "authority-seeker" as one of the main motivations for attending a fundamentalist church.

Fundamentalist religions often consider mystical or paranormal experiences as delusions or dangerous events. Pentecostal and charismatic religious movements emphasize "gifts of the spirit," including prophesy, healing, recognition of spirits, performance of miracles, wisdom, and knowledge (Roberts, 1995, p. 370; Rosten, 1975, pp. 591–592). Christian fundamentalists frequently have conflicts with Pentecostals and charismatics because fundamentalists give primacy to the inerrant authority of the Bible rather than to direct spiritual experience (Roberts, 1995, pp. 370–371).

Tensions between those who give primacy to the authority of tradition rather than to direct mystical and miraculous experiences have occurred for centuries, as would be expected if personality dispositions have a role. The life and death of Jesus were based on conflicts between those who maintained rules, authority, and superiority of past traditions versus proponents of inspired teachings supported by claims of paranormal phenomena. Such tensions were also apparent in the re-actions within Christianity to the desert ascetics and in the Protestant Reformation (Woodward, 2000). One argument that goes back to at least the sixteenth century is that the miracles described in the Bible were real and were needed to establish the authority of the Bible, but once that authority was established, miracles were not needed and claims for post-biblical miracles are fraudulent or the work of the devil (Mullin, 1996, pp. 12–16). The variation in beliefs among individuals and groups should also be kept in mind. Some of those who focus on authority also believe that supernatural interventions sometimes occur in post-biblical times.

The hostility of some extreme skeptics toward those who believe in paranor-mal phenomena has noteworthy similarities with religious fundamentalism and appears to be a manifestation of dominance and superiority (Kennedy, 2003c). Like fundamentalists, these skeptics believe that people and organizations which have different beliefs and values are a threat that must be vigorously fought and deserve ridicule and hostility. "Feelings of threat, hostility, and lack of respect for those with different beliefs and values are prominent with both fundamentalists and extreme skeptics" (Kennedy, 2003c, p. 30).

Skeptical writers generally view science as authoritative and consider religious and paranormal beliefs as indicating an immature stage of cognitive development that is in opposition to rational scientific theories (e.g., Kurtz, 2001; Schumaker, 1990; Vyse, 1997; Zusne & Jones, 1989). This perspective implies superiority of the skeptics and is based on philosophy and personal values that may reflect tem-perament and are far outside the domain of established scientific evidence.

SUPERIORITY WITHOUT AUTHORITY AND DOMINANCE

Religion and spirituality can also provide a sense of self-worth and superior-ity for those who do not have social status and dominance. Baumeister (1991) pointed out that the religions of slaves typically glorified meritorious rewards in an afterlife and punishment of oppressors. Glorification of rewards in the afterlife and of austere living in the present are also apparent in the religions of the less affluent whereas the religions of the more affluent tend to view material success in the present world as blessings from God (Roberts, 1995).

More subjective forms of spirituality can also provide a means for establish-ing a hierarchy of superiority. Characteristics and criteria for determining who is more spiritually advanced are often proposed (e.g., White, 1972; Wilber, 2000). The claim that one is among a small minority of highly evolved people and that everyone should strive to be like him or her is a common symptom of the drive to achieve a sense of superiority.

Certain religious traditions have included the belief that the occurrence of miracles was a sign of divine favor or of the holiness of those involved (Mullin, 1996). In addition, mystical or transcendent experiences have been widely interpreted as evidence of high spirituality and sought through practices such as meditation (Kornfield, 2000; Spilka et al. 2003, pp. 259–263, 297–298).

Psi experiences are sometimes presented as associated with an advanced state of spiritual development (Grosso, 1992; Murphy, 1992; Ring, 1984; Thalbourne, in press). Traditional yoga writings similarly proposed that paranormal abilities are associated with developing spirituality (Prabhavananda & Isherwood, 1981). Gopi Krishna (1974) claimed that his kundalini experiences (which resembled a mental health breakdown) made him a highly evolved "genius" and gave him psychic powers. However, that appears to have been a self-evaluation with no objective or tangible evidence to support his high opinion of himself.

It is now widely recognized that the occurrence of transcendent and related experiences do not necessarily indicate ethical behavior, compassion, wisdom, integration, or other characteristics normally associated with spirituality (Kornfield, 2000; Zweig, 2003). In fact, the sense of superiority from such experiences may promote self-serving abuse of power. The most conspicuous evidence for this point comes from the numerous cases of spiritual leaders who claim many transcendent experiences but have a lavish lifestyle and use their position of authority for sexual activity with people they are supposedly spiritually guiding. Sexual exploitation has happened much more widely than is generally acknowledged in both eastern and western spiritual organizations (Gonsiorek, 1995; Kornfield, 2000; Neimark, 1998; Roemischer, 2004; Zweig, 2003). Such behavior appears to have occurred in the majority of prominent yoga and meditation organizations in the U.S. As discussed in the references above, the sexual exploitation has resulted in numerous lawsuits, but even when consensual, it still appears to be an abuse of authority and trust. In an important discussion of the realities of spiritual pursuits, Kornfield (2000) described the common error of mistaking charisma for wisdom.

SUMMARY

Some people build superiority hierarchies in the material world and some build them only in their minds. Those who build superiority hierarchies in the material world tend to have more negative attitudes toward the paranormal. Paranormal and mystical experiences may sometimes be pursued or claimed in an effort to achieve a sense of superiority. Tensions between people with authoritarian and

transcendent dispositions have occurred throughout history and appear to underlie many religious and social conflicts.

THE MOTIVATION FOR CONNECTEDNESS

For some people, belief in psi may be motivated more by a need for a sense of
interconnectedness rather than for control and superiority. Social connections and
support are one of the widely recognized functions of religion (Spilka et al. 2003).
Women, in particular, tend to value social and emotional connections (Campbell,
2002; Geary, 1998; Gilligan, 1993). Religious, supernatural, or paranormal beliefs
may be held primarily to fit into a social group or organization. Alternatively, the
beliefs themselves may reflect and reinforce the motivation for interconnectedness. Blackmore (1994) noted that belief in psi may be more common among
women because of their greater sense that the world is interconnected. White
(1997b), Braud (1997), and Tart (2002) have discussed the sense of interconnectedness that results from psi experiences.

The relationship between interconnectedness and transcendence merits investigation. Deacon (1997) suggested that humans evolved an innate motivation to
become part of something larger than oneself. This motivation promotes social
organization. Deacon also suggested that this motivation, combined with a propensity to find meaning or symbolic relationships in all experiences, underlies
mystical or religious beliefs.

People with a strong sense of connection may view the world as an interconnected whole that is meaningful and benevolent. These views are similar to the
"assumptive worldviews" that initial research suggests may be related to belief in
paranormal phenomena (Irwin, 2003). This holistic worldview may also lead to
altruism because the world is not divided into an in-group versus outsiders.

THE HEALING FACTOR

McClenon (1994, 2002) proposed that paranormal demonstrations and beliefs
promote healing through placebo and hypnotic effects. He argued that these healing benefits may have been the foundation for the evolution of religion and paranormal beliefs. He also noted that these benefits apply even if psi effects are not
real, and that deception has been widely practiced to induce such beliefs.

Schumaker (1995) similarly argued that transcendent myths and religious beliefs
are important for mental health. He proposed that the decline in the role of religion in culture has greatly hindered the ability for mental health healing and that
a new balance between myth and reality needs to be found. This appears to be
a change from his earlier view that paranormal and religious beliefs were driving
humanity down a road of irrational self-destruction (Schumaker, 1990).

These ideas are closely related to the motivation for efficacy and control. Placebo effects are basically self-healing by the body. It has long been thought that expectation has a major role in placebo effects (Hyland, 2003; Shapiro & Morris, 1978; White, Tursky, & Schwartz, 1985). Certain modern medical practices may reduce expectations. In particular, legal obligations for full disclosure and informed consent can be expected to reduce optimism and expectations. The circumstances of psychic, spiritual, or alternative healing techniques may optimize self-healing in ways that are difficult to achieve in the standard medical profession.

However, placebo effects have always been controversial. After decades of research and experience, some investigators question whether placebo effects exist at all (e.g., Hrobjartsson & Gotzxche, 2001). Placebo effects and their relationship to other variables are inconsistent and unpredictable, even when procedures and subject populations are as similar as possible (Hyland, 2003; Shapiro & Morris, 1978). Conditions for reasonably reliable results have not been identified. Hypnosis also has a long history of controversy, including whether it actually exists and whether responses to suggestion are primarily limited to individuals with certain personality characteristics, notably fantasy proneness (Baker, 1990; Spanos & Chaves, 1989).

The controversies about placebo and hypnotic effects raise questions about whether they are sufficiently powerful to have the role in evolution McClenon proposed. It may be difficult to distinguish the evolutionary role of healing beliefs from other factors such as the motivations for meaning and purpose, efficacy, and superiority. It is also possible that healing beliefs have a role primarily for certain personality types, such as fantasy proneness.

Placebo effects have many parallels with psi effects. Both have inconsistent experimental results and controversy about whether the effects are real. The mechanisms of action for both effects are not known, resulting in negative definitions based on what they are not rather than what they are. Also, the initial research efforts on placebo effects were focused on identifying the characteristics of certain individuals who were "reactors"; however, those efforts were not sufficiently successful to maintain the interest of researchers (Shapiro & Morris, 1978; White, Tursky, & Schwartz, 1985), which is similar to the experience with efforts to identify special subjects for psi experiments (Rao, 1965).

Despite their similar properties, placebo effects have become much more widely accepted among scientists than psi effects. In fact, controlling for possible placebo effects is a standard design criterion for medical research. A more comprehensive comparison of the characteristics and scientific acceptance of placebo and psi effects might be revealing.

FEAR OF PSI

The usual explanations in parapsychology for the inability to obtain reliable psi effects involve speculations about unconscious, instinctive fear of psi (e.g.,

Batcheldor, 1984; Braude, 1997; Ehrenwald, 1978; Eisenbud, 1992; Radin, 1989; Tart, 1984) and suppression of psi to prevent information overload (e.g., Bergson, 1914; Ehrenwald, 1978; Koestler, 1972).

However, the widespread interest in psi and the extensive efforts of some people to cultivate psi abilities are not consistent with these speculations about fear of psi. It may be true that some people fear psi, but there is strong evidence that many others do not, and, in fact, some people desire to develop useful psi abilities, as evidenced by the perpetual popularity of books and courses on developing psi abilities (e.g., Robinson & Carlson-Finnerty, 1999) and the continuing existence of commercial psychics. Similarly, the speculations about information overload overlook the fact that instances of striking psi occur without information overload. These speculations do not explain why instances of striking psi do not occur more frequently and with greater control.

The speculations about fear and information overload, combined with the unreliable, unuseful nature of psi effects, imply that psi has more adverse effects than benefits. Experimental parapsychology assumes that psi is a widespread human ability; however, psi would not be expected to evolve as a human ability if it caused substantial adverse effects and little benefit.

The arguments about unconscious fear of psi have direct spiritual assumptions that are rarely acknowledged. Given the implausibility of evolution producing an ability that has the characteristics of psi, one possibility is that the source of psi is supernatural or external to living people. The instinctive propensity to fear snakes (Tallis, 2002, pp. 135–138) provides a useful comparison. Such instinctive fears make sense for reacting to external threats like snakes but do not offer a rationale for the evolution of an ability that appears to have negligible material benefit and serious adverse effects that need to be suppressed. Following this line of thought, an instinctive fear of psi would imply that the source of psi is external to people. Alternatively, psi could be a pre-existing, innate spiritual ability that is detrimental in the material world, as suggested by Bergson (1914). Either of these approaches identifies psi with a dualistic spiritual realm rather than as a human ability that emerged through evolution.

In terms of motivations, the lack of control of psi is the main theme emerging from empirical findings on fear of psi (Siegel, 1986; Tart, 1986; Tart & Labore, 1986). The need for research on various aspects of the motivation for control and attitude toward psi was noted earlier. Given the human need for control, fear of psi is probably a result of the lack of control rather than a cause, which is contrary to the rationale that fear causes psi effects to be unreliable.

CONCLUSIONS

The efforts to achieve control of psi in experimental parapsychology have not produced significant scientific progress. When psi phenomena are examined without the implicit bias for control, the relationship with spirituality emerges as the central organizing factor. The primary effect of psi experiences appears to be enhanced spirituality and meaning in life. Reliable use of psi for material self-interest in a manner that is scientifically convincing has not occurred and, at this point, does not seem likely.

It is not surprising that those who are by disposition materialistic, pragmatic, and rational find the evidence for psi not to be remotely convincing. If psi phenomena had a degree of predictability and usefulness, the scientific community could assign a label to the unknown process and begin developing methods for its control and practical application. That would not be noticeably different from the situation with the established physical forces. People with pragmatic, materialistic values cannot be expected to be interested in something that has no pragmatic, materialistic use.

People more attracted to transcendence continue to have experiences that they describe as providing absolutely certain knowledge that there is a spiritual realm (James, 1902/1982; Miller & C'de Baca, 2001; Ring, 1984). These people find substantial commonalities among their experiences and the after-effects. The fact that others with more externally focused, materialistic dispositions do not have such experiences and are skeptical is irrelevant to the interpretation of their experiences. They feel that they are dealing with direct experience and knowledge, not philosophical theories, academic rationalizations, or speculations. As William James (1902/1982) noted, there is no point in trying to convince them that their experiences are not real.

Paranormal and mystical experiences have several characteristics in common, including the ability to inspire a sense of meaning and purpose in life. Science, on the other hand, is often described as fulfilling the needs for control and efficacy but not the needs for meaning, purpose, values, and self-worth. However, this perspective may not fully take into account the diversity of motivations associated with different personality types. Some people may find meaning and purpose from scientific understanding, others from transcendent experiences, and others from enforcing the authority of tradition.

Objective scientists must recognize that they cannot prove scientifically that reports of subjective transcendent experiences do not have some validity that is beyond current scientific understanding. Paranormal phenomena that are viewed as miracles initiated by supernatural powers to inspire spiritual growth are largely outside the domain of science, as are many other religious beliefs. The extent to which attitudes toward such matters are based on personal dispositions rather than scientific knowledge deserves recognition.

Tensions among those with transcendent, authoritarian, and scientific dispositions have been common in the history of paranormal and religious beliefs. The motivation for superiority is not limited to authoritarian personalities and can contaminate both science and spirituality. This motivation can prevent proponents of science from being objective and rational, and it can prevent proponents of spirituality from being compassionate and ethical. The aggressive promotion of a particular belief system can be a form of competition and dominance similar to sports. Such aggressiveness can be seen on both sides of psi beliefs but is particularly strong for some of the skeptics. Persons on each side can see the irrational drive for superiority in their opponents, but they have difficulty acknowledging it in themselves.

Science can do much to sort out the web of motivations and to create better understanding among people with different dispositions. The ideas presented here provide a plausible beginning and have some initial empirical support.

A useful next step would be to develop measures that address various factors, including motivations for transcendence, connectedness, control and efficacy, superiority, authority, and healing. Measuring exposure to basic social and cultural factors related to belief in the paranormal would also be useful, particularly for identifying people who do not have strong personal motivations and tend to go along with social and cultural influences. The mix of factors could be characterized for an individual and for different types of paranormal experiences and beliefs. For example, it would be useful to measure the mix of factors associated with (a) experiences that could be actual psi, (b) experiences that appear to be misinterpreted as psi, and (c) skepticism about psi. The motivation for superiority, in particular, has been underappreciated in research, perhaps because many scientists prefer to overlook that aspect of their own personality.

Exploring factors of humility and gratitude versus efficacy and superiority may be particularly valuable. The tangible lesson from the failure to develop useful applications of psi is that motivations for efficacy and superiority may not be applicable in this domain. Successful research strategies in this area must identify and adapt to the properties of the phenomena. The evidence for psi and its association with transcendent experiences may hint that there is a spiritual realm that tentatively encourages development in a transcendent, humble, non-self-serving, nonmaterialistic direction.

REFERENCES

Alcock, J. E., & Ottis, L. P. (1980). Critical thinking and belief in the paranormal. *Psychological Reports*, 46, 479–482.

Altemeyer, B. (1996). *The authoritarian spector*. Cambridge, MA: Harvard University Press.

Archangel, D. (1997). Investigating the relationship between Myers-Briggs Type Indicator and facilitated reunion experiences. *Journal of the American Society for Psychical Research*, 91, 82–95.

Baker, R. A. (1990). *They call it hypnosis*. Buffalo, NY: Prometheus Books.

Barbuto, J. E., & Plummer, B. A. (1998). Mental boundaries as a new dimension of personality: A comparison of Hartman's Boundaries of the Mind and Jung's Psychological Types. *Journal of Social Behavior and Personality*, 13, 421–437.

Barna, G. (1991). *What Americans believe: An annual survey of values and religious views in the United States*. Ventura, CA: Regal.

Batcheldor, K. J. (1984). Contributions to the theory of PK induction from sitter-group work. *Journal of the American Society for Psychical Research*, 78, 105–122.

Baumeister, R. F. (1991). *Meanings of Life*. New York: Guilford.

Baumeister, R. F. (2005). *The cultural animal: Human nature, meaning, and social life*. New York: Oxford University Press.

Bergson, H. (1914). *Presidential address*. Proceedings of the Society for Psychical Research, 27, 157–175.

Blackmore, S. J. (1994). Are women more sheepish? In L. Coly & R. White (Eds.), *Women and parapsychology* (pp. 68–84). New York: Parapsychology Foundation.

Blackmore, S., & Troscianko, T. (1985). Belief in the paranormal: Probability judgements, illusory control, and the "chance baseline shift." *British Journal of Psychology*, 76, 459–468.

Bouchard, T. J., & Hur, Y. M. (1998). Genetic and environmental influences on the continuous scales of the Myers-Briggs Type Indicator: An analysis based on twins reared apart. *Journal of Personality*, 66, 135–149.

Braud, W. (1997). Parapsychology and spirituality: Implications and intimations. In C. T. Tart (Ed.) *Body, mind, spirit* (pp. 135–152). Charlottesville, VA: Hampton Roads.

Braude, S. E. (1997). *The Limits of influence: Psychokinesis and the philosophy of science*. New York: University Press of America.

Broughton, R. S. (1991). *Parapsychology: The controversial science*. New York: Ballantine Books.

Campbell, A. (2002). *A mind of her own: The evolutionary psychology of women*. Oxford, England: Oxford University Press.

Cary, G. (2003). *Human genetics for the social sciences*. Thousand Oaks, CA: Sage.

Collins, W. A., MacCoby, E. E., Steinberg, L., Hetherington, E. M., & Bornstein, M. H. (2000). Contemporary research on parenting: The case for nature and nurture. *American Psychologist*, 55, 218–232.

Deacon, T. W. (1997). *The symbolic species: The co-evolution of language and the brain*. New York: W.W. Norton and Company.

Donald, M. (2001). *A mind so rare: The evolution of human consciousness*. New York: Norton.

Dossey, L. (1999). *Reinventing medicine: Beyond mind-body to a new era of healing*. San Francisco, CA: HarperSanFrancisco.

Egger, M., Smith, G. D., Schneider, M., & Minder, C. (1997). Bias in meta-analysis detected by a simple graphical test. *British Medical Journal,* 315, 629–634.

Ehrenwald, J. (1978). *The ESP experience: A psychiatric validation*. New York: Basic Books.

Eisenbud, J. (1992). *Parapsychology and the unconscious*. Berkeley, CA: North Atlantic Books.

Francis, L. J., & Jones, S. H. (1998). Personality and Christian belief among adult churchgoers. *Journal of Psychological Type*, 47, 5–11.

Francis, L. J., & Jones, S. H. (1999). Psychological type and tolerance for religious uncertainty. *Pastoral Psychology*, 47, 253–259.

Francis, L. J., & Ross, C. F. J. (1997). The perceiving function and Christian spirituality: Distinguishing between sensing and intuition. *Pastoral Sciences*, 16, 93–103.

Fudjack, J., & Dinkelaker, P. (1994). Toward a diversity of psychological type in organization: Part 3. Paper presented at the First Annual Antioch University Management Faculty Conference, October, 1994. Retrieved January 3, 2005, from http://tap3x.net/ENSEMBLE/mpagelc.html

Gallup, G., & Castelli, J. (1989). *The people's religion: American faith in the 90's*. New York: Macmillan.

Geary, D. C. (1998). *Male, female: The evolution of human sex differences*. Washington, DC: American Psychological Association.

Gilligan, C. (1993). *A different voice: Psychological theory and women's development*. Cambridge, MA: Harvard Press.

Gonsiorek, J. C. (Ed.) (1995). *Breach of trust: Sexual exploitation by health care professionals and clergy*. Thousand Oaks, CA: Sage.

Gow, K., Lurie, J., Coppin, S., Popper, A., Powell, A., & Basterfield, K. (2001). Fantasy proneness and other psychological correlates of UFO experiences. Queensland University of Technology, Brisbane, Queensland, Australia. Retrieved October 5, 2005, from http://www.anomalistik.de/gow.pdf

Gray, T., & Mill, D. (1990). Critical abilities, graduate education (Biology vs. English), and belief in unsubstantiated phenomena. *Canadian Journal of Behavioral Science*, 22, 162–172.

Grosso, M. (1992). *Frontiers of the soul: Exploring psychic evolution.* Wheaton, IL: Quest Books.

Haight, J. (1979). Spontaneous psi cases: A survey and preliminary study of ESP, attitude, and personality relationship. *Journal of Parapsychology*, 43, 179–203.

Hammer, A. L. (Ed.) (1996). MBTI applications. Palo Alto, CA: Consulting Psychological Press.

Hammer, D. (2004). *The God gene.* New York: Doubleday.

Hansen, G. P. (2001). *The trickster and the paranormal.* Philadelphia: Xlibris Corporation.

Hartman, S. E. (1999). Another view of the paranormal belief scale. *Journal of Parapsychology*, 63, 131–141.

Hartmann, E. (1991). *Boundaries of the mind: A new psychology of personality.* USA: Basic Books.

Harvey, R. J. (1996). Reliability and validity. In A. L. Hammer (Ed.), *MBTI applications* (pp. 5–29). Palo Alto, CA: Consulting Psychological Press.

Heath, A. C., Cloninger, C. R., & Martin, N. G. (1994). Testing a model for the genetic structure of personality: A comparison of the personality systems of Cloninger and Eysenck. *Journal of Personality and Individual Differences*, 66, 762–775.

Hornsey, M. J. (2003). Linking superiority bias in the interpersonal and intergroup domains. *Journal of Social Psychology*, 143, 479–491.

Houran, J., Thalbourne, M. A., & Hartmann, E. (2003). Comparison of two alternative measures of the boundary construct. *Perceptual and Motor Skills*, 96, 311–324.

Hrobjartsson, A., & Gotzxche, P. C. (2001). Is the placebo powerless? An analysis of clinical trials comparing placebo with no treatment. *New England Journal of Medicine*, 344, 1594–1602.

Hunsberger, B. (1996). Religious fundamentalism, right-wing authoritarianism, and hostility toward homosexuals in non-Christian religious groups. *International Journal for the Psychology of Religion*, 6, 39–49.

Hyland, M. E. (2003). Using the placebo response in clinical practice. *Clinical Medicine*, 3, 347–350.

Irwin, H. J. (1993). Belief in the paranormal: A review of the empirical literature. *Journal of the American Society for Psychical Research*, 87, 1–39.

Irwin, H. J. (2000). Belief in the paranormal and a sense of control over life. *European Journal of Parapsychology*, 15, 68–78.

Irwin, H.J. (2003). Paranormal beliefs and the maintenance of assumptive world views. *Journal of the Society for Psychical Research*, 67, 18–25.

James, W. (1982). *The varieties of religious experience.* New York: Penguin. (Original work published 1902)

Keirsey, D. (1998). *Please understand me II.* Del Mar, CA: Prometheus Nemesis Book Company.

Kennedy, J. E. (1995). Methods for investigating goal-oriented psi. *Journal of Parapsychology*, 59, 47–62.

Kennedy, J. E. (2000). Do people guide psi or does psi guide people? Evidence and implications from life and lab. *Journal of the American Society for Psychical Research*, 94, 130–150.

Kennedy, J. E. (2003a). The capricious, actively evasive, unsustainable nature of psi: A summary and hypotheses. *Journal of Parapsychology*, 67, 53–74.

Kennedy, J. E. (2003b). Letter to the editor. *Journal of Parapsychology.* 67, 406–408.

Kennedy, J. E. (2003c). The polarization of psi beliefs: Rational controlling masculine skepticism versus interconnected, spiritual, feminine belief. *Journal of the American Society for Psychical Research*, 97, 27–42.

Kennedy, J. E. (2004). A proposal and challenge for proponents and skeptics of psi. *Journal of Parapsychology*, 68, 57–67.

Kennedy, J. E. (in press). What is the purpose of psi? *Journal of the American Society for Psychical Research*. (also at http://jeksite.org/psi.htm)

Kennedy, J. E., & Kanthamani, H. (1995). An exploratory study of the effects of paranormal and spiritual experiences on peoples' lives and well-being. *Journal of the American Society for Psychical Research*, 89, 249–264.

Kennedy, J. E., Kanthamani, H., & Palmer, J. (1994). Psychic and spiritual experiences, health, well-being, and meaning in life. *Journal of Parapsychology*, 58, 353–383.

Koestler, A. (1972). *The roots of coincidence*. New York: Hutchinson and Co.

Kornfield, J. (2000). *After the ecstasy, the laundry*. New York: Bantam Books.

Krishna, G. (1974). *Higher consciousness and kundalini*. Norton Heights, CT: The Kundalini Research Foundation.

Kroeger, O., Thuesen, J. M., & Rutledge, H. (2002). *Type talk at work: How the 16 personality types determine your success on the job* (revised ed.). New York: Random House.

Kurtz, P. (2001). *Skepticism and humanism: The new paradigm*. Piscataway, NJ: Transaction Publishers.

Lange, R., Irwin, H. J., & Houran, J. (2000). Top-down purification of Tobacyk's Revised Paranormal Belief Scale. *Personality and Individual Differences*, 29, 131–156.

Lange, R., Thalbourne, M. A., Houran, J., & Storm, L. (2000). The Revised Transliminality Scale: Reliability and validity data from a Rasch top-down purification procedure. *Consciousness and Cognition*. 9, 591–617.

Lawrence, T. R., Roe, C. A., & Williams, C. (1997). Confirming the factor structure of the Paranormal Belief Scale: Big orthogonal seven or oblique five? *Journal of Parapsychology*, 61, 13–31.

Lester, D., Thinschmidt, J., & Trautman, L. (1987). Paranormal belief and Jungian dimensions of personality. *Psychological Reports*, 61, 182.

Macdaid, G. P., McCaulley, M. H., & Kainz, R. I. (1986). *Myers-Briggs Type Indicator atlas of type tables*. Gainesville, FL: Center for Applications of Psychological Types.

Makarec, H. B., & Persinger, M. A. (1989). Temporal lobe signs and Jungian dimensions of personality. *Perceptual and Motor Skills*, 69, 841–842.

Mathews, R. (2004). Parapsychology special: Opposites detract. *New Scientist*, 181, 39–41.

McClenon, J. (1982). A survey of elite scientists: Their attitudes toward ESP and parapsychology. *Journal of Parapsychology*, 46, 127–152.

McClenon, J. (1994). *Wondrous events: Foundations of religious beliefs*. Philadelphia: University of Pennsylvania Press.

McClenon, J. (2002). *Wondrous healing: Shamanism, human evolution, and the origin of religion*. DeKalb, IL: Northern Illinois University Press.

McConnell, R. A., & Clark, T. K. (1991). National Academy of Sciences opinion on parapsychology. *Journal of the American Society for Psychical Research*, 85, 333–365.

Miller, W. R., & C'de Baca, J. (2001). *Quantum changes: When epiphanies and sudden insights transform ordinary lives*. New York: Guilford.

Monaghan, R. R. (1967). Three faces of the true believer: Motivations for attending a fundamentalist church. *Journal for the Scientific Study of Religion*, 6, 236–45.

Mullin, R. B. (1996). *Miracles and the modern religious imagination*. New Haven, CT: Yale University.

Murphy, K., & Lester, D. (1976). A search for correlates of belief in psi. *Psychological Reports*, 38, 82.

Murphy, M. (1992). *The future of the body: Explorations into the future evolution of human nature*. Los Angeles: Jeremy P. Tarcher.

Musella, D. P. (2005). Gallup poll shows that Americans' belief in the paranormal persists. *Skeptical Inquirer*, 29(5), 5.

Myers, D. G. (1992). *The pursuit of happiness*. New York: William Morrow.

Myers, I. B., & McCaulley, H. (1985). *A guide to the development and use of the Myers-Briggs Type Indicator*. Palo Alto, CA: Consulting Psychologists Press.

Myers, I. B., & Myers, P. (1995). *Gifts differing: Understanding personality types*. Palo Alto, CA: Davies-Black Publishing.

Neimark, J. (1998). Crimes of the soul. *Psychology Today*. Retrieved November 2, 2005, from http:// cms.psychologytoday.com/articles/index.php?term=pto-19980301-000043.xml

Palmer, G., & Braud, W. (2002). Exceptional human experiences, disclosure, and a more inclusive view of physical, psychological, and spiritual well-being. *Journal of Transpersonal Psychology*, 34, 29–61.

Palmer, J. (1971). Scoring on ESP tests as a function of belief in ESP. Part I. The sheep-goat effect. *Journal of Parapsychology*, 65, 399–408.

Palmer, J. (1979). A community mail survey of psychic experiences. *Journal of the American Society for Psychical Research*, 73, 221–251.

Pittinger, D. J. (1993). The utility of the Myers-Briggs Type Indicator. *Review of Educational Research*, 63, 467–488.

Prabhavananda, & Isherwood, J. (1981). *How to know God: The yoga aphorisms of Patanjali*. Hollywood, CA: The Vedanta Society of Southern California.

Radin, D. (1989). The tao of psi. In L. A. Henkel & R. E. Berger (Eds.), *Research in Parapsychology 1988* (pp. 157–173). Metuchen, NJ: Scarecrow Press.

Rao, K. R. (1965). The place of psi in the natural order. In J. B. Rhine & Associates (Eds.), *Parapsychology from Duke to FRNM*. Durham, NC: Parapsychology Press.

Rhine, J. B. (1973). *Extra-sensory perception*. Boston: Branden Press. (Original work published 1934)

Rhine, L. E. (1981). *The invisible picture: A study of psychic experiences*. Jefferson, NC: McFarland.

Richards, D. G. (1996). Boundaries in the mind and subjective interpersonal psi. *Journal of Parapsychology*, 60, 227–240.

Ring, K. (1984). *Heading toward omega: In search of the meaning of near-death experiences*. New York: William Morrow.

Roberts, K. A. (1995). *Religion in sociological perspective* (3rd ed.). New York: Wadsworth.

Robinson, L. A., & Carlson-Finnerty, L. (1999). *The complete idiot's guide to being psychic*. New York: Alpha Books.

Roemischer, J. (2004). Women who sleep with their gurus—and why they love it. *What is Enlightenment*, Issue 26. Retrieved October 20, 2005, from http://www.wie.org/i26/women-who-sleep.asp?pf=1.

Ross, C. F. J., Francis, L. J., & Craig, C. L. (2005). Dogmatism, religion, and psychological type. *Pastoral Psychology*, 53, 483–497.

Rosten, L. (1975). *Religions of America: Ferment and faith in an age of crisis*. New York: Simon and Schuster.

Rutter, M., Pickles, A., Murray, R., & Eaves, L. (2001). Testing hypotheses on specific environmental causal effects on behavior. *Psychological Bulletin*, 127, 281–324.

Schmiedler, G. R. (1964). An experiment of precognitive clairvoyance: Part V. Precognition scores related to feelings of success. *Journal of Parapsychology*, 28, 109–125.

Schumaker, J. F. (1990). *Wings of illusion: The origin, nature and future of paranormal belief*. Buffalo, NY: Prometheus Books.

Schumaker, J. F. (1995). *The corruption of reality: A unified theory of religion, hypnosis, and psychopathology.* Amherst, NY. Prometheus Books.

Schumaker, J. F. (2001). *The age of insanity: Modernity and mental health.* Westport, CT: Praeger.

Shapiro, A. K., & Morris, L. A. (1978). The placebo effect in medical and psychological therapies. In S. C. Garfield & A. E. Bergin (Eds.), *Handbook of psychotherapy and behavior change* (pp. 369–410). New York: Wiley.

Siegel, C. (1986). Parapsychological counseling: Six patterns of response to spontaneous psychic experiences [Abstract]. *Research in parapsychology* 1985 (pp. 172–174). Metuchen, NJ: Scarecrow Press.

Smith, M. D. (2003). The psychology of the "psi-conducive" experimenter: Personality, attitudes toward psi, and personal psi experience. *Journal of Parapsychology, 67,* 117–128.

Somit, S., & Peterson, S. A. (1997). *Darwinism, dominance, and democracy.* Westport, CT: Praeger.

Spanos, N. P., & Chaves, J. F. (Eds.) (1989). *Hypnosis: The cognitive-behavioral perspective.* Buffalo, NY: Prometheus Books.

Spilka, B., Hood, R. W., Hunsberger, B., & Gorsuch, R. (2003). *The psychology of religion: An empirical approach* (3rd ed.). New York: Guilford Press.

Stallings, M. C., Hewitt, J. K., Cloninger, C. R., Heath, A. C., & Eaves, L. J. (1996). Genetic and environmental structure of the tridimensional personality questionnaire: Three or four temperament dimensions? *Journal of Personality and Individual Differences, 70,* 127–140.

Stern, J. (2003). *Terror in the name of God.* New York: HarperCollins.

Stokes, D. M. (1997). Spontaneous psi phenomena. In S. Krippner (Ed.), *Advances in parapsychological research 8* (pp. 6–87). Jefferson, NC: McFarland.

Tallis, F. (2002). *Hidden minds: A history of the unconscious.* New York: Arcade Publishing.

Tart, C. T. (1984). Acknowledging and dealing with the fear of psi. *Journal of the American Society for Psychical Research, 78,* 133–143.

Tart, C. T. (1986). Psychics' fears of psychic powers. *Journal of the American Society for Psychical Research, 80,* 279–293.

Tart, C. T. (2002). Parapsychology and transpersonal psychology: "Anomalies" to be explained away or spirit to manifest? *Journal of Parapsychology, 66,* 31–47.

Tart, C. T., & Labore, C. M. (1986). Attitudes toward strongly functioning psi: A preliminary survey. *Journal of the American Society for Psychical Research, 80,* 163–173.

Taylor, S. E., & Brown, J. D. (1988). Illusion and well-being: A social psychological perspective on mental health. *Psychological Bulletin, 103,* 193–210.

Tellegen, A., Lykken, D. T., Bouchard, T. J., Wilcox, K. J., Segal, N. L., & Rich, S. (1988). Personality similarity of twins reared apart and together. *Journal of Personality and Social Psychology, 54,* 1031–1039.

Thalbourne, M. A. (1998). Transliminality: Further correlates and a short measure. *Journal of the American Society for Psychical Research, 92,* 402–419.

Thalbourne, M. A. (in press). The transhumanation hypothesis. *Journal of the American Society for Psychical Research.*

Thalbourne, M. A., & Delin, P. S. (1993). A new instrument for measuring the sheep-goat variable: Its psychometric properties and factor structure. *Journal of the Society for Psychical Research, 59,* 172–186.

Thalbourne, M. A., & Delin, P. S. (1994). A common thread underlying belief in the paranormal, creative personality, mystical experience and psychopathology. *Journal of Parapsychology, 58,* 3–38.

Tobacyk, J., & Milford, G. (1983). Belief in paranormal phenomena: Assessment instrument development and implications for personality functioning. *Journal of Personality and Social Psychology, 44,* 1029–1037.

Tobacyk, J., & Thomas, A. (1997). *How the big orthogonal seven is really the oblique seven. Journal of Parapsychology*, 61, 336–342.

Vyse, S. A. (1997). *Believing in magic: The psychology of superstition*. New York: Oxford University Press.

White, J. (1972). *The highest state of consciousness*. New York: Doubleday.

White, L., Tursky, B., & Schwartz, G. E. (1985) (Eds.). *Placebo theory, research, and mechanisms*. New York: Guilford.

White, R. A. (1993). About applications. *Journal of Religion and Psychical Research*, 16, 2–4.

White, R. A. (1997a). (Ed.) *Exceptional Human Experience: Special Issue. Background Papers II. The EHE Network, 1995–1998: Progress and Possibilities*. New Bern, NC: Exceptional Human Experience Network.

White, R. A. (1997b). Exceptional human experiences: The generic connection. *Exceptional Human Experience: Special Issue*, 15, 26–33.

White, R. A. (1997c). Exceptional human experiences and the experiential paradigm. In C. T. Tart (Ed.), *Body, mind, spirit* (pp. 83–100). Charlottesville, VA: Hampton Roads.

Wilber, K. (2000). *A theory of everything: An integral vision for business, politics, science, and spirituality*. Boston: Shambhala.

Woodward, K. L. (2000). *The book of miracles: The meaning of the miracle stories in Christianity, Judaism, Buddhism, Hinduism, Islam*. New York: Simon & Schuster.

Zusne, L., & Jones, W. H. (1989). *Anomalistic psychology: A study of magical thinking* (2nd ed.). Hillsdale, NJ: Lawrence Erlbaum.

Zweig, C. (2003). *The holy longing: The hidden power of spiritual yearning*. New York: Tarcher/Putnam.

APPENDIX

SUMMARY OF THE MYERS-BRIGGS PERSONALITY MODEL

The Myers-Briggs personality model (Keirsey, 1998; Myers & McCaulley, 1985; Myers & Myers, 1995) was developed for practical use in occupational settings and interpersonal relationships, and has been widely used in those contexts for several decades. The magnitude of the genetic component is similar to that of other personality models (Bouchard & Hur, 1998).

The Myers-Briggs model utilizes 16 personality categories based on the combinations of four factors. The summary below was taken from Keirsey (1998), whose concepts are largely the same as the original Myers-Briggs model but more clearly separate the E/I and S/N factors that conceptually overlap in the original model.

Extraverted/introverted (E/I) indicates whether a person feels energized (E) or drained (I) from being with a group of people;

Sensing/intuitive (S/N) indicates whether a person focuses his or her awareness and attention more on the external, material world and prefers concrete, observable facts (S) or focuses internally on the self and imagination and prefers abstract ideas (N);

Thinking/feeling (T/F) indicates whether a person tends to value rational thinking and self-control (T) or emotional expression (F);

Judging/perceiving (J/P) indicates whether a person prefers setting and achieving goals and having a sense of closure (J) or spontaneously exploring open-ended possibilities and keeping options open (P).

For example, ESTJ is one personality type and the most different type from that is INFP.

The primary difference between the sexes in personality types is on the T/F factor. About two-thirds of males are T (thinking) and about two-thirds of females are F (feeling) for U.S. data (Macdaid, McCaulley, & Kainz, 1986).

The Myers-Briggs model describes all personality types as being valuable in some circumstances. Presumably, the different personality types have been maintained throughout evolution because they had adaptive value or at least did not inhibit reproductive success. This positive approach may be a significant reason for the widespread use of the Myers-Briggs test in occupational settings. Most personality models have factors that measure neuroticism or similar negative traits that imply a superiority/inferiority ranking of people. When organizations are experiencing tensions between departments that tend to have people with different personalities (e.g., between a sales-marketing group and a data processing group), joint meetings that discuss the existence and value of different personalities may be helpful. However, interjecting a dimension of superiority is counterproductive and inappropriate in these situations. The Myers-Briggs model works well in such cases.

The Myers-Briggs model has been subject to criticism because it was developed over 50 years ago by persons without academic credentials and without fully utilizing the methods and theories of academic psychology (e.g., Pittenger, 1993). The fact that the model is based on types (categories) rather than traits (continuous measures) is one of the more tangible technical criticisms.

A review and meta-analysis of a large number of reliability and validity studies concluded that the Myers-Briggs test performed well and was comparable with other personality tests (Harvey, 1996). In addition to convergent, divergent, and predictive validity, the studies included confirmatory factor analyses. To my mind, the best indication of the validity of a psychological test is useful, practical application for real-world behavior. In that regard, the Myers-Briggs model has good standing because it has been widely used in organizational settings for decades. In addition, consistent, meaningful research results, including studies with large, noncollege student samples, provide further evidence for the usefulness of the Myers-Briggs test (Hammer, 1996; Kroeger, Thuesen, & Rutledge, 2002; Macdaid, McCaulley, & Kainz, 1986). The fact that it may not be fully optimal from an academic, mathematical perspective (e.g., types versus traits) does not mean that it lacks useful validity and reliability.

Although the Myer-Briggs test has been the most frequently used general personality test in research on paranormal and related beliefs, it would be useful to carry out research with other personality models. As noted in the conclusion, the optimal strategy for research on the role of personality in paranormal beliefs may be to develop personality tests that directly measure certain personality factors, including mystical, authoritarian, and scientific dispositions. The value of such a personality test may apply beyond paranormal beliefs and may be helpful for understanding many conflicts among people.

Not All Beliefs Treated Equally[*]

By Kristen Campbell
Religion News Service, November 8, 2008

For some Americans, ghosts—along with extraterrestrials, Bigfoot and UFOs—aren't the stuff of seasonal sightings or tabloid teasers. They're real—as real as a resurrected Jesus and a devious Satan are to millions.

In the United States, though, not all supernatural beliefs are accepted equally. How people seem to parse the paranormal depends in part on religious belief and practice, a survey from Baylor University shows.

"If you are a strong Christian who goes to church a lot, you will likely whole-heartedly endorse the Christian supernatural beliefs but you will stay away from the psychics, the Bigfoots," explained Baylor sociology professor Carson Mencken.

"But if you are someone who reports pretty high levels of conventional Christian belief but doesn't practise that faith, doesn't go to church very often, if at all, you're also very likely to hold other types of paranormal or supernatural beliefs. You're going to believe in a little bit of everything."

Denomination and an individual's self-identification as spiritual versus religious can play a role in such thinking as well, according to Baylor's research.

"Catholics actually score pretty high on paranormal beliefs, which if you look at Catholic theology, that kind of makes sense," said Mencken, citing the role of apparitions, such as those of the Virgin Mary in places like Lourdes or Fatima.

"Most religion, traditionally, approaches faith or approaches God and the divine as something which is a realm that is greater than what we understand or can deal with and is filled with surprises," said the Rev. Christopher J. Viscardi, chairman of the division of philosophy and theology at the Jesuit Spring Hill College in Mobile, Ala. "There is a broad range, including the paranormal, including the supernatural."

Evangelicals, meanwhile, are much more likely to be in line with conventional supernatural thought and much less likely to believe in traditional paranormal ideas, said Mencken, who noted that conservative Christian congregations tend to be at odds with secular culture and "keep a pretty tight rein on their members."

Overall, though, "paranormal beliefs are out there," Mencken said.

Close to 50 per cent of the population believes that places can be haunted, he said, while 20 per cent of the population believes in the ability of psychics.

According to Christine Wicker, author of *Not in Kansas Anymore: A Curious Tale of How Magic is Transforming America*, such beliefs have gone mainstream.

"My reading of history, American history and world history, is that it's a phenomenon of human nature, especially when there is anxiety and fear, or when there's a lack of spiritual depth, a phenomenon to look for things that will either respond to that anxiety or fill that emptiness," Viscardi said.

Wicker, meanwhile, posited that one factor behind the "resurgence of magical thought" is "widespread disappointment with organized religion."

She cited Daniel Maguire, an ethics professor at Marquette University, who said belief in the great faiths is collapsing.

"People are looking for something to replace them, much as they did in the first century as Christianity began to rout paganism. Now it seems to be the other way around," she wrote.

Cecil Taylor, dean of the School of Christian Studies at the Southern Baptist-affiliated University of Mobile, put it this way: "In a post-Christian age, when the Christian consensus is removed, all sorts of paganism rushes in to take its place. And I view most of these things as a renaissance of paganism."

Some of it, though, may simply be a matter of semantics.

While Mencken can't say for sure, he would hypothesize that it's more likely the case that where one person perceives a guardian angel (55 per cent of Americans say they've been protected by one), another may see a UFO (24 per cent say UFOs are probably spaceships from other worlds and 27 per cent are undecided).

But, Mencken said: "If you say you believe in UFOs and you've been abducted by a UFO, you'll get a different response than if you tell people you believe in the resurrection of the body of Christ. And that's the drawing line there, is to what extent society has defined a set of beliefs as OK/conventional versus defined them as kind of out there or kooky or unconventional."

"It's a function of a variety of social processes," he said, "where one set of beliefs has become acceptable and normative over time."

Taylor identified another determining factor: Scripture.

"Evangelicals would look at the Bible to validate experience," he said. "We check the Bible to see: Is this within the realm of possibility? Is this validated by Scripture?"

2

"If You're Here, Please Give Us a Sign":
Ghosts and Haunted Houses

Editor's Introduction

As mentioned in Sharon Begley's article from the previous chapter, neuroscientists have learned that emotions influence how the human brain processes stimuli. That old adage, in other words, is true: People "see what they want to see," or perceive the world in ways that are consistent with their hopes, fears, and expectations. If someone who is deathly afraid of sharks goes for a late-night swim, for instance, he or she might mistake a piece of driftwood for a dorsal fin. This misperception would have less to do with bad vision or poor lighting than the brain succumbing to fear, distorting the image, and literally causing the person to "see" a shark's fin.

Skeptics speak of such misperceptions when attempting to debunk stories of ghost sightings and haunted houses, the types of paranormal phenomena explored in this chapter. Fear, nonbelievers insist, is one of the major reasons that people misinterpret sights and sounds. Under the right circumstances, the hoot of an owl becomes a ghostly howl, while the creaky sound of a house settling into its foundation stirs fantasies of phantoms lurking in the hallway. Of course, fear isn't the only emotion capable of causing someone to think they've seen or heard a ghost. Profound guilt or sadness over a loved one's death might also be to blame, skeptics contend.

Unmoved by these and other "rational explanations," some insist they have had encounters with visitors from the afterlife. In the first piece, "I Ghosthunter," writer Aiesha D. Little joins the ranks of Cincinnati Area Paranormal Existence Research (CAPER), a nonprofit group that investigates people's claims their houses are haunted.

"Supernatural Cleaning Methods," the subsequent selection, finds writer Joyce Wadler running down a list of ways to rid one's home of unwanted spirits. While some "experts" recommend using special herbs and oils, others advocate simply speaking to ghosts and telling them to take their haunting elsewhere. Wadler approaches the subject matter with some degree of bemused skepticism, but she also cites a 2007 Harris poll that suggests 41 percent of adults believe ghosts are real.

In "I Ain't Afraid of No Ghost," the next article, writer and self-professed "big chicken" Eric Nuzum spends a night in suite 870 of the Omni Shoreham Hotel, located in Washington, D.C. The room is thought to be haunted by the ghost of a housekeeper who died there years ago, and while Nuzum reports hearing a few unexplained noises, he emerges from his spectral stakeout shaken but unconvinced. He returns several days later with the DC Metro Area Ghost Watchers, a CAPER-like organization that is unable to turn up any solid evidence of paranormal activity.

In "America's Haunted Army," the following entry in this chapter, Jacqueline M. Hames discusses several U.S. military bases that are especially prone to ghost sightings. At Fort Monroe, Virginia, such notable figures as Abraham Lincoln and Ulysses S. Grant are said to roam the premises, Civil War battle plans in hand.

The final piece, "Ghost Gadgets: Fallible Fun for the Whole Family," serves as a shoppers' guide for amateur ghost hunters, as author Helen A. S. Popkin provides information on where to purchase various types of cameras, thermometers, sound recorders, and other high-tech devices.

I, Ghosthunter[*]

By Aiesha D. Little
Cincinnati Magazine, October 2008

"If you're here, please give us a sign. We aren't here to hurt you. We only want to help you . . . if you want help."

The room is silent. Light from the street lamp throws eerie shadows across the walls as we sit in the dark, waiting for an answer. Michele Hale and Noah Carlisle, members of Cincinnati Area Paranormal Existence Research (CAPER), are sitting on the floor directly across from one another. Hale sighs. Carlisle crosses his legs at the ankles, his fingers locked behind his head, and leans against a couch cushion. There is a tiny infrared camera on top of the television in the corner of the room. This would be a casual setting, this child's bedroom, if the express purpose for being here wasn't to commune with the dead.

"If you'd like to communicate with us, feel free to tap us on the shoulder or arm," Hale says to the air around her. "Or if you get close to the little gray box in the middle of the floor, we'll know you're here."

The green light on the little gray box—an EMF meter, which detects changes in the electromagnetic field—doesn't change colors. If it had, it would be a sign that a spirit is trying to "manifest," that is, gather enough energy from the room to visibly appear. At least that's the theory. In talking to CAPER members about what they do, I quickly come to understand that just about everything is only a theory.

My mind races. *What if something does respond? What will that "something" be? What if it attacks us? What am I doing here!?* It seems like an eternity before my inner monologue comes to an abrupt halt. I feel something touching my back. Poking, really. Fingers. Fingers? I sit up straight and suck in my breath. I don't turn around because I know there's no one there.

I have a love/hate relationship with all TV shows and movies that are meant to unnerve or flat-out frighten. I have a healthy dose of misplaced paranoia, but I find films like *The Shining*, *The Orphanage*, *Dark Water*, and *The Devil's Backbone*—

more psychological horror than actual gore—irresistible. As a child, I remember being mildly creeped out by the music from *Unsolved Mysteries*. In my teens, it was *The X Files* that scared the bejeesus out of me. These days, I can't stop watching shows like *Ghosthunters International, Supernatural,* and *Paranormal State*. Bravo's *100 Scariest Movie Moments*? Love it. But no matter how enthralled I am with what's happening on screen, my finger always hovers over the "off" button on my remote, ready to teleport me back to reality if things get too intense.

For people like CAPER cofounders Joy Naylor and Michele Hale, there is no such button. They've been into the paranormal for years, fueled by their own experiences with the supernatural. After meeting through another ghost hunting group in 2004, the two middle-aged women decided to start their own nonprofit organization with the goal of investigating haunted houses. They created a Web site and set up a phone line so home and business owners could reach them, and set about trying to determine whether those properties are really frequented by spirits. Four years later, they run 12 to 15 investigations a year, each one consisting of multiple visits to the site in question. Once Naylor and Hale determine that the person in need of help isn't a) experiencing things that can be explained away (for instance, a light that flickers on and off could be an electrical problem) or b) mentally unhinged, they agree to help. Depending on what happens while the team is on site—more unexplained activity means a longer investigation—each visit could run from three to six hours. That's a lot of work for a hobby.

"Most people are like, 'Oh, that's creepy.' And we're like, 'Oh, that's creepy—and I want to know exactly why it happened,'" Matt Hoskins, the group's tech specialist, says of ghostly encounters. "The hope is that one day we'll be able to scientifically explain why these things happen."

I contacted the group in mid-July, hoping to tag along on an investigation or two. I don't know if too much TV has made me susceptible to believing in ghosts, but participating in a real, live ghost hunt would put my curiosity about the paranormal to the ultimate test. Honestly, despite my paranoia, I like to be scared sometimes. Just a little bit.

On a humid August evening a couple of weeks later, Naylor, Hale, and I are bringing up the rear in a caravan on its way to a house in Hamilton. This is CAPER's third trip to the home, where the owner has been experiencing strange activity since he started major renovations back in March. He and his wife swear they've heard children's laughter coming from the northern edge of their property. They also claim to have seen shadowy figures lurking in the corners of their bedroom, one dressed inexplicably like a farmer in a plaid shirt, overalls, and a straw hat. They've heard a tapping sound on their walls and on occasion have gotten the distinct feeling of someone climbing into bed with them. Deeply creepy, right? I thought so, too, but for CAPER, investigating is about applying logic at every turn.

"We work on debunking," Naylor says behind the wheel of her blue pick-up. The truck is packed with the gear the group will use for the night: infrared cameras, a monitor, electromagnetic field (EMF) meters. "It's usually something that can be explained," she adds. "We want to help people."

Sarah McEvoy, an investigator-in-training, and Hale are in the back seat nodding in agreement. They're both wearing gray T-shirts that say "Cincinnati Area Paranormal Existence Research" across the back. The words curve upward and then down, outlining the shape of a cartoon ghost. It's Boo, the group's "mascot."

A little later, Naylor discloses how all of the CAPER members feel. "Ninety-eight percent of the time, it's pretty boring," she says with a shrug. "It's that two percent that gets us going. Sometimes it's hard to stay calm when something happens. You don't want to scare the client, but it's exciting. This particular house has got me questioning things."

"Questioning things" is Naylor's way of saying there are things happening that she can't readily explain. The group tells its clients to think about what they're experiencing as logically as possible. They encourage clients to keep a journal of their experiences, noting each one in precise detail. "Do your best to find a rational explanation for what is happening," says the CAPER pamphlet. "Many events, originally thought to be the creations of ghosts, end up with perfectly reasonable explanations."

When we pull into the long driveway of the house we're investigating, it doesn't look out of the ordinary. It's a plain two-story frame house sitting on nearly eight acres of land. There's one house with a large pond to the left of it that sits even farther back from the street; another large house occupies the lot directly across the street. The rest appears to be woods. A U.S. land sale document on file with the county auditor's office tells the investigators that the property dates back to the early 1800s, when the area was nothing more than farmland. In fact, it's believed that the original owner, possibly one of the county's largest landowners, used it to graze cattle. I'm not scared yet, but in the movies, isn't the quiet country home on acres of land always haunted?

The owners (who wish to remain anonymous) greet the CAPER members, show them around again, then leave. Noah Carlisle, another investigator-in-training, tapes down the infrared cameras throughout the house; Naylor and Hale help Hoskins set up the equipment outside while McEvoy and Marie Peterson, the case manager, head inside. They're establishing room temperatures and getting EMF readings so that the base team—the two investigators charged with monitoring activity inside the house from the backyard—will know if anything changes while the rest of the group is indoors.

The investigators then break into teams of two. When the first team is ready to go inside, the last bit of sunlight is fading fast. It's going to be a long night.

The air is stiflingly hot, but a trickle of cold sweat runs down the center of my back. I want to walk out. Stand up, say good-bye to the ghost hunters—and anything else in the room—and leave. I close my eyes, holding my breath.

I'm not being poked I'm not being poked I'm not being poked I'm not being poked I'm not being poked.

I open my eyes and breathe again. The rush of oxygen to my brain makes me dizzy. The sensation on my back stops as quickly as it started and I immediately begin trying to rationalize away what just happened. Maybe it was my muscles relaxing? I had been moving furniture earlier in the day and now, after hours of rest, my muscles were expanding again. Right? It's hard to be irrational when you're hanging out with a group of individuals who are doing everything in their power to debunk the strange phenomena they're encountering. Especially with EMF meters and infrared cameras.

Yeah, that's it. It was my muscles.

We leave the room and I don't speak again until I'm outside. The cool night air is soothing and eases my mind a bit. The monitor glows in the darkness as Hale serves up chocolate chip and raspberry crunch bars, a homemade treat for her fellow investigators. It's a welcomed break. I convince myself that nothing touched me, and don't mention the incident for now. After a short bathroom break another team—McEvoy and Laura Carney, another trainee—moseys inside with no effect. After I alert them that the basement door, which was not open on my first trip inside the house, is now slightly ajar, we spend 15 minutes in complete darkness down there. McEvoy wonders aloud if there are any mice in the basement.

"I'm a bit of a chicken," she says, laughing. The irony of a paranormal investigator being afraid of rodents isn't lost on any of us.

In the living room, McEvoy tries to entice the would-be entities by letting her hair down because the owner told CAPER that something purportedly pulled his cousin's hair while she slept. No response. After 45 minutes she and Carney give up.

It's closing in on midnight and nearly three hours of hanging out in dark rooms, talking to thin air, has made me sleepy. Peterson and Naylor are the last team up tonight, and I tag along. Everything is nice and uneventful until we reach the master bedroom on the first floor. Sitting on the bed with a headlamp strapped to her head, Peterson, who claims to be extremely sensitive to EMF waves, starts asking questions.

"What's your name?"

Nothing.

"What year is it?"

Nothing.

"Do you have any children? What are their—"

That's when it happens. In a flash, the EMF meter jumps from green to yellow to orange!

"Did that just . . . ?" I can't finish my sentence. To finish my sentence would be to verbally admit to what I'd just seen. There's a lump in my throat.

Peterson continues asking questions. When she mentions the current owner's name, the EMF meter spikes again. Naylor, who's standing at the foot of the bed, perks up. "I just saw a shadow go in front of the window."

With great difficulty, I manage to suppress the urge to run. Naylor radios to base and asks Carlisle and Hoskins to come around to the front of the house to "look for deer." Maybe one walked past the window, she says. At the exact time that the EMF meter went off? *Sure.*

A few moments later, Carlisle radios back. No deer. Naylor crosses her arms and then puts her hands on her hips. Peterson is smiling, her eyes the size of quarters.

In a small windowless room at the Sharonville branch of the Public Library of Cincinnati and Hamilton County, CAPER members set up their equipment and prepare to go over their EVP (electronic voice phenomena) readings from the Hamilton investigation. EVPs are recordings of static noise that some investigators believe can capture the voices of the dead. Founded by EVP pioneer Sarah Estep in 1982, the American Association of Electronic Voice Phenomena breaks such recordings into three classes: a Class A recording can be heard clearly without headphones; a Class B can be heard with headphones, though listeners might disagree about what's being said; and Class C, the least conclusive, requires headphones and amplification. It's a few days after the hunt and everyone has had time to examine their own individual recordings, which requires hours of listening to static or, worse, chatty investigators. Everyone naturally has their fingers crossed for a Class A.

Hoskins has isolated three recorded incidents that could possibly indicate paranormal activity. Incident No. 1 happens in the kitchen while everyone except Carlisle is outside. Through the buzz of dead air, a creaking sound comes from the tiny speakers plugged into Hale's laptop computer. Everyone gives quizzical looks and she plays the sound again.

"Did someone move a chair?" Naylor asks.

"It sounds like a zipper," McEvoy says.

We all turn to Carlisle. "No, I wasn't playing with my zipper!" he says, exasperated. Everyone laughs.

They agree that the sound is Carlisle taping down the camera in the family room during set-up and we move on to Incident No. 2, which takes place in the kitchen while no one is in the house. It sounds like the water is running. Peterson says she came in to get water but it was 20 minutes before the recorded incident. Everyone gets closer as Hale plays the recording again.

"Could it be the refrigerator running ice?" Peterson asks.

Hoskins is skeptical of the ice theory. "When you listen to it with headphones, you can very clearly hear water running," he says. "I won't argue it any further, but I just thought it sounded kind of cool."

"I'm gonna have to say no," Naylor pipes up. "I'm gonna have to say it was the refrigerator."

Again, everyone agrees and it's on to Incident No. 3, a series of weird noises picked up on the recorder in the living room, which are quickly dismissed as Michele Hale entering the house to use the bathroom shortly before the first group of investigators set up inside.

"Anyone else have anything?" Naylor asks.

When McEvoy plays what she picked up, I get goose bumps. It's from the master bedroom, where Naylor, Peterson, and I were sitting when the EMF meter spiked into the orange. On the tape, Naylor is talking to Peterson. Suddenly a male voice bursts from the speakers.

It's my house. . . .

The lump in my throat is back. Once again, everyone leans in as close as possible, straining to hear the recording as Hale plays it over and over again. One by one, they each listen to it with headphones.

"You can definitely tell it's male." McEvoy says, her hands clamped over her ears. "It sounds like, 'It's my house.'"

"It isn't a Class A, but it's definitely a Class B," Hoskins says.

Everyone remains calm except Peterson, who's beside herself with giddiness. She slaps her hands together, congratulating herself for asking the questions about the kids. "I'm excited!" she whispers to me, bursting into giggles. "Aren't you excited?"

I'm not sure "excited" is the right word. "Freaked out" is more like it. The EVP coincides with the shadow Naylor saw in front of the window, which coincides with the EMF spike. It's all a little too much coincidence for me to not mention being poked in the back earlier that same evening.

I sigh heavily. "OK, I wasn't sure if I should say anything about this, but, well, it sounds silly—"

"You're hanging out with people who believe in ghosts," Hoskins says. "How silly can it be?"

"Well, I think some . . . *thing* touched me when Michele, Noah, and I were in the upstairs bedroom. It felt like two fingers. Touching my back."

Everyone looks at me inquisitively. Peterson grins. She wants me to be excited, but I just feel uncomfortable.

"Well, that's what we call a 'personal experience,'" Hale says in a very soothing tone. She's good at validating the concerns of others. "We can't prove it."

"It's much more impressive when you can say, 'Listen to this EVP, watch this video, and look at this picture,'" Hoskins says. "We can't say, 'This place is haunted because I feel like I got touched.'"

Which means all I'm left with is my paranoia about what may or may not have happened to me in that upstairs bedroom. I came into this wanting to test my fear of the unknown, and yes, to get a thrill. Now? Not so much. I didn't think that a ghost would reach out and literally touch me, but I find myself reevaluating my attraction to the creepy. In a couple of days, Naylor will tell the homeowner about our findings; I get the impression he doesn't really care. The point of investigating isn't necessarily to "get rid" of whatever's there. (How would you do that, anyway? I mean, unless you think *Ghostbusters* is real.) For CAPER, it's about helping clients "obtain peace of mind." "Politely ask any ghost to leave you, your family, and your home in peace," is another gem from the CAPER pamphlet. "Sometimes that is all that is necessary to bring the undesired paranormal activity to a halt!"

Peace of mind is putting this experience behind me post-haste, but I have a feeling it won't be that easy. Scary movies somehow seem just a bit scarier. Any unexplained noise has me thinking the ghostly farmer from the house in Hamilton is lurking just over my shoulder. Why did I think this was going to be interesting? Clearly, I'm not cut out for paranormal investigations. But I hope that the group from CAPER eventually finds what they're searching for. As long as it doesn't come looking for me, I'll be just fine.

Supernatural Cleaning Methods[*]

By Joyce Wadler
The New York Times, October 30, 2008

The chill of autumn has arrived, and it's time to make your home cozy and snug. Replace those broken shingles, seal the window frames, start the water boiling and throw in some scented nutmegy things, or a rabbit if you've been disappointed in love.

But what to do about that ghost that has been making such a racket, scaring the guests and making it impossible to sleep? Sure, you can kid yourself that it's a squirrel on the roof or a rattling pipe or a fog that comes up from time to time. (On Narragansett Bay? Sure, pal, that's credible.) But eventually, when guests and family members become truly frightened, something must be done.

Such was the case with Kathleen Whitehurst, an artist in Arnaudville, La., who scoured the countryside to salvage materials with which to build her home and guest house, the picturesque l'Esprit des Chenes. Visitors complained of creaking stairs, sounds in the night. Some fled in terror. Finally, Ms. Whitehurst called in a specialist.

"She came all the way from Arkansas," Ms. Whitehurst said in a telephone conversation. "She sat on my couch, and within 30 minutes she says, 'Yes, you do have a ghost in your house.' She goes into a trance, she came back to her body, and said, 'He's a Baptist minister, wearing a white robe, and he's roaming the house.'"

The reason for this problem, incredible as it may seem, was recycling. Ms. Whitehurst had found three Gothic windows in a junk pile at a demolished church, and the ghost had come along with them. The specialist did what is often recommended in these cases, asking Ms. Whitehurst and two friends to make a circle with her around the lost spirit, and tell it, sympathetically but firmly, that it was time to move along.

"All of a sudden, you could feel the electrical energy moving—it was so intense that all the hair on the back of my neck and hands was standing up," Ms. Whitehurst said. "And when she said the final words"—Go, go!—"we got that zapped feeling. And he went up, and he's never been back since."

You don't believe in ghosts? Then you are either tragically out of step with the times or possibly a slovenly spiritual housekeeper looking for an excuse to avoid tidying up. A recent Google Internet search for getting rid of ghosts yielded nearly two million hits. By comparison, a search for cleaning rain gutters yielded 191,000.

In a Harris poll last year of 2,000 adults, 41 percent said that they believed in ghosts. Although the National Association of Realtors says that it is not the legal obligation of a real estate agent to tell a prospective buyer about alleged haunting, many agents, like Diane Ragan of Keller Williams Realty in New Orleans, feel that if they hear of something that may distress a buyer, they have the duty to pass it on.

"Just last week I got a call from a past client who was calling for a friend who'd leased a place and wasn't happy because it was haunted," she said. "He wanted his deposit back. I told him the best thing his friend could do was plead his case."

CAN THESE STUBBORN SPIRITUAL STAINBUCKETS NEVER BE REMOVED?

Before attempting to cleanse a household of ghostlike sounds and scents, the homeowner must first determine whether such sounds and scents are actually of the other world. Happily, there is no shortage of instruction manuals on the subject. One, an e-book called "Is My House Haunted? A Practical Guide," was written by Bonnie Vent, the medium who founded the San Diego Paranormal Research Project. Those who dismiss the paranormal may wish to check out her Web site, sdparanormal.com, and read the transcript of her conversation with the comic George Carlin, which occurred after his death. (Few were as skeptical of the afterlife as he.)

Ms. Vent's guide, which costs $7.97, contains a paranormal activity log in which to record such things as electrical devices going on and off, unexplained noises and cold and hot spots. It lists common misconceptions, including the notion that "paying someone to spread lotions and potion all over the house" will make the spirits go away.

"What does work? Communication!!!" writes Ms. Vent, who is one of those people who is paid; her cleansing services cost $125 an hour. "This does not necessarily mean that they will leave, but you should be able to work out a livable situation."

She also offered a word of warning: "There are people who will take advantage of others by using holy water, burning sage and spreading salt around the perimeter of the house. Spirit people are people—these things have no effect in the long term. You really have to get to the root cause."

ALSO, AS HIS INTIMATES KNEW, UNCLE FRED NEVER FLUSHED

With ghosts so plentiful, it is reassuring to note that most haunting sites, even those with logos dripping blood, take their responsibilities seriously, reminding homeowners concerned about paranormal activity that they should first seek more mundane reasons for strange activity. The tools may include tape recorders, video equipment and infrared photography.

Jason Hawes and Grant Wilson, the stars of the "Ghost Hunters" program on the Sci Fi Channel, have been helped by their expertise as plumbers.

"We had one case, somebody's dead uncle Fred was a plumber and they thought that he was giving them a sign because every morning at 2 A.M. their toilet would flush," Mr. Hawes said. "Come to find out, they would go to bed at about 11 at night and they had a leaky flapper in their toilet. Eventually, after two or three hours, the toilet would drain down enough that the fill valve would kick on, so it would sound like the toilet would flush."

Any other examples?

"We dealt with a case where a guy was actually seeing apparitions in his house," Mr. Hawes said. "It was happening only to him, nobody else was having problems. We found out he was on two medications, including an older one his new doctor didn't know about, and they were making him see things."

Mr. Wilson added: "Another reason we knew it wasn't paranormal was the things he was seeing made no sense. There were grotesque things: flowers wandering across the room, faces turning inside out. Paranormal activity isn't like that. Seeing flowers turning inside out indicates medical or drug problems, not a person without a body walking around your home."

FOR MINOR HAUNTINGS, DO IT YOURSELF

Many hauntings are so slight that the homeowners may feel equipped to handle the problem themselves. This was the experience of Leslie Castay Burkey, a one-time Broadway actress, and her husband, Bryan Burkey, a commercial photographer, who bought an old New Orleans home from the estate of a deceased couple a few years ago. The lady of the house, Ms. Burkey had heard, was "tough, cold and devoted to the house above everything."

Problems began with the restoration of the former master bedroom. Ms. Burkey spoke of bad odors and lights going on and off. Her husband recalled "a definite presence."

"When we started ripping stuff out, it was like the house was saying what are you doing, and would get really persnickety," Mr. Burkey said. "When we started to take up the carpet and put down a wood floor, all sorts of things went crazy."

Incredible! How could anyone have anything against a wood floor?

"What we heard was she had a white carpet in that bedroom that she was very much in love with," he said.

White carpet—the decorating equivalent of falling in love with a married man, an enterprise doomed to failure and heartbreak.

The couple's solution, which proved effective, was to cleanse the home with sage they bought at Marie Laveau's House of Voodoo in the French Quarter.

"The salesperson suggested you burn it and carry it through the house, especially through the doors and windows, and make your own incantations telling the spirits they were free to leave," Ms. Burkey said. "A friend of mine in Connecticut got the idea she should do it in the shape of a pentagram, but that was too black magic for me."

THE SHOCK OF A MAO JACKET MIGHT HAVE KILLED HIM

Guy Clark is an interior designer who restores and sells old properties. Spirits do not trouble him. His current home is a stone house in Bullville, N.Y., which was once owned by the makeup artist Kevyn Aucoin, who died in 2002. As he was lying in bed shortly after he took possession, Mr. Clark had a vision.

"I opened my eyes for a second and someone passed over my head through the window in a blue cabana suit, blue shorts and a shirt, like what people wore in the '60s," Mr. Clark said. "You can't make these things up. I didn't know the man, but I think it was probably Kevyn. He was airlifted out of his front yard and passed away from a brain tumor."

How did Mr. Clark deal with the spirit?

"I said: 'O.K., this is my house. If you need anything, I'm here, but you don't live here anymore, move on.'"

However contradictory the message, the ghost apparently understood, for Mr. Clark never again had a problem.

ENOUGH! NOW, LET A HARDENED REALTOR SET THE RECORD STRAIGHT

"I've had two properties that fall into that category," said Judy Moore, a broker with 23 years of experience who works with ReMax Landmark Realtor in Lexington, Mass.

"The first one was the former parish house where the priest stayed, and it came up at the closing. The home's owner said, 'I just want you to know that there is a priest who haunts this house,' and went on to tell the story that she grew up in the house, and one time her sister had makeup on top of the dresser and he swiped them off. I was horrified. The buyer could have just said, 'That's it, I couldn't live there'—but he was a creative type; he was fine with it.

"The other time was really freaky. This is a house that never did sell. It was built in the 1600s, nobody was living there. The first thing that happened when I walked in, my electronic tape stopped working, and I had the funny feeling that there were spirits in the house, and I don't imagine these sorts of things. I was staging it, there were things that would move, but the worst thing—the really freaky thing—I was putting some dried flowers on the end of this old table and I saw something on the table that was bright red but watery. It looked like blood, but it was too thin, everything on the table was dry. That was the creepiest thing that has ever happened to me in this business."

SUDDENLY, A REPORTER IS AWARE OF HER PSYCHIC GIFTS

It should be noted that when the New England real estate agent mentioned above was reached on her cellphone, it was about 6 in the evening.

"So, are you driving down the Mass Turnpike in pitch-blackness?" she was asked in an attempt to set the mood.

"Oh my God—how did you know?" Ms. Moore said.

OCTOBER AFTER OCTOBER, REPORTERS TRUDGE TO HIS DOOR

Joe Nickell, the ghost hunter for the magazine *Skeptical Inquirer*, has a doctorate in English literature from the University of Kentucky and was once a professional magician. He has, he says, been investigating stories of ghosts for decades.

Ever catch one?

"I have not."

One common reason that people believe they see ghosts is that they are experiencing lifelike dreams, Mr. Nickell said. This is why such visions often occur at bedtime. Also, many people enjoy the notion of being haunted.

"Unfortunately, most people are looking to have their beliefs confirmed, so they bring in ghost hunter types who believe they can get an electromagnetic field meter from RadioShack," he said. "They go into a place and the meter starts going off, whereupon they think they are detecting a ghost. First of all, there is no evidence ghosts exist. Second, there is no evidence that if ghosts exist, they are electromagnetic. These people have no knowledge of microwave towers or faulty wiring in the house or other sources of electromagnetism. It's just too silly for words and it oughtn't be featured on major television shows. It's an embarrassment."

Give us an example of someone who was tricked.

"A young mother called me once very concerned about the possibility of ghosts," he said. "She was getting strange photographs—a sort of curvy stripe, very white and bright. They have since begun calling those ectoplasmic strands. I looked at her camera. Her wrist strap was dangling. The flash was reflecting back the wrist strap, and it produced a great number of these."

FRANKLY, THE BELIEVERS TELL A MUCH BETTER STORY

Brenda is a social worker with a master's degree from the University of Pittsburgh. She lives with her husband, two young children and four ghosts (two adults, two children) in a 99-year-old house in Altoona, Pa. (After receiving death threats when she went public about her home, she prefers that only her first name be used.)

The odd happenings in her household began when her daughter, Anna, 6, was a toddler. Anna sometimes laughed and giggled when nobody was around. "I figured it was an imaginary playmate," she said. "I was not really thinking paranormal."

About this time the name Katie would just pop into her head for no particular reason, she added. "I was potty training Anna, she was sitting with her book. I stepped away for five minutes and I hear her fighting with somebody, saying, 'It's mine, it's mine!' I turned to go back, the book was levitating above her head like it was being held up by somebody a little bit taller."

"That book was huge, a big Christmas flip book," she continued. "She said, 'Mommy, mommy, I'm sharing! I'm sharing with Katie!' Then it clicked. I'm trying to remain calm because we're potty training and anything can throw that off. I said, 'Anna, who's Katie?' She said just a little girl who lives here."

A month or so later, on a Saturday morning when Brenda was doing some dishes, she heard giggling and footsteps around her and saw the girl ghost.

"She had blond hair parted down the middle, the first piece tucked behind her ear like Marcia Brady," Brenda said. "She was neat as a pin, in a little calico print dress that had a pinafore, off-white, all starched, kind of like Laura Ingalls. She had some kind of stockings, boots—that's how long I had to notice what this girl had on. And a Peter Pan collar."

Brenda said she had been doing the dishes, but could she have fallen asleep? There is this dream state an expert mentioned.

"No, no, absolutely not," Brenda said. "The skeptics will pull out every little piddling thing they can. There is no gas leak, we are not sipping gas methane, our furnace is cleaned faithfully."

Brenda now feels it is time for her spirits to be on their way. She has dutifully told them to go to the light. She has tried burning white candles for purity. She even had the people from "Ghost Hunters" in, appearing on their first season. How about sage? Did she try sage?

"I actually have a friend who is a Reiki master who said she would do a house cleansing," Brenda said. "I would rather have somebody come in to guide them."

EVER NOTICE A SPIRIT NEVER WASHES A DISH OR TAKES OUT THE GARBAGE?

The meticulous housekeeper has by now noted that as with so much else, the world of the paranormal is specialized. Ghost hunters often call in others to rid a home of ghosts: so-called house cleaners, perhaps, or, in some cases, demonologists.

Patty A. Wilson, 43, the author with Mark Nesbitt of "The Big Book of Pennsylvania Ghost Stories" and a founder of the Ghost Research Foundation, is both. Ms. Wilson, who says she has been sensitive to the paranormal since childhood, kept quiet about her gifts for much of her life.

"I didn't want to be the crazy lady in the caftan," she said.

The time for homeowners to call for professional intervention, said Ms. Wilson, who does not charge for her services and is suspicious of those who do, is when they feel frightened or threatened.

One such case she had, she said, involved a Penn State student who had written an article about Ms. Wilson for the college newspaper. The girl called her about five or six years ago in an agitated state, saying that the house she was renting with several other girls was haunted by an "obese, overweight black shadow figure," she said.

"He was kind of aggressive, stepping out into the hallways in front of them so they would have to walk through him," Ms. Wilson added. "He physically touched two of the girls. One was sitting on her bed in her underwear. She jumped up screaming, so he let her alone. He also seemed to be around them when they were unclothed."

Talk about your unnatural acts! Are black shadow ghosts considered to be particularly dangerous?

"Some are very aggressive," Ms. Wilson said.

She advised the young woman to do some research on the house, and it was discovered that it had once been owned by two spinsters. They had taken in a neighbor who died of obesity at age 23.

"I thought that kind of fit the bill," Ms. Wilson said.

The house never did get cleaned. The college student's mother moved her out of the house, and that was that.

Does Ms. Wilson recall her name?

"Marianne," she said, adding that she was unable to remember her last name.

Where might she be now?

"She joined Barnum & Bailey, in publicity."

"Ghost stories are not neat and clean," she added. "Everything doesn't always get pigeonholed properly. They're real stories about real people."

After intense corporeal, electronic and audio investigation, Marianne, whose last name is Ways and who did local publicity for the circus as a college intern, is tracked down. Now 28, she works as an associate booker at the Comix comedy club in Lower Manhattan.

She tells a story that confirms much of Ms. Wilson's. Her roommate did see the shadow of an obese man, and he did pop up as the roommate was coming out of the shower.

Ms. Ways never saw the dark shadows herself, but she sometimes heard weird noises and footsteps, and felt as if someone had broken into the house when no one was there, and it frightened her. One day when she was feeling especially anxious, she asked the person who lived in the adjoining apartment if anything weird had ever happened there.

"You mean, like, is it haunted?" the woman said.

Did Ms. Ways ever try to get rid of the ghosts?

"No," she said. "I just left."

DO NOT BE FOOLED BY CHEAP IMITATIONS

The concerned homeowner will know by now that there is dispute about how best to rid the home of spirits. Some tools that the uninitiated might feel would be effective are not. The Ouija board, for example, is considered by many to be a magnet for spirits, the equivalent of spreading a trail of crumbs if you are plagued by ants.

Megan Hoolihan, 28, manager of Marie Laveau's House of Voodoo, has studied the occult for 18 years and seems to take her calling seriously. She says many people in the South believe sage has cleansing properties.

"I recommend making a mixture of powdered sage, holy water and cedar oil, some water from a church or that has been blessed by someone."

What if you're an atheist?

There may be something to this occult stuff, because suddenly the reporter feels a deep chill.

"Cedar oil has cleansing properties," Ms. Hoolihan continued, ignoring the question. "You can also use lavender oil or violet oil. The smells are soothing; it's a comfort."

A bunch of sage costs about $9 at Marie Laveau's. Couldn't you use the stuff from the supermarket instead?

"You can use it; I don't recommend it. It's the same family, but not the same plant. The sage we carry is white sage or gray sage, and is grown organically."

I Ain't Afraid of No Ghost[*]

By Eric Nuzum
Washingtonian, November 2007

You'd think that given an opportunity to stay in a presidential suite, I'd want to take advantage of the amenities. Not this time. I was unshaven, unshowered, and wearing the same clothes I'd slept in—if you can call lying wide awake all night and shivering with fear "sleeping." It was 6:15 AM. I just wanted to go home.

"I hope you enjoyed your stay at the Omni Shoreham," the front-desk clerk said. "Would you like me to print a copy of your—oh, my God, you were in 870!"

Suite 870 at the Omni Shoreham has a couple of things that make it stand out among the thousands of hotel rooms in Washington. First, it has a view—the penthouse suite's terrace offers a breathtaking view of Rock Creek Park, with the Arlington skyline, Air Force Memorial, and Washington Monument peeking above the trees in the distance.

Even more unusual, suite 870 has a ghost.

The clerk's wide eyes went from her computer screen to my face. "Did anything . . . ?" She trailed off, hoping I'd fill in details.

She probably wanted me to tell her about the unexplained noises in the three-bedroom suite or about lights turning off on their own. Maybe she hoped I would tell her I had spent the last hour before dawn on the terrace, hedging my bets that whatever was inside wouldn't step out for fresh air.

All I could think of to say was the truth: "I'm not entirely sure what just happened up there."

"She usually won't let me inside," the clerk said, referring, I assumed, to the resident ghost. "Almost every time I have to go up there, I can't get the key to work. Some folks here won't even go inside."

It isn't uncommon for Omni Shoreham employees to share stories about room 870, also known as the Ghost Suite. They tell tales of faint voices in empty rooms, cold breezes, and televisions and lights turning on and off on their own.

These stories are why I'd forced myself to spend the night there.

A BIT OF BACKGROUND

There are two things to know when reading this story: (1) I am an experienced journalist. (2) I am a big chicken.

The journalist part is relevant because, professionally, I'm a skeptic. I need to have things proven to me. If there was any bias on my part about the Ghost Suite, it was my hope that this assignment would be the most boring, uneventful evening of my life. That's where the chicken part comes in: I am terrified of the idea of ghosts.

The word "terrified" doesn't do this fear justice. Spooky movies, ghost stories, and supposedly haunted houses are verboten around me. I am to "scared of ghosts" what LeBron James is to "competent at athletics."

Whenever my wife has to deal with this fear, she asks: "If you ever saw a ghost, why wouldn't you simply ask it what it wants?"

That's a rational notion, but my fear is irrational, which means there's no place for reasoned thinking and action.

Still, I wanted to confront my fear—and to determine, more for myself than for anyone else, if any of this was real.

A BIT MORE BACKGROUND

During the Shoreham's early years, three people died unexpectedly in the suite, at the time part of an apartment occupied by one of the hotel's owners, Henry Doherty.

One night at 4 AM, Juliette Brown, the family's live-in housekeeper, dropped dead while placing a call to the hotel's front desk. Doherty's daughter and wife also died mysteriously in the apartment. Doherty moved out shortly after the deaths. The apartment remained abandoned for almost 50 years.

Despite its vacancy, something was going on in suite 870. There were claims of doors slamming shut and furniture and housekeeping carts moving on their own. Guests in adjoining rooms would call the front desk in the middle of the night to complain about late-night vacuuming and loud noises coming from the suite. Many of these events seemed to happen around 4 AM, the time of Juliette's death. It's her ghost that's thought to haunt the suite.

In the 1980s, when Omni Hotels bought the Shoreham, it renovated the suite, hoping to use it as an attraction. That didn't play out as planned—maybe because most people didn't want to pay $2,000 a night to stay in a haunted suite.

The Ghost Suite is now the only room in the hotel that the public can't reserve. While it's sometimes used to house dignitaries and guests of the hotel, there's just a simple plaque on the front door identifying it as THE GHOST SUITE.

Even the boss has had a run-in with Juliette. When he was working at another Omni property, current manager Todd Scartozzi stayed in the Ghost Suite with his family while on vacation in Washington. One night his daughter started yelling for him from the other bedroom.

"She cried out, 'Daddy, there's someone in the closet!'" he says. Scartozzi assured his daughter that there was no one in the closet, but she insisted he stay and watch.

The walk-in closets in the Ghost Suite are equipped with motion detectors so that the light will turn on when someone enters. "We were sitting there—the closet door is closed," he says. "I wasn't moving; she wasn't moving. And the light came on."

The light stayed on for a minute, then shut off. A few minutes later, it turned on again, then shut off. The daughter spent the rest of the night in Scartozzi's bed. The next morning he called the hotel's engineers to check the closet lights, but they couldn't find anything wrong with them.

"Sure, it's a little scary up there," Scartozzi says. "But who doesn't like to be scared?"

"I don't," I said.

"Well, then, you're in for quite a night, aren't you?"

GOOD NIGHT

While the National Association of Certified Valuation Analysts was wrapping up its annual convention downstairs, I was settling into suite 870 for the evening.

Despite my anxiety, I fell asleep in about an hour (thank you, Lunesta), although I was still fully dressed, wouldn't get under the covers or take off my glasses, and had turned on every light in the suite. Even with the sleeping pill, I was fully awake 90 minutes later.

I'm not sure what woke me. I was so worked up about being in the suite alone at night that I was hyper-aware of everything. Every noise, no matter how subtle— the click of the thermostat, screams and giggles drifting up from the swimming pool below, water running through the building's plumbing—sounded like a thunderous announcement that some phantom had arrived. All were false alarms— until the creaking started.

It was about 1:45 when I heard the first long, loud *crrrrreeeeaaaaak*, as if someone were opening a noisy door or gingerly walking across an old hardwood floor.

I sat straight up in bed and shouted, "Good golly!"

To be honest, what I said wasn't exactly "Good golly" but a string of colorful metaphors best left to the imagination.

I ran out into the suite's main room. I saw nothing. The noise happened again at 2:15, then 2:50—a total of five times, each with no clue as to who or what was causing it.

I spent most of my time in between creaks wondering what reason Juliette could have had haunting suite 870. You'd think that if it was so important for her to make the living know she was still among us, she'd take the elevator down to the lobby, walk up to a few certified valuation analysts and say, "Hey, I'm a ghost!"

It doesn't make any sense for her to spend her afterlife hanging around in the least occupied room in the building. Plus, what a dull existence—sitting around, doing whatever ghosts do, waiting for a phantom alarm clock to go off every morning at 4 o'clock so you can turn on a TV or run a vacuum cleaner or make a creaking sound.

You'd think this lack of a reasonable case for spiritual presence would make me feel better. It didn't. As 4 o'clock ticked closer, I let go of the notion of getting any sleep and braced myself for whatever might happen.

Four o'clock came and—nothing.

Just as I started to settle down, another creaking noise came from the dining room. Thus my trip out to the terrace to watch the sky turn from black to purple to red to orange and finally to blue.

On one last round through the suite before leaving, I noticed that the lights in the dining room were off. I hadn't turned them off and figured they must have been on a timer, because I hadn't noticed they were off when I'd walked past earlier. I gave the lamp switch a flick, expecting the lights to stay dead.

They came on.

I was out the door and in the elevator in less than four seconds.

CALLING THE PROFESSIONALS

Thinking back to that night, I could come up with nonghost explanations for every one of the few things I'd experienced. The evening felt far from conclusive.

There's no shortage of ghost lore in our area, so I decided to try to experience some other spooks and specters. I roamed the first floor of the Hay-Adams hotel looking for the spirit of a woman who killed herself there, snuck around the National Building Museum in search of General Montgomery Meigs's ghost, and loitered outside some of the spots favored by Lincoln assassination conspirator Mary Surratt, who is said to haunt no fewer than four locations. But these trips yielded nothing, not even an uncanny stiff breeze.

I contacted a group called DC Metro Area Ghost Watchers, or DCMAG. It's led by Al Tyas, a genial, somewhat shy fellow from Falls Church. In addition to investigating alleged hauntings, Tyas collects ghosts. How does one go about "collecting" spirits?

"I buy haunted items on eBay," he says. "But you can't really do it much anymore. It seems that whenever somebody has some junk they can't get rid of, they just claim it's haunted and sell it online."

DCMAG includes retired Navy occupational therapist John Warfield and Lew McClenahan, a law-enforcement officer and firearms instructor. The volunteer group has conducted more than 100 investigations at homes, businesses, museums, and other locations around the area. For its analysis, the DCMAG crew uses an assortment of electronic gadgets that reads like the back half of a Radio Shack catalog: electromagnetic field meters, motion detectors, biorhythm monitors, infrared thermometers.

DCMAG doesn't charge for its investigations and views its work as a community service. The group has been contacted by people who are terrified by something grabbing them while they've slept, making noises, or moving and hiding objects. It has received calls concerning the ghost of a pet rabbit and a haunted mattress. One man claimed ghosts were haunting his wife's vagina. The DCMAG guys declined to investigate that one.

HAVE YOURSELF A SPOOKY LITTLE CHRISTMAS

Al and his crew had an investigation scheduled at the Christmas Attic—a year-round holiday ornament and knickknack store on South Union Street in Old Town Alexandria—and invited me to come along. The Christmas Attic has spent the better part of the past two centuries as a warehouse, at some point picking up a ghost, nicknamed Jack by store employees.

Jack has been known to rearrange displays and throw items that aren't in hue with his decorating taste. He has been seen standing in stairwells and looking out windows. Jack is also, as Al says, "a bit of a perv."

It seems Jack likes to touch the ladies. He strokes their hair or gives them gentle touches. Several female patrons and employees have complained that they feel someone standing close or looking over their shoulder. Employees often leave the store as a group so as not to run afoul of Jack's fingers.

The crew showed up in matching outfits, each with a DCMAG logo embroidered on his chest. While others were scouting the attic and storage areas, Al set up a spirit bell. According to Al, the spirit bell was handmade in Prague to attract ghosts, who then ring it as a way to communicate.

I was dispatched to shadow John as he took electromagnetic-field measurements. The meter rarely registers above 0.2 unless you place it against a wall with old electric wiring, where it may shoot up a few points. Unless you find a ghost, which spikes the meter into the teens to twenties.

John explained that electromagnetic-field meters are used to detect electromagnetic leaks, which can be dangerous. "Anything above a 2.0 is considered a class-B carcinogen," John said. "Wow, look at this," he said, waving the meter at the exposed fluorescent bulb above my head. "6.4, 12.6, 7.3. Huh."

Ghosts versus cancer—it didn't seem like a great tradeoff.

Once Al and the store manager joined us upstairs, I started to hear a faint noise. I didn't say anything at first, but then I heard it a second time a few minutes later.

"What's that noise?" I asked.

"It sounds like some kind of jingling," John said.

All of us looked at one another wide-eyed and whispered, "The spirit bell."

The sound we'd heard wasn't the soft, subtle ring you would imagine from some vaporlike apparition; the spirit bell was ringing as if someone had grabbed it and shaken it hard. We started eliminating other possibilities. Ambient noise from the air conditioner? No. Anyone else in the building? No. Some other bell or ornament in the store? No.

I could feel the color draining from my face as I waited to get felt up by Jack the pervert ghost.

"Eric, now don't freak out," Al said. "Just stay calm."

"I am calm," I said in a tone of voice that demonstrated I wasn't even in the same Zip Code as calm.

Al decided that since Jack was so active, it was time for some EVP recordings. Paranormal researchers believe that ghost voices can be captured on audio recordings even when they aren't heard by the human ear. The process is called EVP, or electronic voice phenomenon.

Al set up his tiny Olympus digital recorder and started asking questions.

"We call you Jack, but what is your real name?" Pause. "Was that you who rang the spirit bell?" Pause. "Is there anything you'd like to communicate with us tonight?" And so on.

To authenticate the results, the DCMAG guys play back the recordings right away, so clients know that any results aren't doctored afterwards. Al did a few recording sessions without picking up much of anything. Then, on the third try, we heard what sounded like a voice whispering a phrase two times.

After several listens, it sounded to me like someone saying "too tart" twice.

After a few more listens, Al and the others argued that Jack had said, "Can't talk, can't talk."

Can't talk? Did Jack have guests over? If I had to go through a sleepless night before coming here, the least he could do was something more than ring a little bell.

"Well, if he won't be talking, I guess we're done here," Al said, packing up his gear.

RETURN TO THE GHOST SUITE

"Who put down the toilet seat?" John asked as he ran into the Ghost Suite's main room. "Did anyone put the toilet seat down?"

"I did," I said.

"Why did you do that?" John asked.

"Well, I was kinda trained to do that," I said.

I don't blame John for being so excited. I had brought the DCMAG crew along for a second night in the Ghost Suite. John and the other guys were trying to draw out the housekeeper-turned-ghost by messing up the suite—spreading magazines on tables, putting towels on the floor, pulling back the bed sheets, lifting the toilet seats.

"We always put those up when we're dealing with female ghosts," he said. "It makes 'em nuts."

Immediately upon entering the Ghost Suite, Al said he could feel a presence in the dining room. He said he could also tell that she—Al sensed it was female—was shy and wasn't all that interested in being documented.

After EMF readings, photographs, biofeedback monitoring, motion detection, and visual inspections, we hadn't found anything. Al tried three different EVP recordings, capturing only one unexplained noise, which sounded like someone saying the word "go" and also like a shoe brushing against a table leg.

After two hours, Al seemed frustrated and felt it best to call it a night.

SCARED OF WHAT?

After the DCMAG crew left, my wife and some friends came over to visit this place I'd been talking about for the past few weeks. When they walked in, they were on pins and needles, expecting a vacuum-wielding apparition to come floating around the corner. I showed them the closet with the light that had turned itself on, the table lamps that had turned themselves off, and the corner of the dining room that Juliette favored.

Later that night I would have nightmares about meters, mysterious voices, and creaking floors, but as I showed them around, I was surprisingly composed.

If anything, my ghostly adventures left me more frustrated than anything else. I had wanted some clarity and closure. Instead, I ended up confused as to what I'm actually scared of.

By any level of journalistic scrutiny, nothing happened in the Ghost Suite. Besides the spirit bell's ringing, nothing happened in the Christmas Attic, either. That doesn't mean I don't have trouble letting go of the idea that something happened in these places. People are often haunted by possibilities, rarely by facts,

As I got ready to leave the Ghost Suite, I wasn't thinking about my fear. I was thinking about Juliette. During the past several weeks, I'd felt strangely connected to her.

If the whole ghost thing is baloney, then Juliette is unfortunate enough to be remembered not for her life but for the fact that she died under unusual circumstances. If her spirit is roaming suite 870, that means she probably was cleaning up after some rich people until the very moment she died, just to end up spending the next 75 years trapped in a string of encounters with strangers who aren't understanding whatever she's trying to tell them.

As I walked out, I turned toward the dining room. "Bye, Juliette," I said. "For both of our sakes, I really hope you aren't here."

America's Haunted Army[*]

By Jacqueline M. Hames
Soldiers Magazine, October 2008

Ghost stories have long fascinated the living. Some seek the thrills, others are searching for answers about the afterlife. People can find both the exhilarating and the enlightening on several Army posts.

Many installations have reported strange occurrences and ghostly activity, ranging from prank-playing poltergeists to terrifying visions. Some bases are haunted by long-forgotten Soldiers, some by civilians, and some are troubled by the unidentifiable paranormal.

NEW JERSEY DEVILS

Fort Dix, N.J., has its fair share of paranormal activity. In addition to sightings of the infamous Jersey Devil by Soldiers during World War II and again in the 1990s, Walson Hospital is said to be haunted.

Walson is one of the most active spots on the installation. Accounts of strange light orbs, unexplained drops in temperature and sightings of ghostly visitors abound. The former basement morgue and psychiatric ward are usually where the eerie stories originate.

Dameyon Beamon, a member of the 305th Medical Group at Walson from 1995 to 1997, said he encountered strange happenings there.

"I worked nights at the primary care clinic," Beamon said. "On many occasions when we would do security checks, the front door that used to be the pharmacy entrance would be unlocked, even if only an hour ago it was locked tight."

One night, Beamon and a co-worker went to the ninth floor, the former psychiatric ward, and noticed an open window in one of the rooms.

"At the precise moment Clark closed the window, the light in the room flickered, turned off and then came back on," he said.

Beamon added that he also came across a supernatural phenomenon while exploring the old morgue. While looking at pictures from events that had taken place in the morgue, he heard "the sound of a grown man crying."

HUACHUCA HAUNTINGS

Several of the more gruesome tales of ghosts come from Fort Huachuca, Ariz., where many apparitions are linked to tragic, untimely deaths. Hangman's Warehouse is reportedly haunted by two Soldiers who were hung in 1942: Pvt. James Rowe and Staff Sgt. Jerry Sykes, who both committed murder within two weeks of each other, according to Cornelius C. Smith's book, *Fort Huachuca: The Story of a Frontier Post.*

Quarters Number 9, Carleton House, has the most documented hauntings on post. Constructed in 1880, it was built as an eight-bed hospital and has since been used as officers' quarters, mess, schoolhouse and chapel. When Carleton House was a hospital, a woman dubbed "Charlotte" died in childbirth there. It is reported that her ghost still wanders the halls, searching for her child. One family who lived in the house had a young daughter who had seen Charlotte, but referred to her as "Barbie." The girl often spoke about Barbie coming to visit, reading her stories or carrying on conversations. A rocking chair in the girl's room was said to move by itself, presumably because Charlotte was sitting in it.

Recently, during a renovation of the building, contractors repeatedly reported finding doors that had been locked at night and open in the morning. Tools that had been put away were found scattered.

VIRGINIA VISIONS

Virginia's Fort Monroe is frequented by many long-dead historical figures, in addition to several Soldier and civilian ghosts. Most of the sightings occur within the Casemate—a moat encircled structure built in the 1800s. The homes within the fortress have been visited by several apparitions, including that of a small child dressed in turn-of-the-century clothing, who can be heard laughing and playing with toys.

Quarters 1, the oldest and most ornate residential structure on post, is said to be haunted by the Marquis de Lafayette, Abraham Lincoln and Ulysses S. Grant. These figures are usually seen reviewing papers that are likely connected to troop movements and battles of the Civil War. Confederate President Jefferson Davis, who had been incarcerated at Monroe, returns to the base and wanders freely atop the ramparts of his former prison.

Tales of strange noises and inanimate objects that move by themselves still exist today. One construction worker swears he heard footsteps and a slamming door while working alone on the 8th floor of the Chamberlin building earlier this year.

Project consultant Larry Knott confirmed that no other workers were on the top floor at that time.

"We're pretty much convinced it was Esmerelda," Knott said, referring to the ghost that is said to reside in the building. Legend has it that Esmerelda's fisherman-father was lost at sea in the 1920s, and she is still trying to find a vantage point that would give her a glimpse of his return.

PRAIRIE PHANTOMS

Several of the most notorious tales of spirits come from Kansas, at Fort Riley and Fort Leavenworth. Leavenworth is home to one of the most famous haunts in Kansas: the Rookery.

Built in 1832, the Rookery is the oldest building on post and currently serving as family quarters. Reports of apparitions of a young girl, an elderly man with bushy hair, and of several older women have been made.

Fort Riley also boasts several buildings troubled by phantoms. McGill Hall, built in 1889 to house Cavalry troops and the oldest building on base, is frequented by a tall figure in a dark overcoat.

During the Cavalry's stay in McGill, residents had a unit photograph taken after formation one day. The Soldiers replaced their rifles in a circular rack after the session, barrels upright and leaning in together. One Soldier did not properly unload his rifle, and as he inserted it into the rack it discharged—killing another Soldier.

In 1997, Spc. Bradley Ehrhardt returned to Fort Riley from deployment and was transferred to the 977th Military Police Company. His barracks were in McGill Hall.

One evening, Ehrhardt returned to McGill before his roommate and was alone in his room. At around 1 A.M., he awoke to discover a figure looming over the foot of his bed.

The apparition was more than six feet tall, and wore a dark overcoat. Ehrhardt described the figure as being like a shadow, though he couldn't see through him. Eventually, Ehrhardt gathered his courage and confronted the phantom, saying he would appreciate it if it just left him alone and "went somewhere." The specter vanished and he never saw it again, but other members of Ehrhardt's unit claim to have seen and heard the Soldier walking around the barracks.

From kindly nannies to brutal criminals, each installation has its own unique, ghostly past. Though some people seek the stories purely for the joy of frightening themselves, others—the ones who have experienced the paranormal—find these tales to be quite real.

Ghost Gadgets[*]

Fallible Fun for the Whole Family

By Helen A. S. Popkin
MSNBC.com, October 31, 2008

If there's one thing for which Steve Gonsalves has irrefutable proof, it's that people want to believe. As technology manager for The Atlantic Paranormal Society (TAPS) on the SciFi Channel documentary-style series, "Ghost Hunters," he's regularly approached by fans bearing that universally understood object of paranormal evidence—The Wonky Photograph.

You know what I'm talking about. Back in the dark ages before digital cameras, every family had a drawer full of "paranormal evidence": The baby with flash-induced "halo," little Timmy with his chronic case of demonic red-eye, bright orbs floating across the family Christmas portrait, that blurry thumb-like apparition you certainly didn't see in the room when you took the picture—and the most frightening of all—the freaky double exposure wherein you and your evil twin or maybe your very soul exist within the same frame.

Still, some people are so anxious to believe, they don't much appreciate it when Gonsalves points out the flaws in their substantiation. "I tell them, you can think it's a vortex, but I can clearly see the strands of fiber from your camera strap," Gonsalves said in a telephone interview. "They get mad—sometimes even angry. They definitely want to have a paranormal picture."

And hey, who can blame them? On the surface, it seems somewhat plausible that the miracle of technology, which provides so much for the living, might also offer some kind of connection to the dead. Heck, even crusty ol' inventor Thomas Edison wanted to build a telephone to the afterlife. (Imagine the roaming charges!)

It's no wonder people consult Gonsalves. He did, after all, leave a profession in law enforcement for a successful TV career ghost hunting with cameras, tape recorders, thermometers and even more complicated gizmo thingies.

If Edison thought about it, and a regular guy like Gonsalves, who by his own admission, has no exceptional technical prowess, it's only natural loads of folks would follow suit.

While a 2005 Gallup Poll revealed that a third of Americans (admitted that they) believe in an afterlife, there are no official numbers to gauge how well the ghost-busting equipment biz fares in revenue. However, a Google search for "ghost hunting gear" reveals plenty of merchants looking to make a dime on wannabe spirit searchers.

You'll find dedicated e-tailers such as GHOST MART (best e-tailer name EVER), as well as plenty of piecemeal offerings on Amazon. Such supernatural sellers hawk anything from basic gewgaws, your run-of-the-mill voice-activated microcassette recorders for instance, to pricey DVR surveillance set-ups for the most serious (or perhaps gullible) ghost hunters.

Meanwhile, Gonsalves' "Ghost Hunters" Gear Guide videos on SciFi.com grab more viewers than even free show excerpts and behind-the-scenes footage. In these brief Webisodes, Gonsalves runs through the basic arsenal of paranormal detection. Here's an abbreviated list with approximate prices (and a few skeptical comments) added:

EMF detector ($25–$400) Detects electro-magnet field fluctuations, which theoretically occur when energy-based spirits are hanging around. Of course, there are lots of other reasons for EMF fluctuations—from exposed wires to the Northern Lights.

Digital video camera (with infrared illuminator) ($35–$3,000) Captures images in dark rooms not visible to the human eye, such as moving objects, forming mists and floating orbs.

Digital thermometer ($70–$200) Reads ambient and surface temperatures, which helps detect free floating cold and hot spots/fluctuations which, as everybody knows, could be caused by a ghostly presence.

Portable tape recorder ($12–$700) Captures EVPs (electronic voice phenomena), such as spirits speaking from the other side which weren't audible during the recording.

White noise generator ($50–$1,400) Creates pure static which is believed to work as a catalyst for EVP recordings by providing noise through which spirits can verbalize. It also filters out background noise for clearer recordings.

Ion generator (TAPS had its custom made.) Allegedly charges the atmosphere, theoretically providing spirits with bonus energy through which they can manifest.

Wireless audio kit with software (Around $800) Transmits audio into a computer where it can be amplified to detect EVP recordings. Baby monitors work, too.

DVR system (with infrared camera, DVR and monitor) ($6,000-$7,000) Digital, time-stamped real-time paranormal surveillance with a whole lot of storage. Runs all night without the need to change tapes.

Thermal imaging camera ($6,000–$50,000) You know, like "Predator" uses. Reveals and records cold and hot spot fluctuations—and you know what that means. *Gho-izzy in the hizzy*!

Polygraph machine ($1,000–$10,000) B.S. detectors that signal when the person reporting the haunting is lying. Oh, wait! Ghost hunters never use those.

Isn't this what ya call pseudo science?

Explaining these items on the Gear Guide, Gonsalves, who says he has worked with Ph.D.-toting scientists to understand the equipment, certainly sounds like he knows what he's talking about—at least to me (who can't do math in my head) and probably to that one third of believing Americans and their silent compatriots unwilling to admit that they also suspect unseen forces—at least to Mr. Gallup.

But not so much to skeptics such as Alison Smith, founder of SAPS (Skeptical Analysis of the Paranormal Society—get it, it's a play on TAPS of "Ghost Hunters" fame), and a research assistant for the James Randi Educational Foundation. She politely pointed out during an extended e-mail interview that all the gadgetry in the world isn't so great at providing proof beyond this one.

"If you think about the application of ghost gear for a long enough period of time (as, I am sad to say, I have) you will eventually come to completely logical reasons why a ghost hunter may use the tools that they do," Smith said.

"Unfortunately, this doesn't mean that the ghost hunters who use them came to the same conclusion for the same reasons—in fact, from the times I've spoken with them, it appears they haven't thought it out very far at all." Smith added, "That could be a misconception on my part, of course."

When presented with the skeptic's side of the argument, Gonsalves . . . well . . . he agreed. "There is no direct link between science and paranormal investigation," he said. "There is no direct link between the paranormal and anything. Science is the only way right now to try and give any validity to paranormal investigators."

Using gadgetry provides better evidence than something along the lines of, "I saw this thing, I have no way to prove it, but that's my story," Gonsalves said.

Makes sense to me—the woman who prefers Macs to PCs because I don't read instructions.

Alas, it does not make sense to Smith, who also pointed out that misreading fallible gadgets is as much a blow to the so-called scientific process of ghost hunting as the gadgets themselves. "An odd EMF reading is never the *same* odd EMF reading," she wrote. "And it's not backed up by anything but a group of (normally) grown men with goatees claiming loudly that they feel a spooky sensation."

Oh you think that's snotty? I dug up this article by Benjamin Radford of the Committee for Skeptical Inquiry and he sure ain't looking to fuel anyone's flight of fancy. In "Reality Check: Ghost Hunters and Ghost Detectors," Radford writes:

> "The uncomfortable reality that ghost hunters carefully avoid, 'the elephant in the tiny, haunted room,' is of course that no one has ever shown that any of this equipment actually detects ghosts. The supposed links between ghosts and electromagnetic fields, low temperatures, radiation, odd photographic images, and so on are based on nothing more than guesses, unproven theories, and wild conjecture."

Dang, buzz kill.

Not that we should, or at least will, pay any attention to what Radford writes. As history reveals, no amount of naysayers can come between Americans and seemingly cool gadgets. Skeptics didn't stop people from buying salad shooters or the first version of the Apple iPhone.

As for Smith, she doesn't have so much of a problem with paranormal documentary-style shows such as "Ghost Hunters," and understands the need for drama and spookiness. "I see nothing wrong with investigating the concept of ghosts either," she wrote, adding that she too goes on ghost investigations and tests out the same equipment used on shows for her own organization, SAPS.

"The only issue I have with any of it is the presentation of the evidence, and that's why having these things on television is a bit of a problem," Smith said. "If the point is spookiness and drama and entertainment, just say so. If it's about real research, perhaps television isn't the best place for it."

Yeah, but where's the fun in that?

3

Are We Alone?
UFOs and Extraterrestrials

Editor's Introduction

One need not be a crackpot conspiracy theorist to acknowledge the possible existence of extraterrestrial life. Given the billions of planets in the universe, it's highly unlikely that Earth, our tiny blue marble, is the only one capable of spawning and sustaining life. This raises the question: If aliens do exist, why haven't we seen them? Wouldn't any extraterrestrial civilization even slightly more advanced than ours have already figured out a way to traverse great stretches of space and make contact with us parochial earthlings?

According to some, aliens have visited the Earth—a theory explored by the selections in this chapter. Believers cite as evidence the countless photographs, home movies, and first-person accounts of UFOs, or unidentified flying objects, that have emerged over the last century. Perhaps the most famous UFO-related event occurred in July 1947, when *something* fell from the sky and landed in the desert near Roswell, New Mexico. At first, the U.S. Air Force issued a statement saying it had recovered from the crash site a "flying disc." The military later retracted that story, insisting the mysterious object had been nothing more than a weather balloon. It wasn't until the 1970s that people began questioning this explanation, and many now speculate that what military officials actually recovered was an extraterrestrial spacecraft, perhaps even the bodies of its alien crew.

In the 1990s, the military admitted that the weather-balloon story had been a cover—not for finding a downed UFO, but rather the remnants of Project Mogul, a top-secret spy program that involved using high-altitude balloons to listen for sound waves produced by Soviet nuclear tests. While this explanation has satisfied some, others maintain it's just the latest in a series of government lies.

The United States hardly has a monopoly on UFO sightings, and people in all corners of the globe have reported seeing strange disc-, saucer-, and cigar-shaped aircraft. Some witnesses even claim to have been abducted by aliens and subjected to invasive examinations. These and other tales are difficult to prove, and for every credible UFO believer, such as former U.S. astronaut Edgar Mitchell, the sixth man to walk on the moon, there are dozens, if not hundreds, of average Joes— folks whose blurry photographs and shaky camcorder footage have yet to confirm what the laws of probability predict: We are not alone.

In "Eyes on the Sky: Some UFOs Are Real, Whether Government Admits It or Not," Harry Willnus casts his lot with those who believe the Earth has been visited. He accuses the U.S. government of attempting to "debunk, make fun of, and discredit" those who come forward with UFO evidence.

In the next selection, "Is There Anybody Out There?" Darren Devine examines the wave of UFO sightings reported in Wales. "The Searcher," the next article, shifts the focus to Texas, where writer Skip Hollandsworth visits the home of Ken

Cherry, a former Wall Street investment banker who now heads the state's branch of the Mutual UFO Network (MUFON), the largest group of UFO investigators in the United States.

In "The Phoenix Lights Explained (Again)," UFO debunker Tony Ortega criticizes NBC's *Dateline* for inaccurately reporting on a pair of March 1997 Arizona sightings—events he says stemmed from two sets of airplanes, one flying in vee formation, the other dropping flares.

Eyes on the Sky[*]

Some UFOs Are Real, Whether Government Admits It or Not

By Harry Willnus
Ann Arbor News, August 10, 2008

The most recent UFO survey of Americans found that about 42 million of us have seen something in the sky that we couldn't identity. UFO researchers generally believe that about 90 percent of sightings can be attributed to natural causes such as meteorites, planets, birds, aircraft, satellites, or the moon shining through clouds. However, the remaining 10 percent of reports cannot be so easily explained away. The most intriguing often include close-encounter events (within 500 feet) with multiple witnesses who often are highly respected members of the community, such as police officers and pilots.

By UFOs I mean "flying saucers" or alien crafts.

The modern wave of UFO sightings and reports began with the July 1947 Roswell, N.M., event. More than 60 years later the phenomenon is alive and well with at least 100 sightings per day around the world. An O'Hare Airport sighting in November 2006 was also given wide press coverage after a story by Jon Hilkevitch was published in the Chicago Tribune. A disc was seen in broad daylight hovering over gate C-17, just below the 1,900-foot cloud ceiling. After some moments the saucer left, leaving a doughnut hole in the clouds for several moments and allowing airport personnel to see the blue sky through the hole that had been created.

The most recent series of UFO events took place in Stephenville, Texas, between December and March. Some of the activity was not far from President Bush's ranch in Crawford, Texas. The most dramatic sighting occurred on Jan. 9. A huge craft, some estimates put it at a mile long and a half mile wide, was reported by dozens of witnesses. The Mutual UFO Network (MUFON) has recently obtained radar readings via the FOIA that show something strange and

---

unexplained was seen on that night in the skies over Texas and that a craft traveled at 1,900 mph without breaking the sound barrier.

Let's not forget a couple of the most well-known UFO cases of all time, one that occurred right in our own backyard, and which remains a true classic UFO event. In 1966 cases in the Dexter and Hillsdale areas created quite a ruckus, and news of these sightings was reported in every major newspaper in the country. The Air Force sent its "front man" for UFO investigations (Project Blue Book), Dr. Allen Hynek, to investigate.

Hynek carried out an investigation and a press conference was held in Detroit. He admitted he didn't know for sure what people had seen in Dexter and Hillsdale but that swamp gas was a possible culprit. This, unfortunately, was what the press picked up on. Hynek became the laughingstock of the nation for a time as the press and citizens just didn't buy that explanation. The Air Force finally got out of the UFO business (publicly anyway) and Project Blue Book was terminated in 1969. The business of publicly investigating UFO cases today is undertaken by individuals and groups such as MUFON.

Hynek eventually became one of the few scientists of the day who saw the need to take the UFO topic seriously and that it needed further study. He eventually came to believe that some UFOs were interplanetary crafts. In 1973, after leaving government work, Hynek founded the Center for UFO Studies (CUFOS). I call Hynek the "grandfather of ufology" and it was an honor for me to work with him as an investigator for a time. Hynek died in 1986.

Many scientists agree that the chances for life existing someplace else in the universe are a slam dunk.

There's a nearby galaxy that's a billion years older than our home, the Milky Way. And if life somewhere else was just a bit more evolved than us, they easily could be thousands of years ahead of us technologically.

Having had a recent online discussion with several skeptics/debunkers, I noted two arguments they continually pointed to. First, they argued, the distances are simply too far and it would take too long for trips between star systems. Second, they seemed to think that UFO sightings are nothing but faraway, hazy lights in the sky. Both arguments demonstrate a lack of knowledge about the phenomena, and narrow thinking.

Some scientists believe that space itself can be bent, warped, or folded and that "worm holes" may allow for shorter space travel times. Time slows as one approaches light speed.

Many UFO reports are not just "hazy lights" in the sky. Some sightings are day-light events. Skeptics/debunkers overlook the landing trace cases on record which show remarkable evidence that a physical object was present. Former NASA astronaut and moonwalker Dr. Edgar Mitchell has just recently claimed that aliens exist and are visiting Earth.

And what of our own military and the UFO phenomenon? Richard Dolan's exhaustive work, "UFOs and the National Security State: Chronology of a Cover-up 1941–1973," is a true eye-opener regarding UFO activity that our military has encountered.

There is not sufficient space herein to answer the $64 question, "why is the government hiding the truth?" Since 1947 there has been a government policy to debunk, make fun of, and discredit people who have had a UFO encounter. However, there appears to be some movement in bringing to light what many of us know to be true: We are not alone in the universe and we are being visited now. Keep your eyes on the sky.

Is There Anybody Out There?[*]

By Darren Devine
Western Mail (Cardiff, U.K.), June 26, 2008

Since the dawn of time, we have looked to the heavens and pondered: "Is there anybody out there?" This basic curiosity has helped fuel the space race, as well as spawning the sci-fi genre and countless conspiracy theories about government attempts to cover up UFO sightings and alien visits, among them the so-called "Roswell incident".

It was here, in New Mexico in July 1947, that US officials found what was initially said to be debris from a "flying disc", but was later described as the remnants of a fallen weather balloon.

The incident later took on the dimensions of a science fiction epic when, in 1978, ufologist Stanton T Friedman interviewed Major Jesse Marcel, who had been involved with the original recovery of the debris.

Marcel told Friedman the military had covered up the recovery of an alien spacecraft.

Two years later, American magazine *National Enquirer* also interviewed Marcel, putting Roswell before a much larger audience, and over the years the story has snowballed into the most famous UFO incident in history.

As new witnesses and reports emerged over the years, the US General Accounting Office launched an inquiry and directed the Office of the Secretary of the Air Force to conduct an internal investigation.

Reports from that investigation concluded the debris from the crash had probably come from a high altitude balloon used in a secret US programme to monitor Soviet nuclear tests.

So-called "alien bodies" apparently recovered were said to be dummies that had been used in military tests.

The explanations were naturally given short shrift by the UFO community, who claimed witnesses had been intimidated and evidence tampered with to keep the truth about Roswell under wraps.

Now, as reports suggest South Wales Police officers in a helicopter gave chase to a "flying-saucer shaped" aircraft after it zoomed over the region last week, has Wales just experienced its own Roswell?

An anonymous source suggested the incident took place while the helicopter was at 500ft and waiting to land at the Ministry of Defence's St Athan base in the Vale of Glamorgan.

The crew claimed to have seen the UFO speeding towards them from below and swerved to avoid it.

They apparently suggested afterwards that a collision and certain death would have resulted had they not taken swift evasive action.

The object, invisible through night-vision goggles but clearly discernible to the naked eye, was later said to have headed off in the direction of the Bristol Channel.

South Wales Police later suggested the skies are cluttered with a whole range of objects that could provide a rational explanation for the helicopter crew's experience.

But within the UFO community, last week's incident is certain to be viewed as yet further evidence that official accounts are inadequate.

Cardiff-based UFO hunters Chris and Jane McCarthy claim to have made numerous sightings of unearthly objects in the skies.

Mrs McCarthy said that around two years ago her 52-year-old council worker husband, along with two colleagues, saw a vacuum cleaner bag-shaped object the size of a small plane floating above Cardiff Bay.

Mrs McCarthy, 54, who used to be a claims manager but who now carries out UFO and psychic research full-time, said: "I have seen things I just cannot explain.

"I was travelling from Dublin to Shannon last September for a UFO conference when we saw a helicopter chasing six or seven silver spheres.

"They were flying in formation and it was almost like the helicopter was transporting them, because it was shining a light in front of them.

"On another occasion I was out around Pontypridd on a UFO hunt with Dave Coggins (a fellow UFO hunter).

"I was taking photographs and a black helicopter came over our heads and we saw it following a UFO."

Mrs McCarthy also claims that when she and her husband moved to their current Cardiff home in the early 1990s she saw three lights in a triangular formation from their bedroom overlooking a school field.

"Nothing got on that field in those days because it was inaccessible to traffic," she said.

"That to me was a UFO. What else can you say? There have been too many incidents around the world for it not to have been.

"I'm not so arrogant as to believe we are on our own.

"Many people believe we're not alone. There's more to life than we know."

As implausible as these incidents sounds some psychologists are not entirely dismissive of those who claim to have seen UFOs or to have had some kind of paranormal experience.

Retired clinical psychologist Dr Peter McCue says though many incidents can be explained through misperception, like mistaking a plane or helicopter for something else, not all can be accounted for in this way, especially incidents where several people claim to have witnessed a UFO or apparition.

Dr McCue's explanation combines hallucinations with telepathy.

He said: "Rather than being the effect of some kind of mass suggestion when people collectively see these things it appears to be the result of genuine paranormal phenomena where minds interlink.

"You cannot attribute everything to misperception or illness. There are circumstances where people have genuine experiences which are collective. And some UFO sightings are of a similar nature."

Dr McCue believes such incidents can occur where a loved one is killed in an accident and a spouse or relative claims to have seen an apparition of them at the moment of their death.

He said: "I'm not suggesting that people are seeing things that are physically there when they see a UFO, but I think they may be having a collective experience that is similar to seeing a ghost.

"When more than one person sees a thing it could involve a coordinated hallucination and can probably be explained by telepathic interaction.

"Several decades ago, a psychical researcher called G N M Tyrrell put forward an interesting theory about apparitions.

"He conjectured that they were hallucinations arising from subconscious telepathic interaction between people.

"Imagine, for instance, that a soldier serving in Iraq is injured in an explosion and, at that moment, he thinks of his wife back in Britain, wishing he could be with her.

"According to Tyrrell's theory, the soldier's crisis might instigate a subconscious telepathic interaction with his wife, resulting in her seeing, hallucinating, an apparition of him.

"Tyrrell suggested that the apparitional process tends to mimic ordinary perception.

"Therefore, during its brief appearance, the figure might look like a real person, and if the soldier's wife happens to be with someone else at the time—her sister, for example—she might be drawn into the proceedings, again, via subconscious telepathic interaction.

"Consequently, both women might see the apparition of the soldier."

THE WELSH ROSWELL

An incident in the Berwyn Mountains of North Wales on January 20, 1974, sparked worldwide speculation and came to be known as the "Welsh Roswell", with claims that a UFO crashed and "bodies" were retrieved and taken away by soldiers.

The incident was triggered by sightings of lights in the sky and a sudden tremor, followed by officials seen combing an area around the villages of Llandderfel and Llandrillo, near Corwen.

People were said to have run from their houses, fearing a second tremor, before seeing a blaze of light on the mountainside.

Some claimed to have seen an egg-shaped craft on the ground with a pulsating orange and red glow.

Some information has since emerged under MoD secrecy rules and the incident has been given an incident number by the MoD—Air 2/19083.

Some information in the file shows how:

- The Gwynedd Police Constabulary major incident log records an explosion at 9.10 PM with an officer receiving 999 calls about a UFO;
- A witness saw an object on the hillside and said: "I saw bright red light, like coal-fire red. It was a large perfect circle. Like a big bonfire. I could see lights above and to the right and white lights moving to bottom. Light changed colour to yellowish white and back again";
- A message recorded in a police log said: "There has been a large explosion in the area and there is a large fire on the mountainside";
- A telex message to the chief constable of the Gwynedd constabulary around 10 PM on January 23 said: "I saw bright green lights, object with tail—travelling west. Saw about Bangor direction—dropped down";
- At approximately 10 PM on the same night a further message said: "Saw a circular light in the sky at an estimated height of 1,500ft. This object exploded and pieces fell to the ground. [Witness] estimates the pieces would have fallen into the sea between Rhyl and Liverpool."

SOME UFO SIGHTINGS IN WALES REPORTED TO THE
MINISTRY OF DEFENCE OR TO UFO WEBSITES

- A pensioner and two other people saw up to 40 lights in a cigar shape in the sky moving down the Garth Mountain at speed for 30 minutes in March 2006. They disappeared then reappeared.
- More than 16 drivers stopped their cars to look at a UFO above a busy road west of Cardiff on October 14, 2004, at 10 PM.
- A silent object was seen in the sky by a couple in their garden in Barry at 3.20 PM on September 5, 2004. The bright, star-like object started coming towards them and looked like a box kite with no fuselage. It flew towards

Cardiff Airport at an altitude of around 3,000ft. Cardiff Airport said nothing was seen at the airport or on radar.

- The MoD confirmed that a green, circular object seen hovering in one position over Mumbles in January 2002 was classed as a UFO.
- The Welsh Federation of Independent Ufologists said a family travelling by car to the Great Orme in Llandudno on November 10, 1997, encountered a UFO. They could not account for several "lost" hours after finding their car engulfed by a purple triangular craft.
- There were several "cigar-shaped object" sightings in Pembrokeshire in the 1970s which prompted an RAF inquiry.
- In 2004, Alison Moore, 26, took footage of a floating disc in the sky above her home in Trehafod, Rhondda.

The Searcher[*]

By Skip Hollandsworth
Texas Monthly, April 2008

On the afternoon of January 9, Ken Cherry, the 61-year-old owner of a prosperous Tarrant County securities firm, was sitting in his home office, studying various stock market reports flitting across his computer screen, when line two rang. Line one is devoted to customers and brokers. Line two is the UFO phone.

Cherry is the Texas state director of the Mutual UFO Network (MUFON), the country's oldest and largest UFO investigation group. He supervises a staff of 41 certified MUFON investigators in the state. These men and women spend their free time interviewing people who have written in to the MUFON Web site or called one of its numbers claiming to have seen a UFO. In an average month, the Texas chapter of MUFON receives between fifteen and twenty such reports. Most of them sound like what Cherry heard on January 9: A woman outside Stephenville, seventy miles southwest of Fort Worth, said she and her teenage son had seen some flashing lights in the sky the previous evening. Cherry asked a few questions and hung up. Since the woman had described seeing the lights for only a few seconds, he didn't figure this would be anything other than a typical sighting.

Then line two rang again. A Stephenville man was calling to say that he had seen something strange the night before: a single bright light hovering over the treetops near his home. Curious, Cherry logged in to the MUFON Web site, where he saw several reports waiting for him, all from residents of the Stephenville area who had seen strange lights on the night of January 8. The next day, Cherry read a front-page story in the *Stephenville Empire-Tribune* about four more area residents who had seen something in the sky on January 8. One of them was Steve Allen, the president and owner of a trucking company in the nearby town of Glen Rose. Allen also happens to be a licensed pilot, comfortable with judging aircraft and flight patterns from the ground, and what he described nearly took Cherry's breath away: flashing lights covering a distance of a mile in length and half a mile in width at an altitude of about 3,500 feet. The lights, Allen said, were "totally silent" and had been racing around the sky at about 3,000 miles per hour until they suddenly turned into "burning flames . . . white in color." Within seconds, the flames had disappeared and there was nothing left to see. But approximately ten minutes later, the lights reappeared, this time traveling to the east. Allen added, "Two military jets, possibly F-16's, were in pursuit."

Cherry walked out of his office and down the hall to find his wife, who's the operations manager for his securities business and answers line two when he's not there. "Dear," he said, "we might be on to something big."

The Stephenville Event, as some have called it, has quickly become one of the most publicized UFO sightings in a decade. The story showed up in newspapers as far away as China. CNN's Larry King devoted two shows to what it all meant. "Do you believe alien beings are out there?" King teased, staring intently at the camera, forehead glistening. "Do you believe they've come to Earth?"

Predictably, there have been plenty of jokes and marketing gimmicks—Stephenville began advertising its upcoming rodeo as "out of this world"—but most locals were more than a little spooked by what took place in their night sky. One eyewitness wondered if he was watching the end of the world.

To add to the mystery, Major Karl Lewis, a spokesman for the 301st Fighter Wing at the Naval Air Station Joint Reserve Base Fort Worth, when asked whether any of his planes could have been involved, initially declared that none of the base's jets had been operating around Stephenville that night. He glibly told reporters that what people had seen was probably nothing more than an illusion caused by two commercial airplanes and the setting sun. But a week later, after more citizens kept coming forward to report that they too had seen rapidly moving lights that could not possibly have been caused by an ordinary airplane, Air Force officials released a terse press release admitting that ten F-16 fighter jets had been training in the area on January 8. When reporters asked what the jets had been doing, Lewis cryptically stated, "What we do down there falls under operational procedures that cannot be released because of operations security for our mission."

Meanwhile, sightings were continuing to pour into the MUFON Web site. One man wrote that he had watched "three distinct sets of lights" for about five minutes; another witness saw "strobing lights"; a man who had been driving with his daughter from Eastland reported, "We spotted two large, bright lights like stars. The two lights moved towards each other very, very fast . . . They looked like they met and then five or six smaller lights dispersed out in a circular pattern away from them and then everything was just gone."

What were those lights, and what were those F-16's doing? For Cherry and his investigators, the answer to these questions has become their holy grail. "It's maybe a once-in-a-lifetime opportunity to solve a mystery," he told me. "Are those lights from some secret military aircraft? Or did they come from somewhere else? And if they did come from somewhere else, then what does the government know?"

Cherry is an unlikely UFO hunter. After graduating magna cum laude in business from the University of Texas at Arlington, he became a star stockbroker in Dallas, eventually working his way up to Wall Street and then to regional vice president of Lehman Brothers in Chicago before returning to Texas in the mid-eighties to start his own securities business. When I went to see him at his home in Keller, he was dressed in a blue blazer, a button-down shirt, jeans, and loafers. As I followed him into his living room, I saw no drawings of triangle-faced aliens with huge eyes. Instead, over the mantel was a framed verse of Scripture that read, "Stand still and consider the wondrous works of God." On his coffee table were copies of *Smithsonian* magazine.

"To be honest with you, I wasn't all that interested in UFOs until I visited that UFO museum in Roswell back in 1991," Cherry said with a chuckle, referring to the New Mexico town where the military reportedly attempted to cover up a 1947 UFO crash. "It was just a little amateur museum, but it did get me to thinking that maybe the government knew more than they were telling us."

This led him to join the three-thousand-member MUFON, which is based in Fort Collins, Colorado. Soon he was named the head of the Texas operations ("I guess they liked my management expertise"). For his lead Texas investigator, Cherry chose Steve Hudgeons, a burly project manager for a Fort Worth glass installation company who shares Cherry's no-nonsense attitude. When I met the 58-year-old Hudgeons for lunch at the West Side Cafe, a working-class restaurant in Fort Worth, he took a bite of ground steak and growled, "Believe me, I'm not a big believer in all that paranormal, *X-Files* kind of stuff. I only do this because I've wanted to know for a long, long time if these supposed UFO sightings are real or just made up."

Since receiving his investigator's certification in 1992—he was required to pass a lengthy test based on the 311-page MUFON Field Investigator's Manual—Hudgeons estimates that he has looked into more than two thousand accounts of UFO sightings in Texas. "And to be honest with you," he said, "I haven't once finished an investigation where I could say for certain that someone had seen a genuine UFO. Ninety percent of the cases I get are explainable, the result of somebody seeing an unusual cloud formation or taking a photo with a bug on the camera lens. The other reports I get are tantalizing, but the people have no evidence whatsoever to prove what they saw." He took another bite of steak. "I'm a nuts-and-bolts guy. If I can't prove something unidentifiable was up there, then I move on to the next case."

When the reports began flooding in from the Stephenville area in January, Hudgeons knew he was about to embark on a different kind of investigation altogether. "Here were dozens of unrelated witnesses—solid, salt-of-the-earth folks spread out over three or four counties—all saying they had seen something."

Hudgeons and Cherry sent word to the news media that they would be setting up at a Rotary Club hall in Dublin (about ten miles from Stephenville) to interview anyone in the area who had seen the lights. On the appointed day more than five hundred people arrived. Many of those, it turned out, had come simply to be part of the hoopla. A couple of teenagers showed up wearing hats made of aluminum foil. Some other teenagers sold T-shirts that read "Stephenville: the new Roswell." Cheerful Rotarians passed out free popcorn and Dr Pepper. At least fifty members of the media milled around, interviewing anyone who would talk to them. One reporter from the *Dallas Morning News* described Hudgeons and the other MUFON investigators in attendance as "a cross between the ghost busters of the movie and the amateur detectives of the Scooby-Doo cartoons."

But by the end of the day, more than two hundred citizens had come forward, completely swamping the eight MUFON investigators, who had brought only fifty questionnaires. There were, certainly, a few oddballs. One elderly man declared that aliens had abducted him in the sixties. Another said his television was on the fritz because of UFO interference and asked the investigators if they could repair UFO-damaged sets.

Still, the number of legitimate-sounding reports were so high (ultimately, MUFON collected around two hundred accounts from the Stephenville area) and they were coming from such credible sources—everyone from a county constable to an anesthesiologist—that Cherry and Hudgeons quickly realized that the Stephenville Event was going to be the biggest mass UFO sighting in the United States since 1997, when Phoenix had a visit. What was especially curious to Cherry and Hudgeons was that the sightings had taken place over a series of days. One of the more flabbergasting accounts, from a Dublin machinist and welder named Ricky Sorrells, dated a week or more before the majority of the reports. Sorrells told MUFON's investigators that he had been out hunting at dusk when he saw a giant gray object in the sky, three football fields in length. He'd looked through the scope of his rifle and noticed that the bottom of the object had no rivets, nuts, or bolts; it did have cone-shaped holes embedded in its surface. The object hovered three hundred feet in the air over the tree canopy, then took off at a terrific rate of speed.

Initially, the problem for the MUFON investigators was that no one had gotten a clear photo or snippet of video. But in early February, Cherry and Hudgeons made an unpublicized trip to Stephenville to view a thirteen-minute home movie that had been shot by a man standing on his front porch on the east side of town. During the first round of hoopla, the man had not gone public with the video because he didn't want to be besieged by UFO fanatics.

"Our experts haven't had a chance to study what he shot in great detail," said Cherry, "but all I can say is that I've never seen anything like it. It's completely unexplainable, the lights constantly changing color and shape every couple of seconds as they move from one part of the sky to another, like some sort of hieroglyphics. Some of the shapes are scorpion like, other shapes wormlike, and even other shapes are like circles. And believe me, the man who shot the video is not sophisticated enough to have faked the footage. He's like just about everyone else out in that part of the state—a respectable, decent, salt-of-the-earth Texan who, up until this moment, thought the whole UFO phenomenon was just for kooks."

It will not be long before we all get to see this video: The respectable, decent, salt-of-the-earth man has reportedly sold his goods to a major television production company. Hudgeons and Cherry warned me, however, that despite its singularity, the video is not the great smoking gun that will finally convince even the most hardened UFO skeptic. "If the video showed some sort of craft behind those lights," Cherry said, "like maybe a craft three football fields in size, then this would be a whole different ball game, the most talked-about event in the world."

A few minutes later a phone began to ring from down the hall. "Line two?" I asked.

"Line two," he said, smiling. He rose from his chair in the living room. "That's what makes this job so interesting. You never know what the next phone call will bring."

The Phoenix Lights Explained (Again)*

By Tony Ortega
Skeptic, October/November 2008

UFOs make great ratings, so it isn't surprising that NBC'S *Dateline* aired a special on Sunday, May 18, entitled *10 Close Encounters Caught on Tape*. To its credit, the NBC program at least made an attempt to provide prosaic explanations for each of the events it presented. In most cases, those explanations were actually pretty good, and the "UFO experts" for the most part came off as yahoos.

But they were saving "the #1 UFO event caught on tape!" for last—the lame Phoenix Lights, the 1997 event that I helped debunk years ago as a reporter in Arizona. I prepared myself for yet another time that so-called journalists wouldn't get even the most basic facts right. I wasn't disappointed.

For starters, there were *two* separate events on the night of March 13, 1997 over the skies of Arizona. The mysterious "vee" configuration of lights that so many people across the state witnessed was seen over Prescott at about 8:15 PM. It traveled south to Phoenix at about 8:30 and passed over Tucson at 8:45. That's 200 miles in thirty minutes which means the vee was moving at about 400 miles per hour. Some early eyewitnesses perceived that it was high in the sky, others swore it was low and moving very slowly. (And I mention "early" purposely. As the months passed, more and more elaborate—and ridiculous—claims were made by eyewitnesses who were clearly trying to one-up each other.) As I've pointed out many times, the eyeball is a poor instrument for judging the altitude of point sources of light in a night sky. Simple physics, however, suggests the vee was high in the sky and moving very fast, even if it looked like it was moving slowly due to the altitude.

As I first revealed in the *Phoenix New Times*, a young man named Mitch Stanley spotted the vee from his backyard. Looking through a 10-inch Dobsonian telescope he saw that it was a formation of airplanes. Using a magnification of 60X—which essentially put him 60 times closer to the vee than people only using their naked eyes—Stanley could see that each light in the sky was actually two, with one light under each squarish wing. The planes still looked small in his scope—suggesting they were flying at high altitude—and he didn't know what type they were. But there was no doubt, he told me, that they were planes.

After his sighting, Stanley tried to contact a Phoenix city councilwoman who was making noise about the event, as well as a couple of UFO flim-flam men working the local scene, but he was rebuffed. I was the first reporter to talk to him, and as a telescope builder myself, I made a thorough examination of his instrument and his knowledge of it. (For the inexperienced: a Dobsonian telescope is much easier to move than the typical department store scope; it's child's play for an experienced observer like Stanley to get a good look at passing planes at altitude.) And he had a witness: he had told his mother, who was standing nearby, that the lights were planes. After my story, the *Arizona Republic* also found his story credible and wrote about it.

On the night of March 13, news of the 8:30 PM sighting traveled fast, so a large number of people were outside with video cameras when the second and unrelated event, at about 10 PM, happened in the sky southwest of Phoenix. A string of lights appeared in the sky, and slowly sank until they disappeared behind the nearby Estrella Mountain range. This was later shown to be a string of flares dropped by the Maryland Air National Guard over the North Tac military range. Dr. Lynne Kitei, featured prominently on the *Dateline* program, can repeat all she wants to NBC and other media that these lights were magical and "intelligent" and later showed up just outside her living room window, but the videotapes taken that night by many people show without a doubt that this was a string of mundane lights that fell and disappeared behind the range, exactly as a string of flares dropped by the military planes would have.

The problem developed later when people conflated reports of the two sightings. For the many people who had seen the earlier vee pass directly over their heads, the explanation of the flares made no sense whatsoever. News organizations didn't differentiate between the two events or report on the Stanley identification—even the *Republic* stopped referring to its earlier solid reporting on the Lights and began promoting it as "unexplained."

To this day, programs like *Dateline* invariably question people who saw the earlier "vee" event, and quote them saying that flares couldn't possibly explain what they saw. They are right. They didn't see flares, they saw a formation of planes. *Dateline* repeatedly showed people talking about their memories of the 8:30 vee *while showing video of the 10 PM flares*. Talk about misleading.

There *was* at least one person who videotaped both the 8:30 vee *and* the later event. I saw his tape myself. It clearly showed the five lights of the 8:30 vee moving *in relation to each other*, exactly as you'd expect in a formation of airplanes.

As for the people who swore they saw a black triangular shape joining the five lights of the vee, that's a classic contrast effect of the human eye. In a very telling case, a man who swore he saw a black shape joining the lights of the vee saw it pass directly in front of the moon. At that point, he saw not a black shape but wavy lines pass over the undimmed moon. But rather than conclude that he'd seen the contrails of planes, the man, whose perception had already been heavily influenced by the UFO explanation concluded instead that the pilot of the alien craft had turned his spaceship transparent right at that moment so the man could see the moon through it. How convenient!

Part of what fueled so much confusion over the Phoenix Lights event was the input from a couple of UFO "investigators" on the scene—one of whom was literally put out of business after my stories about him came out. For example, when it became obvious that the hundreds of people who saw the vee pass overhead had many different ideas about it—some said it was just over their heads, other said it was high in the sky, and no one could agree on the colors of the lights—instead of concluding that human beings naturally come up with different perceptions of the same event, these UFOlogists instead began to promote the idea that everyone had seen different vees! The early reports left no doubt that a single vee crossed over the state that night in about a half-hour. But by the time the UFOlogists were through, the credulous came to believe that Phoenix was practically under attack by dozens of mile-wide triangular space-cruisers!

Also at fault was the local TV news fraternity, which not only couldn't get the basic facts straight, but also cynically exploited the event for ratings. We're still dealing with the misconceptions they promoted, such as . . .

Claim: *The vee made no sound. (Not true. I talked to witnesses in Prescott, a quieter environment, who clearly heard jet noise.)*

Claim: *The vee didn't show up on radar. (None of the UFO investigators bothered to ask for tapes from the FAA in Albuquerque, whose officials at the time told me they only kept tapes for 11 days. So we'll never know what the radar picture looked like that night.)*

Claim: *The 10 PM lights fell in front of the mountain range, so they couldn't be flares dropped in the distance by military planes (Videotapes taken by observers from higher elevations in the Valley saw the flares for a longer period of time than those who were in lower places, confirming that the flares dropped behind the Estrellas.)*

Perhaps it's a good thing that NBC has now declared this the numero uno UFO sighting of all time. Few sightings have been so thoroughly investigated by reporters, and so well explained. But you won't hear that from the networks, who can't get enough of the ratings that come with "the unexplained."

4

Parapsychology

Editor's Introduction

The more scientists learn, the more enamored they become of the human brain, an organ some have labeled "the most complex structure in the universe." According to those who believe in "psi," or psychic phenomena—extrasensory perception, mind reading, and telekinesis, the ability to move objects with the mind, among them—the brain is even more powerful and impressive than researchers realize. The articles in this chapter offer an introduction to parapsychology, the field of study that uses science to investigate the validity of psi.

Historically, scientists have approached psi with skepticism, and for good reason. The world is filled with people seeking hope and validation, and so there's money to be made by declaring oneself clairvoyant and selling bogus predictions. What's more, psi are not easily proved or disproved. If a mind reader fares poorly in a lab experiment, he or she may claim that the stress of being observed by researchers interfered with the psychic process.

Fortune-tellers, meanwhile, escape scrutiny by focusing only on those predictions that come true, ignoring the vague or flat-out incorrect ones that would tarnish their hit-to-miss ratios. Such was the case with Jeane Dixon, the psychic who is famously thought to have predicted the assassination of John F. Kennedy. What people don't remember is that, prior to the 1960 election, Dixon said Kennedy would lose, and that labor issues would dominate the campaign. She was wrong on both counts, but because she was right about the president dying in office—the only prediction people still talk about—her place in history is secure.

In "The Truth is Out There," the first piece in this chapter, Scott Carlson profiles Stephen E. Braude, a professor who, in making parapsychology his focus of study, has drawn scorn from fellow academics. In such books as *The Gold Leaf Lady and Other Parapsychological Investigations*, Braude has spoken out against believers and skeptics alike, and as he tells Carlson, he thinks it's important to always keep an open mind.

In "I See a Psychic in Your Future," the next selection, Danielle Murray writes of being amazed by psychic Mandy Horton, who delivers a rather accurate telephone reading.

"Enemies in the Mind's Eye," the subsequent entry in this chapter, discusses the U.S. military's Star Gate program, which entailed using "remote viewers"—people who claim to be able to view far-off locations—to carry out intelligence missions. In the next piece, "Psychic Power? Not a Ghost of a Chance," Lynne Kelly casts doubt on Dixon and other psychics.

The chapter proceeds with "How Did He Know That?" in which Bill Heavey considers the Reverend Reed Brown, a Washington, D.C., "spiritual counselor" who claims to communicate with his clients' dead relatives. Brown also offers advice for the future, though he doesn't see himself as a fortune teller. "I deal in possibilities and probabilities," he says. "The future is never decided beforehand. We make our own future."

In the final piece, "How Psychic Are You?" Sarah Reistad-Long discusses several women from different walks of life who have experienced psychic phenomena. She also provides pointers on how to improve's one's psychic ability.

The Truth Is Out There[*]

By Scott Carlson
The Chronicle of Higher Education, January 11, 2008

The pivotal moment of Stephen E. Braude's academic career happened when he was in graduate school, on a dull afternoon in Northampton, Massachusetts, in 1969.

Or, at least, what follows is what he says happened. Readers—skeptics and believers both—will have to make up their own minds.

Braude and two friends had seen the only movie in town and were looking for something to do. His friends suggested going to Braude's house and playing a game called "table up." In other words, they wanted to perform a séance.

They sat at a folding table, with their fingers lightly touching the tabletop, silently urging it to levitate. Suddenly it shuddered and rose several inches off the ground, then came back down. Then it rose a second time. And again and again. Braude and his friends worked out a code with the table, and it answered questions and spelled out names.

Braude says he had not given much thought to the paranormal before that afternoon, but the experience shook him to his core, he says, sitting in an easy chair in his immaculate home in suburban Baltimore. He insists there was no way his friends could have manipulated the table, adding, "I should tell you, we were not stoned."

Today Braude, 62, is one of the few mainstream academics applying his intellectual training to questions that many would regard at best as impossible to answer, and at worst absolutely ridiculous: Do psychic phenomena exist? Are mediums and ghosts real? Can people move objects with their minds or predict the future? A professor of philosophy at the University of Maryland-Baltimore County, Braude is a past president of the Parapsychological Association, an organization that gathers academics and others interested in phenomena like ESP and psychokinesis, and he has published a series of books with well-known academic presses on such topics.

His latest, *The Gold Leaf Lady and Other Parapsychological Investigations* (University of Chicago Press), is sort of a summing up of his career, filled with stories of people who claimed to have otherworldly abilities. The writing is so fluid that the book at times seems made for a screen adaptation. (In fact, Chris Carter, creator of *The X-Files*, contributes a blurb to the back of the book. Braude advised Carter on a screenplay he is writing.) But Braude also includes some dense philosophical arguments—especially in a chapter about synchronicity, in which he ponders whether humans can orchestrate unlikely coincidences through psychokinesis, the ability to move or influence objects with the mind.

"He is setting the standard for how an analytic philosopher who takes this stuff seriously should proceed," says Raymond Martin, chairman of the philosophy department at Union College, in New York, who formerly worked at the University of Maryland at College Park and met Braude then. "He's very thorough in informing himself about what has been shown empirically, and he is cautious. He is usually skeptical in the end, but he is not dismissive."

Martin thinks philosophers are often too quick to dismiss anything that smacks of exotic phenomena because they want to protect the integrity of the discipline. "A lot of people just don't want this stuff on the table, because they regard it as an embarrassment to philosophy," he says. "Steve does take it seriously, and he has paid a price."

Greg Ealick took several of Braude's classes 20 years ago when he was an undergraduate at UMBC, and he is now Braude's colleague as an adjunct instructor in the philosophy department there. He says the philosophical aspects of Braude's work are "first-rate," although he's not convinced of the science of researching paranormal phenomena.

Braude's explorations could be seen as thought experiments, he says. Common in philosophy, such experiments pose odd scenarios to test arguments. A particularly well-known one asks: What if your brain were pulled out of your skull, put into a vat, and hooked up to a computer that could keep it alive and simulate external stimuli? Would you know that you were no longer inside your body? Therefore, can you know anything about the external world? "A lot of first-rate philosophy of mind comes from wildly speculative thought experiments," Ealick says. "I don't think that Steve's are really any wilder than the rest."

After his experience with the table in Northampton, Braude says, he put the event out of his mind for almost a decade. He got a job at the University of Maryland in 1971, and he went about publishing articles on the philosophy of time and the philosophy of language for the next seven years, until he got tenure.

Then he came out, so to speak. He knew that philosophers, like William James and later H. H. Price, had studied paranormal phenomena such as spiritualism and life after death. He thought he could demonstrate to colleagues that such phenomena were still worth studying. "To show you how naïve I was, I actually thought that they would be pleased to discover that they were wrong, so long as that brought them closer to discovering the truth." Instead, many shunned him.

"It clarified for me a lot about the scholarly community generally, something that has been confirmed over and over and over," he says. "It's not the haven of intellectual freedom that it is often cracked up to be."

Some of that jaded perspective comes through in *The Gold Leaf Lady*, which Braude describes as his "kiss-and-tell book" about his paranormal research. He trashes plenty of people in the book, including supposed psychics and their handlers who appear to be frauds. But he saves his sharpest barbs for prominent skeptics, like Paul Kurtz, a professor emeritus of philosophy at the State University of New York at Buffalo and founder of the Committee for Skeptical Inquiry, and James Randi, a magician better known as the Amazing Randi. Randi is described as a "publicity hound" who "weaseled out" of a challenge to explain phenomena produced by Ted Serios, who some believe could make odd and spooky images appear on Polaroid film. Kurtz is described as "disreputable" and sloppy. The skeptics, Braude says, pick out the weakest cases and demolish them, then use those spectacular debunkings to persuade the public that all exotic claims are bosh.

Braude believes that most people who dismiss the possibility of paranormal phenomena simply have not considered "the best cases" in parapsychology—cases like that of D. D. Home, which Braude summarizes in *The Gold Leaf Lady*. Home, a medium who lived in the mid-1800s, allegedly performed several fantastic phenomena under strict observation. He once held an accordion by one hand inside an electrified cage, and the instrument played all by itself—or so several observers documented.

Another "best case," according to Mr. Braude, is the real-life gold-leaf lady of the book's title. She is an allegedly illiterate Florida woman named Katie who goes into trances and writes in French, has predicted events for police detectives with stunning accuracy (like the time she predicted that bales of marijuana would wash up on a particular beach on a particular day, and they did), and occasionally finds flakes of paper-thin brass growing on her body. Braude believes that he saw a piece of brass appear spontaneously on her face during an interview. (He has kept some samples of the brass leaf in Ziploc bags.)

But other chapters of *The Gold Leaf Lady* describe the difficulties of putting strict controls on tests of "psi" abilities (like psychokinesis or ESP) and the inconclusive results that follow. Braude tells the story of Dennis, a fellow who showed potential in psychokinesis and was in many ways an ideal test subject. He was easy to work with, and he had no problem stripping and changing into inspected garments in front of a camera (a standard test procedure to make sure a subject isn't hiding any trick devices). But each time Dennis traveled from California, he traveled on a red-eye flight and arrived tired and flustered, like an athlete who hadn't rested before a big game. That, Braude believes, may explain in part why Dennis could not do much during the controlled tests.

Or it could have been the disdain a colleague showed for Dennis, which may have undermined his confidence before the tests. While observers want to apply strict controls, they don't want to squelch phenomena by applying pressure or making test subjects feel badgered. "That would be like saying, 'Let me see an erection'," Braude says.

Or it could have been a "source of psi" problem—that is, the unconscious, latent psi abilities of the testers could have interrupted the movement of the objects.

(Sadly, Dennis could not continue his tests under better conditions. After he traveled back to California the second time, he was bitten by an opossum and died of a heart infection.)

Even to consider the question of psychic ability, never mind going through the trouble of testing people like Dennis, takes a leap in faith that psychic ability actually exists—a leap that many people aren't willing to make.

And some people at UMBC seem to not want to be associated with his research, or even talk about it. Senior members of Braude's own department either did not reply or did not want to comment about his work when contacted by *The Chronicle.*

In 2002 Braude gave a lecture to the physics department, where he says he was shouted down by other professors. Lynn Sparling, an associate professor of physics at the university, doesn't remember the substance of the talk, but she remembers her impression of Braude. "I came away feeling that this guy was kind of an embarrassment to the university," she says. "I just thought he was a total goofball. I couldn't believe some of the things that I was hearing."

"If you're going to talk about that stuff, you really need to know what the physical laws are," she says. "If something is defying gravity, you have to have a reason for defying a law that has been proven over and over and over again."

In an e-mail message, Braude responds that so little is understood about psychokinesis (if indeed psychokinesis is real) that a levitating table does not necessarily defy laws of physics. And, he says, we don't necessarily have to understand and explain a phenomenon to know that it is real. "This matter could only be a problem for those who naïvely believe that physics must have an explanation for everything that happens," he says.

Larry Wilt, library director at UMBC, who has a doctorate in philosophy, has read much of Braude's work and admires its philosophical rigor. "My sense is that he is well respected by people on campus who have read his work," he says. "Those who haven't read it will dismiss it out of hand."

Braude will retire within a few years, and he's not sure to what extent he will continue to study the paranormal after he leaves the university. He is a pianist trained in classical music and jazz—a beautiful grand piano sits in his living room—and he plans to devote lots of time to playing and performing with groups.

He is also a stereoscopic photographer, with a collection of antique equipment, some inherited from his grandfather. His photos of landscapes pop to life in three dimensions when placed in a viewer. His portraits of people are so lifelike they are eerie—human beings locked in time, almost like wax figures.

But there may also be new horizons for him in parapsychology. Djurdjina Ruk, his wife of five years, studies astrology. Once a professor of psychology at the

University of Novi Sad, in the former Yugoslavia, she supported herself during the recent civil war by providing astrological predictions for European and Chinese soccer teams and for the Serbian mafia. She wanted for nothing and was even offered a Ferrari by the mob while the country around her imploded, as Braude details in the last chapter of *The Gold Leaf Lady*.

Braude says that during their time together she has been uncannily accurate, determining, for example, the time of the birth of one of Braude's friends down to the minute. The couple plan their trips and vacations around her astrological charts. They also gamble based on her predictions; their winnings during the 2005 football season paid for a summer vacation.

He's still not sure what to make of it. He once regarded astrology with the sort of disdain that others bring to his work, but now he thinks he should have an open mind. One thing is certain: He doesn't care what other people think.

"I stopped worrying about trying to convince other people," he says. "I'm in this to try to figure out things for myself."

I See a Psychic in Your Future[*]

By Danielle Murray
Montreal Gazette, October 20, 2007

I didn't want my fortune told. The only time I'd seen a clairvoyant, it was all good and I didn't want to mess things up.

But when interviewing a psychic, it's hard not to want to know. Just a few things, for the sake of integrity. So I asked her to tell me something about myself, something not so obvious.

She could have had me checked out. You can Google anyone nowadays. Instead, she asked me why my knees hurt.

Which indeed they did. Having just spent the morning at the computer, I'd been sitting on my knees since breakfast, the way I usually do when I write. Even people who know me very well don't know that.

Mandy Horton never saw me walk and she never saw me sit, though. We were talking by phone. So how did she know about my knees?

From an early age, Horton knew she was different. Not just a black sheep, but "very out of this world."

She says she could sense spirits around her, see accidents before they happened and knew when others were going to die.

Mediums, ghost whisperers, diviners, fortune tellers. Call them what you will, but long before Nostradamus arrived on the scene five centuries ago, there have been people who claim to see things others cannot.

Back in the 1960s, when Horton was growing up, people thought folk who could do that sort of thing were downright peculiar—or evil—and nobody dared really talk about it.

Now they do.

Hit TV series (*Medium, Ghost Whisperer*) and movies ("I see dead people") explore the topic, and psychic expos are common.

Plenty of people are still skeptical, though the naysayers are losing ground.

Back in 2002, a public-opinion poll found just 40 per cent of Canadians believed in extra-sensory perception (and 30 per cent of us had consulted a psychic at least once).

But now, according to research by University of Lethbridge sociologist Reginald W. Bibby, almost 60 per cent believe and 31 per cent think it's possible to communicate with the dead. Two-thirds also believe in life after death.

James Randi of the James Randi Education Foundation in the U.S. is not one of them. The Toronto-born magician has offered a $1-million "paranormal challenge" to anyone who can prove they possess supernatural powers.

The catch? He gets to control the setting. He says that if one is truly psychic, test conditions shouldn't matter. No applicant has agreed to his conditions.

"Belief in such obvious flummeries as astrology or fortune-telling can appear—quite incorrectly—to give confirmatory results, and that can lead to the victim pursuing more dangerous, expensive, and often health-related scams," Randi says on his website to explain why he believes psychics are dangerous. "Blind belief can be comforting, but it can easily cripple reason and productivity, and stop intellectual progress."

Englishman Ian Rowland is so good at faking psychic ability, setting up clients, influencing dialogue, enthusiastically following up on hits and quietly ignoring misses, that people quite often don't believe he's not the real deal. Instead, Rowland is the author of the *Full Facts Book of Cold Reading*, an account of techniques he says are used by psychics.

"Cold reading is also often used by people who pretend they give 'psychic' readings, and it enables them to give 'amazingly accurate' readings to complete strangers," he writes.

But why are we so willing to believe?

Well, according to Richard Wiseman, we just want to.

The British psychologist, well known for his research into the paranormal, told the BBC that humans, especially in times of stress or bereavement, often take what is said by psychics, no matter how general, and make it fit.

"I think the mediums are fairly sincere, but the person is reading a lot into what are fairly ambiguous comments," he says.

"We want to believe that a statement is true, that it applies to us. So we tend to buy into it."

After more than a century of research carried out in all corners of the world, not one organization has proven the existence—or non-existence—of the paranormal.

It used to bother Horton, but not now. "I'm not here to change anybody's opinion," says the 48-year-old mother of two. Sharon Cheney feels the same. She not only trusts her own psychic ability but feels we are all capable and it's just a matter of plugging into it.

Cheney knew early on she saw and felt things other people didn't. And like Horton a decade or so later, it wasn't discussed—not even with her mother, who used to talk to her dead grandmother.

As she became better able to master her abilities, people came to her for guidance often enough that she decided to make a living from it. To cover all bases, she earned a degree in applied social science and has a masters in counselling psychology.

In addition to doing psychic readings and public speaking engagements, she is an author, trained hypnotherapist and life coach and also practices animal communication, business forecasting, dream interpretation, past-life regressions and energy healing. And like Horton, she takes messages from beyond.

It's an iffy business.

Despite the Hollywood star treatment, psychics get a whole lot more bad press than good. They can claim a third eye or second sight but most can't seem to stop the bad stuff from happening to them any more than the rest of us. And none has come up with one of those great predictions that rocks the world—and comes true.

Yet man has toyed with the notion of a sixth sense for centuries. Common sense tells us it's absurd. But we continue to believe—in growing numbers.

We can't quite shake it. I can't quite shake it. Even my mother doesn't know about my knees.

Enemies in the Mind's Eye[*]

By Marianne Szegedy-Maszak and Charles Fenyvesi
U.S. News & World Report, January 19, 2003

His name would eventually be revealed as Joseph McMoneagle, but for the purposes of the Army's psychic intelligence unit, he was simply Remote Viewer No. 1. One fall day in 1979 he reclined in an easy chair in an office at Fort Meade, Maryland. The lights were dim. Sitting nearby was an interviewer, who gave him a series of geographical coordinates that were supposed to be his mind's destination. After about 20 minutes, McMoneagle brought himself out of a deep meditation and, as he describes it, "opened my mind." Gradually images began to appear: A low, windowless building; a smokestack. He smelled "a strange stink," a mixture of sulfur and natural gas. There was also a "smelting or melting activity." After an image came to mind, he drew it roughly on a piece of paper. Another viewer, No. 29, could "see" heavy metal equipment, including tubes conducting a "heat exchange." For him, the site emanated a "sense of power."

Far-fetched as it sounds, the remote viewers at Fort Meade were engaged in deadly serious work—an odd marriage of American intelligence-gathering and paranormal experimentation. Unbeknownst to themselves, viewers No. 1 and No. 29 seemed to be describing Lop Nor, a Chinese nuclear complex.

The experiment was only one episode in a remarkable research program run by the Defense Intelligence Agency and CIA from 1972 until 1996. The project, known variously as Grill Flame, Sun Streak, and finally Star Gate, explored a variety of parapsychological phenomena but especially one known as "remote viewing," the process by which someone in, say, Maryland visualizes an office in the Kremlin and describes it both in words and drawings. The viewers were shadowy and unacknowledged participants in the quest for intelligence about a range of security concerns: nuclear weapons sites, the Iranian hostage crisis, the kidnapping of Gen. James Dozier by the Red Brigades, the location of Col. Muammar Qadhafi during the raids on Tripoli in 1986, and the espionage case of Aldrich Ames.

The outlines of Star Gate have been sketched before, but new details of the project have come to light in 73,000 pages of previously classified records released by the CIA last November and made available just this month. (An additional 20,800 pages are undergoing review, and 17,700 pages were deemed too sensitive to release.) The documents illuminate a chapter of spying that bears closer resemblance to Miss Cleo than to James Bond.

In a sense, it was inevitable. From the early 1950s on, United States intelligence explored psychic research, hoping to use extrasensory perception (ESP) for intelligence operations. After all, the Soviets were doing it. Nonetheless, officials were torn between worries that the Soviets—and later the Chinese—were ahead of the United States in the psychic arms race and the skepticism of many American officials about spending money in the field seen as dominated by kooks.

Even such hardheaded operatives as Richard Helms, who later became the director of the CIA, were intrigued. The declassified documents reveal a memo written when Helms was deputy director for plans in 1963. For 10 years a small group in the Technical Services Division had been studying hypnosis and telepathy for use in clandestine operations but concluded that these fields were not ready for operational applications. Helms disagreed and sent a memo suggesting more research in "this somewhat esoteric (and perhaps scientifically disreputable) range of activities." He argued that given the Soviet preoccupation with "cybernetics, telepathy, hypnosis, and related subjects—recent reported advances—may indicate more potential than we believed existed."

Remote viewing was added to the roster of psychic phenomena in 1972 when the CIA became interested in the published viewing experiments of Hal Puthoff at the Stanford Research Institute. In 1972, the CIA gave the institute $50,000 to study remote viewing. Russell Targ, who joined the project in 1972, recalls a CIA official telling him: "You are wasting your time looking at churches and swimming pools in Palo Alto." Two years later, the institute received the geographical coordinates of a "Soviet site of ongoing operational significance."

"Turning point." The target was Semipalatinsk, in what is now Kazakhstan. Aside from suspicions that the site was important, nothing was known about it. Given the coordinates, a remote viewer provided a layout of a cluster of buildings and drew a puzzling, "damned big crane." He identified the underground facility as storage for Soviet missiles. Satellite photos verified the viewer's report, according to Donald Jameson, then a senior CIA Soviet specialist, who called the event a "turning point." One group within the agency refused to look at the Semipalatinsk data, objecting to the unscientific methodology. Another group allowed that the data might be real but called the process "demonic."

Still, officials were convinced enough of the program's potential that a training program was designed, as well as an ESP teaching machine. Questions designed to detect ESP talent supplemented the standard personality test used by the CIA. Some employees were deemed psychically gifted. When the CIA cut the program in 1975, the funds shifted first to the Air Force and then, in 1980, to the Defense Intelligence Agency. The military also looked for potential talent. That meant, says

Paul H. Smith, a retired intelligence officer who spent seven years in Star Gate, "certain odd proclivities, like a creative pursuit in music or art, an interest or aptitude in foreign languages. They were also looking for people who didn't report any ESP experiences."

Between 1979 and 1994 Fort Meade's viewing site conducted roughly 250 projects involving thousands of missions. One, in 1987, was an attempt to find a mole in the CIA. The viewers came up with a composite: The man lived in the Washington area, drove an expensive foreign car, perhaps gray, lived in a palatial home, was intimate with a woman from Latin America, possibly Colombia. Aldrich Ames lived in a palatial house in the Washington area. He drove a Jaguar and was married to a Colombian. The car was red; the house was gray. Not that the information was used; Ames was apprehended in 1994. By 1995, the end of the Cold War, along with increasing concerns about unfavorable scrutiny, drained the remote-viewing program of both its vitality and its supporters, and CIA director John Deutch ended it. All told, it had cost $20 million. The CIA says it no longer funds remote-viewing research, but the military is less emphatic in its denials. In the end, the weakness of remote viewing, says Smith, "is the weakness of any phenomenon that deals with the threshold of human perception. There are false positives, vague notions, and confused data that go with the territory." Paradoxically, for nearly a quarter of a century of American spying, that was also a strength.

Psychic Power?[*]

Not a Ghost of a Chance

By Lynne Kelly
Sunday Herald Sun (Melbourne, Australia), June 6, 2004

What can you do with the anecdotes you hear of apparent ESP? You have three choices. You can reject them as a fabrication or misinterpretation. That would be naive, leaving you with no chance of glimpsing some new wonder.

You could unquestioningly accept the anecdote. That would be equally naive, leaving yourself vulnerable to every scam and delusion on offer.

Or you can investigate. You can find out exactly what did happen, all that preceded the incident and how much the story has altered with each retelling. You will also need to find out details that you have not been told, due to the narrator's belief that they were insignificant.

They may well lead you to a different interpretation. Such an investigation is, in most cases, impractical if not impossible. So what can you do with an anecdote? Listen politely. It is of no more use to you than that.

So much of the evidence of psi (psychic abilities) is anecdotal evidence. When quoted out of context and in retrospect, coincidences always sound far too unlikely to be mere coincidence.

In fact, rare events are very common. Does this sound like a contradiction? Let's try a simple experiment. Take a pack of cards. Shuffle well and deal out four bridge hands, each of thirteen cards. Pick up the hand in front of you and look at the particular thirteen cards. The chances of you having exactly that hand are over 635,000,000,000 to one against. The dealing of that exact hand is an exceedingly rare event and yet you just did it. And you can go on performing such rare events all day long.

Beware of statistics of the likelihood of an event observed only in retrospect. Had you predicted exactly that hand in writing before it occurred, then I would be mightily impressed.

---

* Excerpt from *The Skeptic's Guide to the Paranormal*, by Lynne Kelly. All rights reserved. Reprinted by permission.

Premonitions of disasters are commonly quoted by distressed family members. Ask yourself how many times has a mother or father imagined an accident involving a child late home, or has someone seen, in their mind, a plane crash when a loved one is about to fly or a derailed train when a loved one is about to travel by rail? Given the millions upon millions of such images playing in heads every day, is it any wonder that a few prove to predict a real tragedy?

The millions of premonitions which failed to eventuate are soon forgotten, dismissed as natural worry. The few which, sadly, eventuate are recounted over and over, the images become more firmly fixed and the story unintentionally embellished and more firmly embedded in family folklore.

Unless such incidents are written down in advance and the number which prove accurate outweigh the number which prove false, such anecdotes provide no evidence at all.

PRECOGNITION

Psychic predictions are interpreted in retrospect and announced as astounding premonitions. One significant success by a media psychic can establish credentials for life. The woman who saw Kennedy's death. The man who named the child's murderer. But no one checks up on all the failures, do they?

No psychic warned us about the attack on America on September 11, 2001, Afghanistan's horrors or the Bali bombings. As each major event is reported on the news, ask yourself: Did a psychic tell of it beforehand?

Every year we are blessed with the predictions for the following year by those who make a living as media psychics. A royal will marry and another one die. A plane will crash and a city will flood. Weather will be extreme and an actor will be caught being naughty. Then we get the claims of accuracy during the year, if there are any. A psychic gets a hit and it is lauded loud and clear. The misses are forgotten.

There is a simple test. Collect all the published predictions next year. Check them regularly and tick those which are hits. You will then get a firm feeling for playing the psychic statistics game. Hits will be rare, misses and vague statements common. That I will confidently predict.

THE JEANE DIXON EFFECT

Sometimes the retelling of the evidence enhances its effect. Jeane Dixon made predictions about the election and assassination of President Kennedy which are often quoted. Typical is this account:

> Jeane Dixon, a Washington real-estate dealer and highly talented psychic, had long been startling friends and acquaintances with uncanny predictions that had, often unfortunately, come true. As early as 1956, she had predicted that the 1960 presidential election would be won by a Democrat who would die in office. By November of 1963,

Dixon was experiencing increasing feelings of foreboding concerning the Massachusetts Democrat, who had won the 1960 election. The Sunday before the assassination, she said, she felt a 'black veil' closing in on the White House and it continued to draw closer in the following days. On Tuesday, she told her luncheon companions, 'Dear God, something terrible is going to happen to the President, soon'. On Friday, President Kennedy was murdered in Dallas.

In this retelling, you have no way of checking the claims. Almost all is anecdotal and provided by the claimant herself.

Even the printed claim is difficult to verify. The source of the prediction was the May 13, 1956, edition of *Parade* magazine and said: "As for the 1960 election, Mrs Dixon thinks it will be dominated by labor and won by a Democrat. But he will be assassinated or die in office, although not necessarily in his first term." This is the basis for her claim of accurately predicting Kennedy's murder.

Given the assassination threats to US presidents, the likelihood of 10 years in which to do it and about a 50 per cent chance of a Democrat being in office, she was on reasonable odds.

Labor did not dominate the election. It is not mentioned that in 1960 she also predicted: "John F. Kennedy would fail to win the presidency".

Despite the wide belief that she is one of the world's most gifted psychic seers, she predicted, among many other flops, that the Russians would beat the Americans to the moon, World War III would begin in 1958 and a cure for cancer would be found in 1967. In fact, the "Jeane Dixon Effect" is a term used to describe the tendency for the mass media to exaggerate the few correct predictions of a psychic while ignoring the multitude of misses.

THE FRAUD OF TAMARA RAND

Most psychics are not perpetrating deliberate fraud. They genuinely believe in their gift and have many reasons to explain the frequent failures. Tamara Rand was different. Her prediction was amazingly accurate—and totally fraudulent.

On a talk show tape, dated January 6, 1981, KTNV talk-show host Dick Maurice interviewed the well-known Los Angeles psychic about her prediction that there would be an assassination attempt on President Reagan by an assassin with the initials "JH" and a surname something like "Humley". The assassin, with sandy hair and from a wealthy family, would shoot the President in the chest. This would happen, she revealed, in the last week of March or the first week of April. On March 30, John Wayne Hinkley did as predicted. On April 2, 1980, the tape was shown on three major US networks to an audience of millions with the astounding claim it was filmed in January.

Associated Press reporter Paul Simon was sceptical. His research soon revealed that the recording was faked by Maurice and Rand on March 31, making the previous day's events vague to make them sound more authentic.

How many people saw the original telecasts or heard of them over coffee the next day? How many of these have still not heard that the predictions were a fraud? How many of us have the opportunity to investigate as Paul Simon did? How do we know with whom to trust our precious beliefs?

CLAIRVOYANCE, CLAIRAUDIENCE

Clairvoyance is the ability to see people and events beyond the range of the five senses. Yet no one has truly displayed clairvoyant abilities under strict test conditions.

One of the best-known clairvoyants of recent years was Doris Stokes (1919–87). To be accurate, Stokes only claimed to use clairvoyance occasionally. Predominantly, her skills were clairaudient. She claimed to be able to hear voices which could not be heard using the normal sense of hearing.

Stokes came from a poor, working-class family living in Lincolnshire, England. The death of her father when she was only 13 had a profound effect on her. After marrying paratrooper John Stokes, she endured his return from World War II permanently impaired after a head injury. She then suffered the loss of her only biological child, a son, John Michael, and adopted a son, Terry.

Stokes, understandably, became fascinated by death, attending seances and consulting mediums. While qualifying as a nurse, she also trained as a medium. Later in life she performed to packed audiences, filling venues such as the London Palladium and the Sydney Opera House.

A witness account from paranormal researcher and author Ian Wilson describes what he witnessed at the London Palladium on November 16, 1986, after Stokes had taken her seat on the gilded, red velvet chair centre stage: "Almost immediately she reported hearing from the 'other side' someone whose name seemed to be Kelly or Kerry, with a surname sounding like Stennett. It was enough for a gasp to come from a smartly dressed, mid-thirtyish woman in the front row. Ushered to the nearby microphone, this woman emotionally explained that her name was actually Stenning, and that Kerry was her daughter who had been critically injured in a road accident, and had recently died from her injuries. Then the detail seemed to come thick and fast.

Stokes produced more names, then addresses and details of the accident. She predicted that Mrs Stenning, or her sister sitting next to her, was wearing something of Kerry's, which was correct. This is the usual practice of someone seeking to contact a loved one. Stokes offered the comforting words that Bill, Kerry's dead grandfather, was with her.

Stokes moved on to other audience members. Elderly Elsie Scott acknowledged Bill and Irene as her deceased husband and daughter.

Graham started to talk from the other side. His wife, Dawn, again sitting in the front, confirmed the many details about his accidental fall and subsequent death.

The rest of the show consisted of responses to the general audience, which appeared to be the standard cold-reading show. But the audience was now convinced. It was powerful, emotionally charged and convincing stuff.

Ian Wilson is a firm believer in the afterlife. But he also approaches the paranormal with a degree of scepticism. Here is what he said about his investigations that night:

"With me on that occasion, in a theatre box from which the whole show could be carefully observed, were television journalists Beth Miller and Siobhan Hockton, deputed merely to the task of collecting names and addresses of those audience members for whom Doris Stokes produced her communications, the intention being for these to be interviewed afterwards in depth.

"But within a matter of a mere 15 minutes, Beth and Siobhan learned far more than they had expected, and on their return their reactions were of shock, disbelief and downright anger. For as they had questioned one after another of those for whom Doris Stokes had produced messages, it emerged that there was nothing either psychic or coincidental in the fact that these were mostly seated close to, if not actually in, the theatre's front row.

"Not only had the key individuals been known to Doris beforehand, each had been specifically invited to the show by none other than Doris herself

"As Mrs Stenning disclosed, a friend had written to Doris Stokes on her behalf, telling her of Mrs Stenning's loss of her daughter Kerry."

The researchers had also discovered Elsie Scott was a regular at Doris Stokes's shows, always trying to get a seat near the front. Bill and Irene had come through to her at least three times before.

Dawn had sought guidance at a very vulnerable time in her life. Her husband's fall had left him on life support in hospital. Staff had suggested Dawn talk to someone about the issues surrounding the cessation of life support as he was brain dead. Dawn asked to speak to Doris Stokes, who returned the call after contact was made through a social worker. Stokes had talked to Dawn and her mother a number of times then sent free front-row tickets to her London performance.

As long as we have pretence masquerading as ESP and pretenders masquerading as psychics, it is almost impossible to find out if there really are people with such abilities.

I will leave it to you to decide whether the audience at Stokes's other performances were witnessing true clairaudience or pure exploitation.

How Did He Know That?[*]

By Bill Heavey
Washingtonian, July 1999

There are unseen forces tugging at the Reverend Reed Brown's body. "I feel spirit pushing me forward," he says, speaking rapidly and intently, eyes shut. "I feel someone pressing me on this arm here," he says. "But it's a little lopsided, this push. I would feel much better if it were one of these jobs," he says as he mimes two hands pushing forward evenly.

"So things may feel off-kilter to you. But it's okay because you're moving forward and it's. . . ." He stops mid-sentence and his eyes pop open.

"You want to be a dad, don't you?"

I nod, not trusting my voice because of the lump rising in my throat. I want to be a dad more than anything. My wife and I have just been through a year of fertility treatments that didn't take. Now we're trying to adopt a baby.

"Have you ever thought about adopting?" he asks. I nod again. "Because I'll tell you something. I've never been married, but I've helped raise two children that I was extremely close to. And I believe that it's not chance that the children we get are ones we've been connected to in a past life."

He sees my eyes roll at the mention of former lives, and he smiles. "This is all sort of new to you, isn't it?" he says. I nod. "It's okay," he says. "Everything works out."

Reed Brown doesn't look like a kook. He's an affable, middle-aged guy in a tweed jacket who could pass for a college professor. We're seated in a room off the front hall of the Arlington Metaphysical Chapel, a little white church with stained-glass windows and Methodist hymnals in the pews.

The chapel is part of the United Metaphysical Churches, a spiritualist organization headquartered in Roanoke, Virginia, with 13 churches across the nation. The organization is nothing if not inclusive: Members believe in Jesus and the Bible but also in other holy men—from Buddha and Mohammed to the 19th-century Hindu mystic Ramakrishna—and other sacred texts, such as the Bhagavad Gita of Hinduism and the Torah. Members also believe in means of divination, from tarot cards to numerology.

I'm here because I heard about Brown from friends and because I am curious but very skeptical. I grew up here in the most cerebral city in the country, a place that hums on policy and intellectual horsepower. The IQ is to DC what beauty is to LA, money is to New York, and owning the biggest snow blower on the block is to Buffalo. I have witnessed grown men at Washington dinner parties comparing SAT scores in a ritual reminiscent of Masai warriors seeing who can jump the highest from a standing position. And now, after waiting four weeks for a half-hour appointment and paying $100 (cash only) I am talking to an ordained minister who believes in astrology and reincarnation—and who seems to know things about me that defy explanation. What I find truly strange is that I'm starting to believe he's for real.

I'm not alone in my quest. Whether it's the coming millennium or a generation of baby boomers who've grabbed the brass ring and found it was only brass, there is a resurgent interest in the paranormal. A Yankelovich poll in 1998 compared current patterns with those 20 years ago. It found that 52 percent of us believe in spiritualism, the idea that our spirits live on in a different form after we die. That's compared to 12 percent in 1976.

Television shows with paranormal themes reflect the obsession: From *Touched by an Angel* and *Sabrina the Teenage Witch* to *Profiler* and *The X-Files*, the fascination with things that defy rational explanation keeps viewers glued to the tube. The hero of *Early Edition* is every Washington insider's dream: a guy who gets tomorrow's newspaper today.

Even here in cerebral central, there's a growing core of customers who support Reverend Reed Brown, Reverend James DiBiasio at the Institute for Spiritual Development in DC, and psychics like Beverley Newton in Fredericksburg. It's a word-of-mouth community from which you can glean a few basic rules.

"Anyone in the Yellow Pages is a fake," says a Virginia interior designer who has been going to a psychic in New York and to Reverend DiBiasio once or twice annually for about 20 years. "Anyone with an 800 number or, God forbid, a 900 number is a fake. Generally, anyone who says they're a psychic is a fake."

"The good ones are generally involved in some kind of a church, in helping people," says the interior designer. "The bad ones—and the field is loaded with crooks—are in it for money." Reverend DiBiasio, she points out, has at least an eight-month waiting list and charges $80 for a session. He could easily get more, she says.

Before I enter the room with Reed Brown, his receptionist tells me to take two index cards. On one, I am to write down questions I want answered about my life. On the other, I am instructed to write the names of three dead people I want to know about.

I sit in the middle of the chapel—far from the reach of any cameras that could be spying on me—and cup the cards close to my chest as I write. I then fold the cards in half, then in half again.

Inside the room, Brown lets me pop a blank cassette in the machine he keeps for people to record their sessions. I tell him my birth date and first name, nothing else. He has me hold the cards in my hands, then places his hands over mine with his eyes closed.

He tells me to forget everything written on the paper and just to think, "I am here. Now what?" He says a short prayer, asking that "the doorway between the two worlds be opened and that the loved ones and teachers of this, our brother, will come here now and give him that which will uplift him, guide him, and direct him." Then he waits for whatever comes into his mind.

The next thing he says is, "Wow," like my hands are electrified. "I'm feeling a lot of spirit energies around you. Well-meaning people who say you should be doing this or you should be doing that. And it's strange to me, because as soon as I say that, I'm feeling earmuffs. And that means to me that you need to do it your way."

I'm working to suppress a smile. I have some good qualities, but taking advice from other people is not among them.

He asks me to say, "It's a beautiful day." I do. "The name 'Bill' just came right up off that card," he says. "There's a Bill in spirit around you."

It's the name of my grandfather, who died 30 years ago, whose name is in fact one of the three on the card. Because Brown knows my name is also Bill, it could be an educated guess.

"He's sending you a lot of affection," Brown says. "He's looking out for you." A few minutes later, he mentions that he's getting another name, "Meme or Nini." I don't say anything, and he drops it. But Meme is another name on the card, my grandmother. Meme was the heart of the family, and though she also died long ago, we still talk about her.

"What are we seeing here. . . ." His voice trails off. "It's like a medallion around your neck and someone brushing your forehead, like they're trying to clear your third eye." Now he's speaking not to me but to whatever else is in the room. "Yeah, but what is it?" he asks. "But what is it?"

After a pause, he says, "I'm seeing a jewel around your neck, sort of like what they have in fraternal orders. Mayors sometimes have it, a sign of their political station. I don't know what all this is about; I don't know even what I'm saying here.

"And I hate to throw this out to somebody who doesn't believe in reincarnation, but you're an old soul. You've been places and seen things. And I can feel that in both of these pieces of paper. And I want to say this to you: If you're not involved in the humanities as a vocation, you need to find a way to be involved as your avocation."

I have not told Brown I'm a writer.

"I believe it's through service that we progress as beings," he says. "And there are many kinds of service."

He closes his eyes again and sits very still. Then he opens them and asks, "You ever do any writing?"

Maybe the old soul stuff is because I'm prematurely bald. The jewel business makes no more sense to me than it does to him, though I'm partial to his candor in admitting he doesn't understand it.

Maybe the reason Brown can't see my third eye, the "psychic-energy center" between one's physical eyes, is because there's a big "sucker" label plastered over it. But he's been right about too many things for me to believe he's just throwing darts.

It was easy to be skeptical from a distance. Now that I'm here, I'm of two minds. Part of me thinks there's got to be a trick. And part of me is enthralled.

I have the feeling that once he's off and running, he's just reporting what he sees and hears, a human antenna, and that he's not particularly attached either to what he's saying or to how I receive it.

"The good ones don't even remember what they've told you," the woman who has been visiting psychics for 20 years tells me. "It just sort of passes right through them. They'll be the first ones to tell you they don't own the information."

There's also a warmth to the guy. There is something almost playful about his manner, and it invites your trust. Of course, gifted con men have the same traits.

Other people who've visited Reed Brown report similar instances of his inexplicable accuracy.

One woman was told that there were two spirits watching out for her. "Reed Brown said to me, 'I'm getting the name Robert. Does Robert mean anything to you?' Robert was one of my grandfathers," recalls the woman. "Then he said, 'I'm getting the name Dominic. Does Dominic mean anything?' Dominic was my other grandfather. Robert is a common enough name, but Dominic? You can't guess that one. How do I explain it? I don't. I can't."

Brown told another woman that he saw her mother standing behind her holding the reins of two horses and saying not to worry, that she'd be there waiting for the daughter in heaven.

"That was a perfect image of my mother," she says. "We kids used to joke how she loved those horses more than she did us."

Howard E. Lallande, an asphalt contractor in Annandale who has visited Brown several times, says that Brown at first had difficulty contacting Lallande's dead father and that when he did, the spirit apologized, saying he'd "been working on a project." The funny thing is, Lallande says, those were invariably his father's words when he showed up late.

Brown's "summoning" of dead relatives—or at least their names—may be what first-time visitors remember most. But others, especially those grappling with problems, have come away with more.

"I was having a lot of health problems at the time, and I was beginning to worry," says the woman whose grandfathers were Dominic and Robert. "Reed Brown asked me, 'You're worried about your health, aren't you?' Then he said, 'Don't worry, everything will be fine. You're going to turn to holistic medicine, and you're going to live a long life.'"

The woman made an appointment with a holistic doctor. Though her chronic health problems didn't disappear, she says she now knows how to control them.

Tom, 43, is a Brown follower, and he fits the brainy Washingtonian profile to the letter. Director of finance at a telecommunications company, he was skeptical four years ago when a friend told him about Reed Brown. But he decided to go.

"I was determined to volunteer as little about myself as I could," he says. "I didn't want to give him anything to feed off."

By the end of the half-hour session, Tom was astounded by what he'd been told.

"He knew the health of family members. He named a good friend who had recently died young. He knew about a Catholic monsignor who was my guardian and whose health was failing. He said, 'His spirit is weakening, but don't worry. He's at peace.' He even knew that my grandfather had been a glassblower."

Dr. John Palmer is a psychologist with the Rhine Research Center in North Carolina, an organization that conducts research on reported cases of ESP, or extrasensory perception, and psychokinesis, the influencing of material objects through mental power.

Like most scientists, Palmer is reluctant to say whether he believes in psychic ability of the type that Reed Brown appears to exercise. He says tests have revealed that some self-proclaimed psychics are nothing more than people who are adept at reading clues from body language, clothing, and facial expressions.

"You'd be surprised at how much you reveal about yourself without ever opening your mouth," he says. A woman with expensive jewelry but modest clothes, for example, is likely to be someone who had money at one time but has lost it.

On the other hand, Palmer has studied the results from hundreds of experiments that do indicate abilities that science can't explain. One study involved putting a subject in front of a machine that randomly generates zeroes and ones and having the subject try to make the machine produce more of one number than the other.

"The weight of evidence shows that people can significantly affect the outcome of these machines," Palmer says. "Not everyone, and not all the time. But enough so that we are left with a puzzle: How do you explain this without somehow revising the physical laws we have now?"

Palmer cites an experiment in which subjects looking at pictures or film clips in one room try to "send" the image to another subject in a room elsewhere in the building, who then tries to match the received image with one of four choices presented. The odds for random success are one in four.

"But what we find over thousands of times is that it works out to about 33-percent success," says Palmer. "Enough to be statistically significant. Again, it's a puzzle. And our efforts to explain these results by standard scientific hypotheses have so far been inadequate."

Brown rejects the label of psychic. "I'm a minister with a spiritual gift," he says when I call a week later and identify myself as a reporter.

"I grew up in old-time spiritualism. They were called mediums then and were always associated with churches. I am not a fortuneteller. You know, that 'Will I meet a man?' sort of thing. I've had plenty of people get mad and storm out when I couldn't contact Aunt Sally on demand or tell them what their next job would pay. That's what some people expect.

"I just start rambling and things come to me and sometimes I'm not even aware of what I've said," Brown continues. "It's a counseling session to find out what the problem is and what to do about it.

"I deal in possibilities and probabilities. The future is never decided beforehand. We make our own future. I think people should be skeptical. It's healthy. And I won't see people more than once or twice a year. You don't want to be someone's command center. You would not believe how many people are dying to pawn off the responsibility of making their own decisions onto somebody else. People need to know that they have to make their own decisions."

He says he discovered his gift when he was three, when he predicted that his mother, who thought she was past childbearing age, would have another baby girl and that both that child and his other sister would come down with whooping cough. All, he says, came to pass.

Asked what he does when he feels negative energies or premonitions, Brown says it's a judgment call whether to reveal what he's sensing.

"First of all, it's just a premonition. Nothing's written in stone. So it may not happen. Second, there's a kind of self-fulfilling prophecy you have to watch out for. If I say, 'I think you might get into an accident with a red car,' a person is likely to be so worried every time they see a red car that they'll eventually hit one.

"I'm not a gypsy but a spiritual counselor. If there's something off in your life that I pick up on, it doesn't mean someone's out to get you. It means there's something you're doing to cause it. So there's a lesson for you to learn. I'm trying to nudge you down the path. The truth is that good comes out of everything."

Back in the room, as my 30-minute session with him winds down, he tells me I'm in the midst of a tremendous "accruing time," when things are going to be coming to me. That everything around me is changing for the good.

"You've really got a lot going for you, a lot of people pulling for you. Now you just have to go make it happen. That's really all I can tell you."

I thank him, shake his hand, get my cassette, and go. Walking to my car, I feel strangely happy and hopeful. It's not just a question of Brown's "score"—though I cannot account for how he knew about Meme or wanting to adopt or that I was a writer. It's something else. A sense of having been recognized and affirmed.

At this moment, I don't care whether it's a con. Right now I'm thinking that believing only in what we can see or touch is a con, too.

How Psychic Are You?*

By Sara Reistad-Long
Marie Claire, March 1, 2006

If you think ESP, mediums, and reincarnation are for the birds (and flighty ones at that), read this article—it just may make you a believer. Five women share their supernatural experiences, from seeing ghosts to seeing the light. Plus, how to tap into your inner psychic.

LESLEY 32, SPECIAL-EVENTS MANAGER

About five years ago, I was working for a small company owned by a married couple. The wife was pregnant and was scheduled to have her labor induced. They went in at 9 A.M., and the husband said he'd call to check in once everything was over. The whole day went by, and people at the office were talking about how strange it was that we hadn't heard from him.

Suddenly, I just kind of sat up straight and blurted out, "Well, the baby was born without fingers." Dead silence. Nobody knew what to say. I didn't even know where those words had come from! I was so embarrassed.

The next day, my boss came in, and it was clear that something bad had happened. He looked really worn out and tired. After apologizing for not having been in touch the day before, he told us the reason: The baby had been born without fingers. Everyone turned and stared at me.

I still don't understand how I knew, though I've experienced plenty of situations where I can sense something is wrong. Or a person will be on my mind, and that's when they'll call me. I believe we're all intuitive—it's just a matter of tapping into our sense of awareness. Case in point: Parts of the house I grew up in always felt as if there was a separate presence there. Then, when my parents did some remodeling, they saw that the walls in one hallway were all singed. It turned out there had been a fire there. And in the bathroom, they found three bullets lodged in the wall!

DAVIDA 32, ACCOUNT DIRECTOR

When I was little I used to have out-of-body dreams. I'd just sort of hover around the house, and at breakfast, to everybody's consternation, I'd rattle off things that had happened after my bedtime. I didn't know this until much later, but apparently, my grandmother used to have dreams like this, too. I was 14 when my grandmother died, and before anyone told me about her death, I just knew.

In college, I once dreamed of a bunch of kids running around my dormitory courtyard. One boy really stood out, right down to his name and the numbers on his jersey. Two years later, I became a summer-program counselor at my school, and one day, after a nap, I went to the window and actually saw the scene that I had dreamed of two years before. Even the jersey numbers were the same! I met the boy, but nothing profound happened. Maybe he has a role in my future.

Being a little bit psychic has always been a positive for me. I dreamed about someone who looked exactly like my son years before he was born. I still have a drawing I did when I was 11 years old that looks eerily like the restaurant my husband owns today. My premonitions have been going on for so long that they seem really natural. I can't control them. Sometimes I wish I could—then I would be able to talk to my grandma again.

KELLY 26, GRAD STUDENT

I was in a major car accident with my mother when I was 13. We hit a deer, and our car flipped over twice. Miraculously, concussions were our only injuries. But during the few seconds in which the car was flipping, I had what I thought was a dream. My body stayed in the car, but the thinking part of me went really high up, watching the whole scene. It was as if I was in "Superman mode." I saw the ambulance arrive, my twin sister, Sarah, picking up the phone at home and finding out what had happened, the people in the nearby farmhouse coming out to look. I heard the deer panting as it ran away. I was just all-knowing. And I had no fear.

Then, it was as if somebody pressed "download," and I was aware of every detail of my life. I didn't see anybody, but there was a presence with me, and we went through my whole life, pausing at certain moments. The presence didn't judge, but listened as I evaluated those moments. At the end of my "dream," I saw my funeral. Then I heard—or felt, rather— a voice say, "It could end this way, but there's more for you to do. We're putting you back in." Suddenly, I was zipped back into my body, and the car had stopped spinning. I never told my mother what happened.

Years later, in college, the story came up for the first time. My boyfriend, who'd been reading up on this sort of thing, gave me a book called *The Light Beyond*, by Raymond Moody. It was basically a psychiatrist's record of the countless, almost identical near-death experiences his patients had described. I was shocked to discover that other people have had the same "dream" I had. Comparing my experience with those of so many others awakened my curiosity. To me, it proves there is something beyond what we know.

SARA 26, GRAD STUDENT (KELLY'S TWIN)

Kelly, my twin sister sent me a book called Many Lives, Many Masters, by Brian Weiss. It deals with a psychiatrist whose patient regresses into past lives during hypnosis. I'm not a particularly religious person, and I had certainly never had anything paranormal happen to me, but when I started reading the book, I couldn't put it down.

I was a little skeptical but ultimately curious enough to go to a past-life regression class. It's a lot like meditation: You focus on relaxing every part of your body, then you visualize yourself walking on a beach—that kind of thing. Finally, the past-life therapist counts backward, telling you that when she's done, you will begin your regression. At the end of the counting, she starts asking questions about what ever you might be seeing.

Under hypnosis, my most vivid memory was of giving birth. I knew the woman was me, even though she didn't have my features or body. I awoke from that vision with a thorough understanding and detailed recollection of the physical sensations of labor and delivery, even though in this life, I've never given birth.

The majority of my regressions have been good. Then, during a weeklong retreat with Kelly, I experienced a regression in which I was a young man in Manhattan who died after getting hit by a car. At my funeral, I saw my son—who is now Kelly's fiance. I felt terrible abandoning him. I know that on the face of it, knowing my "son" is going to marry my twin sister sounds entirely bizarre. But I'm quite comfortable with it, actually. After all, I feel like I know him so well already!

SUE 43, WRITER

Once, when I was a kid, I was at my paternal great-grandfather's house, sitting alone. I was probably being punished for something, because I remember feeling sorry for myself. An unfamiliar woman walked into the room. She introduced herself as my great-grandmother and told me that, whatever happened in my life, she'd always be there for me.

Years later, when my grandmother died, my grandfather and I were looking at a bunch of old pictures. I saw one of a woman I recognized immediately. My grandfather didn't seem surprised that I knew who she was—he'd seen her that same day, and she'd told him she was taking me under her special care. Apparently, I'm her spitting image—in looks and personality.

That's not the only time a dead person has visited me: Somebody once died in the house where my husband and I live. Since we have to—and want to—live there, we don't really want to know how he died. For a long time my husband worked nights, and often, I'd wake up seeing somebody sitting on his side of the bed. I just assumed it was my husband, and I'd lean over to touch him. But instead of feeling a body, my hand would hit the bed, and the person would immediately get up and walk out. It spooked me. My kids saw him, too. So we named the guy Fred—he was, after all, part of our household. My husband was the last one to see Fred. He was alone in the kitchen. At first he thought he heard the dog, but then he saw this being walk by. He was dumbfounded. Prior to that, he'd been very skeptical.

WANT TO HONE YOUR SIXTH SENSE?

We asked Georgia Rudolph, widely credited as one of the country's first psychic crimebusters, what it's like to have her unusual gift—and how you can become more intuitive.

How did you start working on criminal cases?

About 20 years ago. I was talking to a cop about a series of break-ins. I suddenly knew he needed to be careful for the next few days. I told him, "It's going to be dark, and you'll be stooped down, and if you're not prepared, he'll shoot." Right after that he was in a stakeout, hunched over, and remembered what I'd said— just in time to dodge a bullet. He was amazed, and word started to spread.

What was your most memorable case?

The most notable one involved a killer named Jack McCrady, who shot his wife, then reported her missing. The Ohio cops were stumped and tracked me down in Pittsburgh. I asked them to tell me her name, and instantly, I knew that she had been shot and buried. Then, I got a feeling that the killer's name was John but that he went by Jack. I was hesitant to say the next bit—that he was a cop. Even though I'd never been to that region, I was able to give the cops directions to the spot where the body was buried.

Are you frightened, knowing about all those crimes?

I'm not afraid to know about crimes—sometimes before they even happen— because I'm a firm believer that everybody has a specific lifeline.

What actually happens when you channel?

It's like a mind's-eye thing. There will be a little voice in my head, and I'll just know. Each time I do it, I get better and have more knowledge.

Can anybody be a psychic?

Everyone is born psychic, but we're taught to ignore it. Think about how intuitive kids are. I'm convinced I'm this way today because, when I was little, I was shuffled around a lot—so I never had an authority figure telling me my clairvoyance was bogus. I'd liken it to a window with the shades down: With conditioning, you can teach your self to pull up the shade. We're made up of mind, body, and soul. Being psychic is very much about having an awareness of all three. How can we improve our intuition? I recommend meditation, yoga, and listening to New Age music. Everything is connected, so paying more attention to earth sounds is a great way to tap into "higher forces."

5

Cryptozoology

Editor's Introduction

Thought to roam the forests of the Pacific Northwest, Bigfoot is a famously elusive creature. If, indeed, it's real, the giant ape lives deep in the woods, far from the prying eyes of humans. It occasionally leaves behind footprints or allows itself to be photographed, but by and large, it leads a life that leaves skeptics questioning its existence. The same goes for the Yeti, sometimes referred to as the Abominable Snowman, a Bigfoot-like creature rumored to dwell in the mountains of Tibet and Nepal. "Nessie," the Loch Ness Monster, is every bit as shy. This alleged beast—which many believe to be a holdover from the days of the dinosaurs—rarely grants people a glimpse, choosing instead to swim beneath the surface of Scotland's legendary loch.

Bigfoot, the Yeti, and Nessie are but three of the "cryptids" long pursued by cryptozoologists—individuals committed to finding animals whose existence science has yet to confirm. The term cryptozoology—the focus of selections in this chapter—was coined in the 1940s by the Scottish researcher Ivan Sanderson. Many of the discipline's leading figures are trained zoologists and naturalists, and even though they've devoted their lives to searching for animals naysayers dismiss as myths, they scoff at the suggestion they're involved in the paranormal. "[Our members] have to have a scientific disposition," John Kirk, head of the British Columbia Scientific Cryptozoology Club (BCSCC), tells Rebecca Caldwell in "Beasts that Bear the Burden of Proof," the first article in this chapter. Among the critters sought by the BCSCC are the Sasquatch, another name for Bigfoot, and the aquatic Cadborosaurus.

In "Tracking the Elusive," the second entry, Tom Bell profiles Maine resident Loren Coleman, a veteran cryptozoologist who has penned more than 20 books and runs his own museum. Asked by Bell whether he believes in Bigfoot, Coleman affirms the scientific nature of his field: "Belief is the province of religion. Belief is about faith. As a scientist, as a cryptozoologist, I see that we need to base our conclusions on evidence." Based on what he's seen, he says, there is a large, unclassified primate lurking in the woods of the United States and Canada.

"The Scientist and the Monster," the next entry, focuses on Bob Rines, a successful inventor and attorney who has chosen to spend his twilight years searching for the Loch Ness Monster, which he claims to have seen in 1972. Amazingly, at the time of his sighting, Rines had in his hand a Super-8 movie camera, though he was too enthralled by Nessie to take his eyes off the lake and start shooting footage.

In "Hairy Scary Stories Linger in the Thin Air," Troy Lennon traces the histories of the Yeti and Bigfoot legends, offering possible explanations for the strange footprints long associated with both cryptids. "The Myth Hunters," the final piece, finds writer Kim Knight joining New Zealand cryptozoologists as they search for several bashful beasts, two of which—the moose and the South Island kokako, a songbird—are viewed by skeptics as merely extinct, not mythological. Still, New Zealand is home to legends of more exotic cryptids, such as the moehau, a Bigfoot-style ape, and the Canterbury black cat, a fearsome feline one witness describes as "an Arnold Schwarzenegger of a cat."

Beasts That Bear the Burden of Proof*

By Rebecca Caldwell
Globe and Mail (Toronto, Can.), May 17, 2003

I've personally never seen a real, live whale. But I believe in whales and I don't mock people who say they've seen whales, and not just because I belong to some sort of Cartesian blubber-worshipping cult. I was taught about whales in school, a reasonably credible source. I've seen whales in documentaries. I've even read most of Moby Dick.

Now I have never seen Bigfoot, either. And while I can read reports of people who claim they have, or at least had a look at its gigantic footprints or a whiff of its odour that allegedly takes the fun out of funky, it's still a little more difficult for me to make the case for its existence.

But this weekend, 250 scientists, outdoorspeople and the plain curious from all around the globe will do just that, as the International Bigfoot Society holds its annual convention in its headquarters of Hillsboro, Oregon, with lectures, panels and exhibits on the subject of Bigfoot's being.

And it's not just Americans who are obsessed with these allegedly mythical beasts. Scotland has turned Loch Ness into an international tourist attraction with the monster that allegedly lurks within. In British Columbia, there's the British Columbia Scientific Cryptozoology Club, formed in 1987 by John Kirk. At the time, Kirk was on holiday at Lake Okanagan in B.C.'s interior when he says he saw the Ogopogo—a giant fresh-water serpentine creature that is Canada's answer to the Loch Ness Monster. Although a writer, not a scientist, by profession, Kirk was fascinated by what he saw and what it meant.

"It started a domino reaction: What is this animal? What does it feed on? What's its reproductive life? How does it manage to survive in a contained body of water? How has science missed this animal?"

Since its inception, The BCSCC has evolved into a sort of scientific-adventurer's club with a view of tracking down "cryptids": Creatures such as the Ogopogo,

Sasquatch, the ocean-going Cadborosaurus and the fresh-water Black Salamander. It's an exclusive group: Its 100-plus members are carefully veiled to avoid including crackpots and protect the society's credibility in the woolliest of fields.

"[Our members] have to have a scientific disposition. They have to realize that we're not a paranormal society—we're not *The X-Files*, we're not looking for ghosts and goblins—which we always get lumped in with unfortunately.

"And you have to be able to testify that you've got a good character: No criminal record. You're not a troublemaker. You don't harass people."

And while the environment can blossom a romance—Kirk met his wife at a Sasquatch conference—cryptozoology can be as vicious as a Bigfoot bite. The children of Ray L. Wallace were roundly dismissed when they announced earlier this year that their recently deceased dad had been Bigfoot's inner self. B.C.-resident Chins Murphy created a rill in the community after he claimed to have debunked the 1967 Patierson-Gindin film (the Bigfoot equivalent of the Zapruder film) that purports to show a few seconds of Sasquatch.

And then of course, there's a lot of competition and one-upmanship to be the first to find a new animal to add to the kingdom.

"There's not so much in the broader field of cyrptozoology—but my gosh, there is rivalry in the Sasquatch field," Kirk says. "A lot of smaller groups are very possessive about information they have."

While the BCSCC doesn't hold regular meetings, it does conduct regular expeditions on the trail of their quarry. Lake Okanagan is a regular site of their investigations: Occasionally it gets more adventurous. Two years ago, members of the group travelled to Cameroon on a CryptoSafari, searching for the Mokele-mbembe, an elusive creature that is said to resemble a sauropod dinosaur.

They didn't find it. But, says Kirk, they did find anecdotal evidence seemingly by different sources, some from tribes that had no contact with each other.

"They started describing the animal's features that only someone who had seen it would know about. We spoke to dozens of people, and we were struck that they all had the same details."

As for skeptics, they do exist. The cryptozoologist takes it in stride, since it's all in the name of science. Because sometimes natural scientists do find something. Recently, a new species of jellyfish has been discovered. Last year, a new type of beaked whale was identified.

"There continue to be new discoveries all the time, so the cynics who say there are no new animals to be discovered are off their rocker. To discover a new species of whale is pretty substantial," says Kirk.

"The validity of anecdotal and eyewitness evidence as far as science goes is pretty muted, but you get such a huge consistency in what the witnesses see that you realize, yes, something is out there. Let's figure out what it is."

Tracking the Elusive[*]

By Tom Bell
Portland Press Herald (Portland, Me.), October 30, 2005

Loren Coleman is a world-renowned expert on the creatures that exist in the imagination but have yet to be documented by scientists. Bigfoot, the Loch Ness Monster and the Abominable Snowman are some of the stars in the field.

The Portland resident has written more than 20 books and more than 500 articles on the subject. He was in the news earlier this month when the makers of the Duel Masters trading card game offered a $1 million bounty for the safe capture of one of these alleged creatures.

Coleman helped the company with publicity when it launched the bounty, but Duel Masters quickly canceled the stunt after lawyers concluded that somebody could get hurt in the frenzy to capture Bigfoot or Nessie.

Coleman is a cryptozoologist. He says people like him are often maligned as crackpots until a real discovery is made and previously skeptical scientific authorities shamelessly celebrate the find, as in the cases of the giant panda and the Komodo dragon.

In his home, Coleman has established a cryptozology museum which contains items such as a life-size model of Bigfoot, a resin bust of the Feeje Mermaid, props from such movies as "The Mothman Prophecies," and Coleman's extensive collection of cryptotoys.

To protect his privacy, Coleman only opens the museum to people he knows.

Coleman spoke at a symposium on the relationship between cryptozoology and art on Friday and Saturday at the Bates College Museum of Art in Lewiston. His blog can be read at cryptomundo.com.

We met with Coleman at his home and talked to him about his work.

Q: What is a cryptozoologist?

Cryptozoology is the study of a hidden or unknown animal not as yet classified or verified by zoologists. A cryptozoologist is a person who studies these cryptids, as they are called, gathers information, whether they are eyewitness accounts, archival news articles, native traditions, photographs or footprints.

About 80 percent of the things that are shown to me are misidentifications, mistakes, outright hoaxes or obviously not an unknown creature. But the core of the other 20 percent is what I investigate and share worldwide with other cryptozoologists.

A lot of people now call me the world's leading living cryptozoologist because my mentors, like Bernard Heuvelmans and Ivan Sanderson, the fathers of cryptozoology, have died. Since I've been doing it for 44 years, even though my background has been in zoology, anthropology and psychiatric social work, it is a title that sort of has been bestowed upon me, more than one that I have picked out.

Do we have any cryptids in Maine?

There is one I call Cassie, or the Casco Bay Sea Serpent. I interviewed an old Norwegian fishermen who had seen one (in 1958) near the Portland Light Ship off Cape Elizabeth. . . . When he told me the story, he was like someone who had seen the JFK assassination. It (the serpent) was so vivid and so alive in his eyes. It looked like a big sea serpent with one big hump. . . . He said something that an eyewitness wouldn't make up, which is that the creature was going along and every time the light ship blew its foghorn, it turned its head slowly and then turned it back.

Have these serpents been seen by someone else?

Commander Preble (former commander of the *USS Constitution*) actually shot a cannonball over one of them. There is a whole history from colonial times until now.

Any other Maine cryptids?

There are black panther reports from the Damariscotta area on up to New Brunswick. And there are some old legends of a Bigfoot-type creature around Mount Katandin by the native peoples up there. In Durham, Maine, in 1977, a gorilla-like creature was seen along the Durham Road. There is one man who lives in Sydney who collects footprints and says they migrate.

The best place for a Bigfoot sighting obviously is the Pacific Northwest. But there does seem to be an Eastern variety, and I documented this in my book "Bigfoot." I really look at it in a scientific way, in which I took all the reports, and (the Eastern Bigfoots) are much more aggressive. There are many more dogs killed and many more conflicts with humans. Almost as if it is reflecting a sense on the sparser numbers, and they are feeling more encroached by humans.

Do some people think you are crazy?

I am actually a skeptic of what comes across my desk. I really know a lot about animals. I know a lot about different things. And the ridicule factor is used by people who don't know. A lot of people who talk about Bigfoot don't know where (these creatures) live or their habits, or that there is a long history of reports. Or the evidence. They have never considered the thousands of miles of tracks.

So do you believe in Bigfoot?

My routine answer is that I don't believe in Bigfoot. Belief is the province of religion. Belief is about faith. As a scientist, as a cryptozoologist, I see that we need to base our conclusions on evidence. I accept or deny evidence. I see if there is a pattern there. I analyze it. And based on what I have seen in the evidence for Bigfoot, I believe there is an authentic, unknown primate in some of the deeper wilderness areas of this country and Canada.

Have you ever been on the "Art Bell Show?"

Yes. I have appeared on Art Bell six times. I've been on Larry King. I have been a consultant on "In Search Of." I was the senior series consultant and was involved in many of those programs. And on "The Mothman Prophecies" I was the publicity person. I was on 300, 400 radio shows in one month.

What is your favorite holiday?

Halloween. (Laughs). I like that it is kid-oriented. I am very kid-oriented. I'm president of the booster's club for baseball at Portland High. But I like it because the ridicule level really comes down. And people can talk about topics like this without feeling they are being laughed at. At this time of year, people who have real sightings feel more comfortable coming out and understanding that they are not alone.

The Scientist and the Monster[*]

By Billy Baker
Boston Magazine, December 2008

As dusk fell on June 23, 1972, Bob Rines was a former war hero, a noted MIT scientist, a celebrated attorney, and an accomplished inventor who'd spent his multiple careers following success with more audacious success. He was 49 years old, his legacy already assured. Then he saw the hump.

Rines and his wife had been enjoying the evening with Scottish Wing Commander Basil Cary and his wife, Winifred, at the Carys' home on a hillside overlooking Urquhart Bay, on the northern shore of a remote Highland lake known as Loch Ness. After tea, Basil Cary stepped outside to the porch to smoke a pipe and saw something moving in the water below. "My dear," Rines heard Cary say, in what Rines describes as typical British understatement. "That couldn't be an upturned boat."

Rines had visited Loch Ness the previous year, on a lark, to investigate the age-old reports of a large unknown animal living in the murky water. Like many scientists who've been drawn to the mystery of Loch Ness, Rines, a pioneer in sonar technology, was playfully skeptical of the monster stories. But he'd met enough eyewitnesses, and picked up enough unexplainable images on his sonar, that by the time he returned for this second round of searching, he was, at the least, open-minded. When Cary made his offhand pronouncement, Rines's heart leapt into his throat.

The foursome dashed off the porch, through the yard, and across a two-lane road to a shoulder atop a steep bank that led to the loch's edge. There, trading turns with a telescope and binoculars, they watched a large grayish hump with the texture of an elephant's skin move across the bay. Rising at least 4 feet out of the water, the hump seemed to be about 25 feet long and attached to a creature of indeterminate size. Spellbound, they saw it plow against the current before it changed direction and began moving toward them. Then it submerged and disappeared.

The event would change Rines's life. With the water still rippling from the creature below, he vowed he would confirm what he'd seen. No matter the beating his reputation might take. No matter how long the search would drag on.

"I'm excited," Rines told me this past summer as we sat in the living room of his Harbor Towers apartment discussing the plans for the latest expedition to Loch Ness (about his 20th overall, he guessed). "I'm not always excited because I don't always have a detailed plan. It's a needle-in-a-haystack search. But this year, I know where to start. Or at least I think I do." With that, the 86-year-old rose from his deep leather couch—swatting my hand away when I moved to help—and shuffled off to the so-called Nessie room he maintains in one of the other units he owns on the 24th floor.

The Nessie room, which overlooks the opaque waters of Boston Harbor, is a celebration of Rines's three decades exploring the loch. The first thing that catches a visitor's eye is also Rines's greatest success to date: a series of grainy underwater photographs he took in the mid-1970s, which he believes show a diamond-shaped flipper, a gargoyle-like head, and the entire underbody of a long-necked, dinosaur-like animal. The photos, which all correspond with large objects recorded on sonar at the same time, were published around the world and prompted the Scottish Parliament to pass a conservation act protecting whatever might be in Loch Ness. After his pictures hit the media, Rines slowed his quest. He thought the hunt was about to come to an end; that scientists would flock to the lake and coax the mystery from its 700-foot depths. But that, of course, never happened. Since 1985, when he resumed the search again in earnest, Rines has enjoyed little success. His biggest remorse, he says, is that he didn't devote himself to the pursuit when the trail was hot.

In the early years of his Nessie hunt, Rines would regularly pick up large moving objects on his sonar. But the instruments haven't recorded anything like that in more than two decades, and the eyewitness accounts, which once flourished, have been in decline. A couple of years ago, Rines came to a sad conclusion, and shifted his approach. He believes that Nessie, like his friends from the tea party, is dead. So he's looking for skeletons.

"These are very odd shapes," he said as he opened the white binder, labeled "Loch Ness 2008," and began handing me fuzzy sonar printouts. The images, he said, represented his last chance. Rines suffered a stroke two years ago, and his health is failing. He had one final Nessie expedition in him, and a final grand idea. Before his stroke, he had made a detailed sonar map of the loch's bottom, identifying more than 100 suspicious targets. One, he hoped, would be the remains of Nessie. As his frail fingers combed through the printouts, he spotted a long, angular image. He turned toward me and, with an infectious hope in his eyes, said, "There aren't many long-necked animals."

For 45 years, until he retired last spring, Rines taught classes at MIT that centered on innovation and discovery—a fitting assignment for an inventor with over

100 patents to his name who also happens to be an attorney specializing in intellectual property. Though he's been guided in both professions by a singular belief that reason and intellect can solve problems, even reveal hidden truths, the lawyer in him has also been frequently frustrated by the standards of science—a discipline where, unlike in a courtroom, eyewitness testimony means nothing. Indeed, if Rines were called to court to argue Nessie's existence, he's certain he could marshal more than enough evidence to convince a jury. Science, he's well aware, requires more than that. It requires physical evidence. And until Rines finds it, his own credibility is at stake. Bob Rines is not trying to make his name by finding the monster in the lake; he's trying to save the staggering reputation he's earned elsewhere.

Rines, a native of Brookline, got his start at MIT, where, as an undergrad in the late 1930s, he began the work on high-definition sonar that eventually led him to invent the foundations for the technologies used to locate the sunken wreckage of the *Titanic* and the *Bismarck*, as well as those in the guidance systems on the Patriot missiles used in the first Gulf war—innovations that would get him inducted into the National Inventors Hall of Fame. During World War II, he was sent by the Army to erect an emergency radar system on Saipan, an island in the Pacific where Japanese bombers had been destroying American B-29s on the ground. "My little radar put a stop to that," he said; it also got him inducted into the U.S. Army Signal Corps Wall of Fame. After the war, Rines earned a law degree from Georgetown and went into practice with his father, whose Boston patent law firm worked to protect inventors—an ideal Rines brought to MIT when he returned to the university to begin teaching there in 1963. A decade later, concerned that the rights of patent holders were endangered, Rines founded (and went on to teach at) his own law school, the Franklin Pierce Law Center, in Concord, New Hampshire. Like many polymaths, Rines has also indulged a talent for music. As a boy, he impressed Albert Einstein when the two played a violin duet at a summer camp in Maine, and, later in life, he found time to compose a handful of Broadway scores, several of which made it to the stage. In 1987, he won an Emmy when *Hizzoner the Mayor* was made into a TV movie.

Still, the first line of his obituary will identify Bob Rines as the man who tried to prove the existence of the Loch Ness monster. He's accepted this. He says that he's only snapped at a naysayer once, a British customs agent who teased him after he declared the intentions of his visit. He asked the man if he believed in God and when he said he did, Rines asked him if he'd ever seen Him. "And I said nothing more," Rines remembered, somewhat embarrassed by his tactic. "They can just call me crazy, and that's okay by me. At least I won't go to jail for it, like Galileo."

Loch Ness is the largest body of fresh water in the United Kingdom, larger than all of the lakes and reservoirs in England and Wales combined. It's been calculated that you could fit every man, woman, and child on earth in its depths three times over. A mile wide and 24 miles long, the lake sits in the heart of the Scottish Highlands, and the lush green hills that roll gently along its banks can inspire an illusion of intimacy from shore. That is, until a boat passes and a sightseer can once again gauge how grand those hills are, how massive the water is, how large Rines's task has been.

On a warm day this past September, the *Udale*, a 45-foot boat Rines had hired for his final attempt to find Nessie, motored down the center of the lake. It was halfway through the two-week expedition, and the *Udale* was patrolling above one of Rines's sonar targets as I wound along the highway on the northern shore with Rines's grandson, David. It was my first glimpse of Loch Ness, and I glued my eyes to the water, afraid I might miss something. David gave the lake only a passing glance.

In addition to David, Rines would be joined on this trip by another grandchild, his youngest son, and his wife, Joanne, the former editor and publisher of *Inventor's Digest*. They're all unquestionably devoted to Rines, but when it comes to this monster business the family's emotions are mixed. David, who pointed out that Rines required his relatives to always have a camera with them while at Loch Ness, made the journey mostly because it was his grandfather's last expedition and he wanted to be there with him for the milestone. But he was avoiding much direct involvement, largely, he said, "out of fear that I might see it and be equally consumed." Yet while David is dubious about his grandfather's theory that the monster may have been some kind of plesiosaur, a dinosaur holdout that found a refuge in the loch, he's not skeptical about his grandfather's belief that he saw *something* in 1972. "Hardly a day goes by without him talking about it," he said. "You're going on 40 years now, without ever flinching."

Watching Rines spend a good deal of his time and fortune pursuing the Loch Ness monster has, if nothing else, inspired those around him to chase wild dreams. "His law clients are crazy scientists with crazy ideas, and time and time again he's seen these crazy ideas come to fruition and have an impact on the world," David said. "For him, the pursuit of the impossible is irresistible."

David slowed the car as we arrived in Drumnadrochit, the undisputed capital of Nessieland. One expects Niagara Falls, a giant tourist trap with electric signs. Instead, it's a quaint Scottish village that treats its most famous resident and chief attraction with equal parts pride and restraint. The most significant structure is the Drumnadrochit Hotel, a stone lodge in the Victorian Baronial style. The hotel has been at the center of the Nessie legend since a local gamekeeper walked in the door in 1916, "his face as white as paper," and reported that a huge animal had surfaced by his fishing boat.

Reports of lake monsters have floated around the Scottish lochs for centuries, dating back to the kelpies and water horses of Highland folklore. In 565, Saint Columba reportedly saved the life of one of his followers who was being attacked by a "ferocious monster" in Loch Ness. The stories really got going in the 1930s, when road-building along Loch Ness improved access and thinned the trees that blocked sightlines. In 1933, the *Inverness Courier* ran a story about Mrs. John Mackay, the manager of the Drumnadrochit Hotel, who reported seeing something resembling a whale. There were several other sightings that year, including the first descriptions of an animal with a long neck. That year also saw the first of many hoaxes when M. A. Wetherell, a big-game hunter sent by the *London Daily Mail*, produced a set of giant footprints that would turn out to have been made with a trophy from a previous hunt—a hippopotamus foot that Wetherell used as an ashtray.

These days, the Drumnadrochit Hotel is under the control, ideologically speaking, of Adrian Shine, the most famous skeptic in the Nessie game. A 59-year-old Englishman with a great big Rasputin beard and a way of speaking that oozes professorial authority, Shine has built his name poking holes in the theories of Rines and the other believers. His Loch Ness Exhibition Centre, which now fills the original hotel building, features a 30-minute-long multimedia attempt to discredit claims of the monster's existence. (Rines calls Shine a "dear friend," though the scientist with a wall full of diplomas always qualifies any praise by sliding in the fact that Shine is a "self-trained" naturalist.)

Shine admits that there is a mystery in Loch Ness; even he cannot dispel what he says are 1,000 documented sightings. (Others put the figure at 2,000; some as high as 5,000.) People have seen something, Shine agrees, but that doesn't mean they've seen a prehistoric monster. What they've glimpsed, he believes, can be explained as either biological, physical, or psychological: They've seen some other, known animal; they've been fooled by a wave or a wake; or they see something because they *expect* to see something.

Like Rines's, Shine's quest began with an encounter. In 1969, he set out to investigate a mystery at Loch Morar, a lake to the west of Loch Ness that has its own tradition of curious sightings, and where, allegedly, a boat had recently been attacked by a water monster. Shine rented a rowboat and paddled around Loch Morar one night with a camera. As he was rowing along the dark northern shoreline, he saw a hump, "very much like the ones I'd seen drawn in books of sightings," emerge from behind a promontory. "I stopped rowing. It stopped moving. I took a photograph . . . and waited for it to move." It didn't, so he rowed toward it.

As Shine drew near it, the hump began to look like a huge, submerged head. "I got closer," he said, inserting a pregnant pause. "It was a rock"—another dramatic pause—"so all my perceptions had actually been wrong. And I vowed that night that if I couldn't believe my own eyes, I wasn't going to believe anybody else's, either. And that has no bearing on the integrity of the person, but only the fallibility of perception."

David Rines describes his grandfather's expeditions as "a cross between *National Geographic* and *The Life Aquatic with Steve Zissou*"—rigorous science mixed with daydream whimsy. In the '70s, Bob Rines had a New Jersey perfumer create a chemical that he hoped would act as a pheromone to attract the animal. Another time, he trained two dolphins in Florida to carry cameras. He was constructing a saltwater pool he planned to float in the loch that would allow the dolphins' skin to recover from the freshwater exposure when one of them died on a stopover at the Hull Aquarium. Rines believed the dolphin, who had never before been separated from its handler, had died of "a broken heart." He was so upset that he shipped the other dolphin back to Florida and called off the scheme.

While he may have failed to locate Nessie, Rines is quick to point out that his attempts have not been without scientific success. He's an MIT guy with MIT friends, and together they've found the deep, peat-stained waters of Loch Ness, where visibility is only a few feet even with powerful lights, a perfect place to innovate. Charlie Wycoff, a colleague who created the dynamic film stock used to capture early atomic bomb explosions and the moon landings, came on several expeditions. He and Rines invented a buoy-mounted mechanism that triggered an underwater camera when sonar detected an object (this is how they captured the famous 1970s photos). Another associate, celebrated MIT scientist Harold "Doc" Edgerton—who pioneered high-speed strobe photography and worked with Jacques Cousteau to develop underwater imaging—was skeptical of the monster. But Edgerton nonetheless lent his expertise to a couple of Rines's expeditions, and also joined him in an unsuccessful hunt for King Solomon's lost fleet off the coast of Israel. Just like Nessie, Wycoff and Edgerton are gone now, too. "I'm the last of the dinosaurs," Rines likes to say.

Measured against his past expeditions, this year's was comparatively simple. Rines had hired two local boats, from which operators from a Louisiana-based company called Seatrepid—which normally does oil rig inspections in the Gulf of Mexico—would pilot a pair of small submarines. The remote-operated vehicles (ROVs) were each outfitted with cameras to find Nessie's bones, and a claw to haul them to the surface. On account of his health, Rines mostly stayed off the boats, and instead spent most of his time at Tychat, a postcard estate where he's stayed since the '70s (and which he's owned since the mid-1990s). The house has a giant picture window that offers a panoramic view of Urquhart Bay, and from it, Rines monitored his team's progress. Several times, I spotted Rines sitting alone at the window, slumped deep into an armchair, binoculars by his side, staring at the water or across the bay toward the Carys' home, where his adventure began.

For the first week or so, the ROVs investigated the more promising spots on Rines's sonar map. The only interesting things they found were a couple of old rifles. On the 10th day of the expedition, the sun was shining and the water was smooth. Sightings almost always occur in flat water; this was, as the locals say, "Nessie weather." Rines called the *Udale* to shore, had the crew lift him aboard on a plastic lawn chair, and took his place in front of the monitor that displayed the camera feed from one of the submarines.

Almost immediately, they got lucky. The camera spotted something on the bottom that had not been on Rines's sonar map, something long and fleshy-looking. Rines pulled himself close to the monitor. What he saw appeared mottled, like a tentacle, or maybe rotting skin. It didn't resemble a log, which is what many of the sonar targets had turned out to be. To Rines, it had all the characteristics you'd expect of something that had lain dead on the bottom for 20 years, in temperatures about the same as a refrigerator's.

The crew radioed to the second boat, the *Highland Park*, which was trolling a far-off stretch of water, and had on board a stronger ROV with a bigger grabbing claw. It took nearly two hours for the vessel to move into position. While he waited, Rines kept his eyes focused on the monitor and wondered, aloud, if he had finally found his monster.

After the *Highland Park*'s ROV brought the object slowly to the surface, the sub was hoisted up by a crane. As Rines watched expectantly, the claw dropped its payload into the arms of a crew member. It was a tire. An old leather tire from a Model T that had been cut so that it was unfurled like a hose.

"If anyone wanted to fake the neck of a plesiosaur," Rines said that night, staring into the fireplace at Tychat, "use a cut tire." Then he turned to me and winked. "I certainly thought that was it."

The expedition's final sweep of the loch, everyone thought, was to be simply ceremonial. Since his stroke, swallowing has been difficult for Rines, and eating his biggest daily challenge, but he spent the last morning determinedly fueling up to convince Joanne he was strong enough for the boat ride.

For Rines, it was a special day. Justice, his youngest son, had arrived early that afternoon. (He was given his name after his father lost a case shortly before he was born. Dismayed at the courts, Rines vowed that he'd know justice in one way, shape, or form in his life.) Justice had grown up on the lake; the summers spent on the Nessie quest serve as his strongest childhood memory. There were definitely times, Justice admits, when he wished his father wouldn't come to his school and talk about the monster, but he has a deep faith in his pursuit. Still, though he's capable of delivering his father's arguments, he doesn't sell them with the same preacher passion. Even when he had his own unexplained sighting, it didn't stir in him the same restless desire that his father's had.

It was 1991. Justice was on the patio at Tychat when he saw two objects about a mile away in the center of the loch, moving next to each other and plowing a wake. He called to his parents, and they trained a video camera on the objects. The distance was too great to show more than a speck, but on the tape Rines's voice could be heard clearly in the background. "He was excited that three members of the family had now seen something," Justice remembered. "This is it! This is it!" his father yelled. "You've seen it." What he saw, Justice won't venture to say.

When it was time for the valedictory cruise to begin, the family members made their way to the *Udale*, which was tied up at the pier below Tychat. David Rines had come up with a plan to take a quick tour of Urquhart Bay, maybe drop the ROV where Rines had taken his "flipper" picture. And that would be it.

But right after the *Udale* coasted out onto the loch, the vessel unexpectedly turned east and suddenly picked up speed, splashing Joanne with its spray. Rines had gotten a whiff of this "funeral," David would later tell me, and decided he wasn't having it. He ordered the captain to head to the "circles," a strange collection of dots that had shown up on the sonar maps.

Joanne thought the markings were probably the remnants of an old wartime experiment in sending Morse code underwater—a explanation she adopted after a bit of Internet research, and which pleased her because she didn't want the crew distracted from the mission. "I wanted them looking for Nessie bones," she told me. But Rines wanted to investigate for himself. There was, he declared, room for only one mystery in Loch Ness. When the submersible reached one of the circles, its lights shone on an insulated cable. That was enough to convince Rines that Joanne's theory was correct. "Honey," he said, patting his wife on the shoulder, "you've made a discovery!"

In the late 1950s, Rines, then still practicing law with his father, took a boat to Scotland for a vacation with his late first wife and their two small children. Aboard the ship, he met Sir James Miller, who would later become lord mayor of London. Miller insisted Rines visit the Highlands and offered his driver to take the family north. It was there, while staying in Fort Augustus at the southwest end of Loch Ness, that Rines came across a book titled *More Than a Legend*. It had been published roughly a year earlier by Constance Whyte, whose husband oversaw the Caledonian Canal, a 62-mile stretch of man-made locks and natural lakes— including Loch Ness, the system's longest waterway—that allows boat passage between the Scottish coasts. Whyte's book was a landmark in that it collected for the first time many of the eyewitness accounts of Nessie. To Whyte, Nessie was a zoological riddle, "a really super 'whodunit,' the murder without a corpse, or to put it more exactly: The witnesses have seen the corpse, but cannot produce it." Rines was transfixed by the stories and more than a bit curious. He immediately sent a copy to Doc Edgerton at MIT, asking if he'd like to use his strobe cameras to have a look at the lake. Edgerton, who'd require several more years of cajoling before he'd agree to help his friend with his quest, returned the book without comment.

In Whyte's introduction, the author shares an insight—or maybe a warning— that could not have been lost on Rines when he read it: "To announce to all and sundry that you have seen the Loch Ness Monster involves a step which cannot lightly be taken." As the chronicler of Nessie-spotters, she writes with sympathy for the true believers, noting that the "ingenuity [used] in discrediting eyewitness accounts has been quite astonishing." After three decades building his case, Rines is undeterred, and has fashioned a closing argument to focus squarely on those eyewitnesses. "Are they all liars? All drunks? I don't believe that about human nature," he said. The human brain, he'll concede, is not 100 percent trustworthy. "But it's not zero, either."

The conundrum remains a lack of evidence, a fact uniquely clear to the lawyer whose ceaseless obsession has been to obtain it. Interestingly, Rines's best chance might have been on his first encounter back in 1972. As he stood atop that hill watching the hump, Rines held a Super-8 camera in his hands. But—as he told me, several times—he was so captivated, so gripped by what he was watching through the binoculars, that he couldn't bring himself to put the ocular to his eyes. He chose to see it for himself. It is a choice he says he does not regret.

Hairy, Scary Stories Linger in the Thin Air[*]

By Troy Lennon

Daily Telegraph (London, U.K.), December 4, 2007

A documentary team in the Himalayas claim they have new evidence of the existence of the legendary Yeti. Also known as the Abominable Snowman, the creature has reputedly lived in the mountains for centuries.

While most people scoff at such stories, legends about large ape-like creatures roaming the wilderness have been so persistent that many think they might have an element of truth. Such people are not deterred by the fact that the evidence consists of ambiguous images, doubtful footprints and other scant clues.

But it all belongs in the realm of what has been called cryptozoology—the study of creatures thought to exist for which no conclusive evidence has been found.

The term cryptozoology was coined by Scottish-born naturalist Ivan Sanderson in the 1940s, but man's fascination with strange beasts goes back much further.

Monks of isolated Himalayan monasteries and other mountain dwellers reported sightings of large ape-like footprints in the snow and visions of hairy wild men living in the icy environment. Although these stories were probably explicable in terms of human footprints becoming misshapen after melting or ill-kempt reclusive humans living in the wild, they snowballed into unshakeable legends.

The West first learned of these legends in the early 19th century. Britain's first representative in Nepal, B. H. Hodson, reported in 1832 that his native guides were attacked by a wild upright walking creature "covered in long, dark hair" with no tail. The men called it a "rakshas" or demon. The natives were shaken by the manifestation.

No doubt the sightings continued but it was much later that the Yeti made another appearance in the British press. In 1889 a British army major and explorer, Laurence Waddell, sighted huge footprints in the snow and his guides explained that they were the tracks of a Yeti—a Sherpa word meaning rock-dwelling creature. Waddell was a professor of chemistry and pathology, as well as writing works

* Article by Troy Lennon, from the *Daily Telegraph*, December 4, 2007. Reprinted with permission.

on history, religion and languages. He was impressed enough by the footprints to report the sighting.

The term Abominable Snowman was coined after reports of the discovery of footprints at high altitudes on Lieutenant Colonel Charles Howard-Bury's 1921 British expedition to Everest. The footprints appeared to be from a group of large creatures who had moved rapidly up the slopes. The guides called the creatures "metoh-kangmi", roughly translated as the dirty snowmen but mis-translated as abominable ones. Howard-Bury said later that they were probably the distorted tracks of "a large, loping, grey wolf" but when the story filtered to the outside world, it was reported as an actual sighting of the creatures themselves and the term abominable snowman entered the English language.

In 1951 Sherpa guide Tenzing Norgay was accompanying Eric Shipton on another British expedition when he saw strange tracks in the snow, which he said were of a Yeti. "It showed three broad 'toes' and a broad 'thumb' to the side," Shipton wrote.

Shipton had never seen such "well preserved" tracks, suggesting that they had not been significantly altered by melting. He said Tenzing claimed he and a large group of Sherpas had seen a Yeti "at a distance of 25 yards (23m) at Thyangboche. He describes it as half man, half beast, about 5ft 6in [168cm] tall, covered with reddish brown hair but with a hairless face. Whatever it was he saw, I am convinced of his sincerity."

A 1953 Indian expedition led by Russi Ghandi found that Pangboche Monastery held what the monks believed to be relics of a Yeti—a conical fur-covered "scalp" and the bones of a Yeti hand. The monks refused to part with either and so could not be studied by scientists.

But the monastery received a visit in the 1950s from a more determined explorer. US adventurer Tom Slick saw the scalp and the hand while on an expedition in search of the Yeti in 1957. Slick was a Texas oil magnate's son who had studied biology at Harvard but whose hobby was cryptozoology.

On a 1959 expedition a member of Slick's team, big-game hunter Peter Byrne, convinced the monks to let him take the Yeti hand bones out of the monastery. He smuggled the Yeti hand out of Asia with the assistance of actor James Stewart, who hid the hand in his luggage. The hand has since disappeared.

Meanwhile, in 1958 a Catholic missionary, Father Frank Eichinger, had returned home to Frankfurt, Germany, from Tibet with a claim that the Abominable Snowmen were really religious recluses living high in the Himalayas.

The vegetarian holy men wore little and walked in the snow bare-footed, not feeling the cold, he said. There have been many expeditions to the Himalayas by cryptozoologists trying to prove the existence of the Yeti, but no conclusive evidence has yet been found. Which does not stop people believing that the creature exists.

The North American counterpart of the Yeti is known by the native American name of Sasquatch, but is known more generally as Bigfoot. Once again, the evidence has mostly been based on large inexplicable footprints, hence the name.

When whites arrived in America they found that many native American tribes had stories about man-beasts who live in forests. One of the first Europeans to claim to have found evidence of the creatures was English explorer David Thompson, who reported having found a footprint in 1811.

Perhaps the most famous sighting, however, was film footage taken in California in 1967. Roger Patterson and a friend, Bob Gimlin, had heard about findings of footprints and sightings of a creature in the Six Rivers National Forest in the late 1950s. They rode on horseback into the forest near a place called Bluff Creek in October 1967 when they captured footage of a loping ape-like creature.

The film was pronounced a fake by many who believe it is merely a man in a costume. But it had some staunch supporters who said that it was definitely not a human. Among them is Jane Goodall, a British expert in studying chimp behaviour. Goodall watched the film, and various other pieces of footage alleged to be Bigfoot, and in a 2002 radio interview pronounced Patterson's 1967 footage to be authentic.

Recently, however, a man named Bob Heironimus admitted he was paid by Gimlin to wear the suit.

This revelation has done nothing to shake the faith of the true believers. Even China has its own version of the Yeti—the so-called Wild Men (Yeren).

They don't live near the Himalayas but, allegedly, in the icy Shennongjia mountain range of central China, descending occasionally to terrify villagers living nearby.

The similarity of reports of ape men around the world led Grover Krantz, professor of physical anthropology at Washington State University, to speculate whether there might be a remnant population of the giant ape Gigantopithecus blacki still existing in some remote parts. The first fossils of G. Blacki were found in South-East Asia in the early 20th century.

It is thought to have died out only 100,000 years ago, which means it once co-existed with humans.

Another expert on the ancient ape, Professor Chris Stringer of London's Natural History Museum, believes the creature may have inspired the Yeti tales.

The Myth Hunters[*]

By Kim Knight
Sunday Star-Times (Auckland, New Zealand), October 26, 2007

It was a dark and stormy night.

OK, says Vicki Hyde, president of the New Zealand Skeptics, so it wasn't stormy. But it was dark.

And there was something out there. Big, black, bulky. Just sitting there, watching.

"We stared. It stared back."

She threw a shoe. It didn't move. "Too big for an ordinary cat. Too still for a dog. Too quiet for a possum."

A quick dash inside and the outside lights went on to reveal: an upended bucket.

"Did we feel silly? You bet."

It can happen to anyone, says Hyde. Mistaken identification leads to incorrect assumptions and misperceptions, she writes in her new book *Oddzone*.

"It doesn't mean you're foolish or stupid or insane. Just human."

And humans love a good mystery. Is there a yeti in the Himalayas? A Nessie in the Loch? A moose in Fiordland?

The hunt for a remnant population of moose liberated in New Zealand bush in the early 1900s is more than three decades old. So is the search for the South Island kokako, last reliably sighted in the 1950s and 60s. Student filmmakers recently went on the trail of a mysterious black cat in Canterbury. And now moa are back in the headlines, with news that next month, an Australian researcher will cross the ditch to find a colony of the giant birds in Te Urewera.

Who are these people who devote lifetimes to the hunt for the unknown?

Ken Tustin, 62, has amassed around 600 nights in the Fiordland bush trying to prove the existence of moose. The closest he has come is the collection of stray hairs, DNA-tested by scientists in Canada, who say his theory is almost certainly correct.

"I read articles saying I'm obsessed," says Tustin. "I think (my story) tells kids, hey, in 2008, there are some great adventures still to be had. There are unsolved things and wonderful mysteries out there."

He knows he'll need photographs to silence the critics—some people say the hairs prove nothing more than that the hunter has been hoaxed. Tustin, and his wife Marg, have had remote cameras in the bush for years. "We've probably put about 10,000 camera nights into it." So far, no moose—"and about 2000 red deer."

He says it's a lovely personal challenge.

"Man thinks he controls the planet but, in effect, we're being outfoxed by a very large, charismatic animal."

For researchers like Tustin, and 60-year-old Rhys Buckingham, who is convinced the South Island kokako still exists, the common thread is begrudging admiration for their prey.

"How come you can't find a thing the size of a horse?" Buckingham asks Tustin.

"How is it you can't find a stupid squawking crow?" retorts Tustin.

What keeps the pair going?

"You've got to have some mystery in your life," says Buckingham—who is fitting in a phone interview around two three-day dance parties.

He says the South Island kokako is an incredible songbird and he believes he has collected numerous tape recordings of the bird that's been dubbed "the grey ghost." Naysayers reckon he's simply recorded tui.

"I used to be more obsessed when I thought there was a chance to save it from extinction," says Buckingham. "I'm getting more disillusioned now, with what appears to be a calamity facing much more common birds, with stoat and rat plagues. I think I'm too late, I haven't been successful . . . it would be so magnificent to save it from extinction."

The moose and the kokako did, at least, once exist. But are there other, more mysterious creatures roaming New Zealand?

In 1966, the *Encyclopaedia of New Zealand* included a section headed "Animals, Mythical." "Numerous tales of monsters, ogres, goblins and fairies, and weird 'hairy men' who devoured unwary travellers and waylaid hunting parties have long been part of Maori lore," it said. "In all probability, such tales of water-dwelling monsters and other huge reptiles known as kumi were nothing more than distorted folk memories of the crocodile of the western Pacific or Asia."

The entry gives slight credence to the waitoreke—an aquatic, otter-like creature. Julius von Haast was believed to have acquired a portion of skin from the supposed animal. Charles Darwin wrote a letter, now held by the Alexander Turnbull Library, querying its existence: "If I have not utterly exhausted your patience, I should be particularly obliged if you would inform me whether you think the evidence is really good that there formerly existed some animal (with hair?) like an otter or Beaver: I am much surprised at this. Could it not have been any water bird or reptile?"

Lemuel Lyes, archival researcher with Natural History New Zealand, says the existence (or otherwise) of the waitoreke is important even if it is now extinct. "If it could be proven to have existed once, then perhaps that would shatter some conceptions about New Zealand's natural history."

Here's a theory: New Zealand is rumoured to have been visited by Tamil explorers. Te Papa Museum records the 1836 discovery of a ship's bell, inscribed with ancient (at least 500 years old) Tamil script, being used by Whangarei Maori as a cooking pot. As it happens, says Lyes, Tamil sailors were known to use tame otters to catch fish. "Maybe, pre-Tasman days, some Tamil lost their otter?"

Lyes says it's feasible a small number of the animals could exist undetected. "We're supposed to have this huge population of stoats and weasels and things, yet how many New Zealanders have actually seen them? What's to stop small pockets of otters living in some sanctuary down south?"

Cryptozoologists—the name given to people who study creatures whose existence has not been substantiated—say there is a very good chance of discovering unknown animals in New Zealand.

According to Hawke's Bay-based researcher Tony Lucas, "We still have many areas in the South Island which remain relatively unexplored. These remote regions hold the best hope of harbouring a new, or previously thought extinct, species."

This is the country, after all, that gave up the takahe half a century after it was thought to be extinct. The Chatham Islands taiko had not been seen for 111 years until it was dramatically rediscovered on New Year's Day in 1978. And as recently as 2003, the New Zealand storm petrel, gone for 150 years, was sighted off the coast of Whitianga.

But how about those reports of a giant black cat in Canterbury? Last year, Mark Orton, a former film student who now works for Natural History New Zealand, trekked the region collecting eyewitness sightings for a documentary called *Prints of Darkness*. "I can only tell you what I saw," Toni May tells the camera. "I can't tell you what it is."

If it was a feral cat, says another interviewee, "it was an Arnold Schwarzenegger of a cat."

The rogue panther is an international cryptozoology mystery—similar stories frequently circulate in United Kingdom and Australian media.

"The characters we featured in our film were not nutters," says Orton. "They firmly believe in what they saw."

His personal theory? "I think there's possibly a rather large breed of feral cats. They've probably thrown up the black gene through years of interbreeding. Through their stealth and willingness to survive, the black cats have had the biggest success and they're the ones thrown up more often than not."

The filmmakers based themselves at Panther's Rock Tavern, Mayfield. The pub got its name in retrospect and now hangs a mock big-cat road sign in the bar. Orton says locals laugh at the story of giant felines. "They've made fun of people in the community who have been open enough to admit the story. Some of the people we ended up putting in the film didn't go to the mainstream media because they didn't want the exposure."

Rex Gilroy knows how they feel. The 64-year-old bills himself as the "father of Australian cryptozoology." Next month, he and his wife Heather will travel to New Zealand to search for moa in Te Urewera—where they claim to have previously found moa tracks and a nesting site.

"A lot of people are frightened to go to the media," says Gilroy. "They (the media) play it up as a joke but it may affect the life's work of some serious researcher. I just say we've got to be prepared to keep an open mind and investigate the evidence.

"You've got to be born for this sort of work," Gilroy tells the *Star-Times*. "As an open-minded field researcher, I prefer to look for the evidence rather than dismiss something out of hand because a textbook says it's extinct."

He will go back to a site he says is home to "maybe half a dozen" small, scrub moa. And that's not all. Gilroy says years ago, he found "tracks of bare human footprints, not too large . . . but I've often wondered who was getting around in the middle of nowhere, in the forest."

Could it be the mysterious Moehau—New Zealand's version of the Big Foot mystery? Gilroy is keeping an open mind.

"It's difficult for me, because I've got to differentiate between hoax sightings and believable ones . . . like some road workers, in the pouring rain, about 10 years ago, in the Eglinton Valley before the Milford Tunnel. They were in a shed, waiting for the rain to stop, and on the edge of the jungle were two birds emerging from the bush, about eight feet (2.4m) in height. And they were chewing leaves off trees . . . I get to know when someone's telling the truth. You can tell embellishments."

Gilroy says "you've got to be a bit eccentric in this business. If people think you're a little bit crazy, they leave you alone so you can do your work.

"I want people to question, to draw their own conclusions. I think you can do no more greater service to man than make him think."

WHAT ARE THE ODDS?

Tony Lucas is a Hawke's Bay student of cryptozoology—the study of creatures or "cryptids" whose existence has not been proven. His work involves sorting through myths, legends, eyewitness accounts and physical evidence before deciding what could be plausible.

"It is harder to prove that something does exist than it doesn't," says Lucas, noting that when it comes to exploring the unknown, "there will always be sceptics, critics and hoaxers".

The *Sunday Star-Times* asked him for an opinion on some of this country's infamous cryptids:

MOEHAU

A gorilla-like animal, New Zealand's version of Big Foot, reported in the Coromandel and the West Coast of the South Island: "Very few reports of vague sightings . . . evidence seems to indicate that these species may have become extinct."

WAITOREKE

An aquatic, otter-like creature, reported mostly in the lower South Island: "I feel this species could have become extinct as a recent expedition by an associate failed to turn up any evidence. The area once inhabited by the waitoreke are apparently now very urbanised and developed . . . gold mining and property development may have been responsible for its loss of habitat and final demise."

SOUTH ISLAND KOKAKO

A songbird last reported in May 2007, near Murchison: "The chances for this bird still existing seem slim. However, there have been physical traces found and a small remnant population may yet be discovered. Recovery of the species would depend on if there were enough still in existence to build a viable breeding population."

CANTERBURY BLACK CAT

Mostly reported in the Ashburton area: "Numerous eye witness accounts and physical evidence seem to back up the existence of this animal. It was only recently that Australia acknowledged there were feral big cats roaming there. It may just be a matter of time before the same happens in New Zealand."

THE FIORDLAND MOOSE

Believed to live in the Dusky Sound area: "This has already been proven to exist with hair samples found and DNA tested. The reason for no actual sightings is, once again, the dense vegetation of the Fiordland area."

6

Ghosts Go Primetime:
The Paranormal in Pop Culture

Editor's Introduction

For nearly a decade, TV has been ruled by "reality shows," programs that purport to portray real people in real situations. Notable among these shows are those that belong to the paranormal subset, series such as *Ghost Hunters*, *Most Haunted*, and *Paranormal State*. Unlike *Laguna Beach*, *The Real World*, and *Survivor*—programs whose appeal largely stems from the interpersonal squabbles of young, attractive cast members—paranormal reality shows are about transcending the mundane and using science to answer a question man has long asked himself: Is there life after death? Some of these shows, such as *Ghost Hunters*, have fared well in the ratings, suggesting that viewers have overcome what programmers say was a post-9/11 aversion to fear and are once again ready to be scared.

The public's current fascination with the paranormal extends beyond reality TV. Stephenie Meyer's "Twilight" novels, which tell the stories of young vampires, have proved wildly popular, inspiring a feature-film adaptation and selling millions of copies. Similarly, Charlaine Harris has found great success with her "Southern Vampire Mystery" books, which are the basis for the HBO dramatic series *True Blood*.

The pieces collected in this chapter examine the paranormal's place in popular culture, considering why so many people are suddenly smitten with spooky subject matter. In the first article, "Networks' Scary Strategy," Anne Becker discusses the success of paranormal reality programs and horror films. Rob Sharenow, a vice president at the A&E network, suggests that viewers' hunger for ghost stories represents a backlash against 24-hour news broadcasting and today's culture of constant information. "So much of the world is known now; there are few mysteries with Google Maps and CNN and coverage of everything," Sharenow tells Becker. "This [programming] is an area that's very mysterious and unknown."

In "When Love Is Strange," Gwenda Bond focuses on "paranormal romance" and "urban fantasy," literary genres that have flourished in recent years, even as the publishing industry continues its downward spiral. Vampires factor heavily in many of the novels Bond cites, as do demons and werewolves. While the stories tend to feature supernatural elements, they're driven by personal relationships, making them especially attractive to young female readers. One publishing executive calls the books "the ultimate escape," and she attributes their popularity to readers' desire to forget about the wars and financial hardships that have dominated headlines of late.

"In Search of Today's Ghost Stories," the next entry, looks at how paranormal reality shows balance skepticism with sensationalism. Writer James Hibberd also discusses allegations the shows doctor their footage. The last article, "'Ghost

Hunters' Redefines Reality TV," an opinion piece by Aaron Sagers, focuses on a show that stars two Rhode Island plumbers-turned-paranormal investigators. Sagers argues the program achieves brilliance through its adherence to classic TV formulas.

Networks' Scary Strategy[*]

By Anne Becker
Broadcasting & Cable, December 8, 2007

Cable networks across the dial and over the Internet are eagerly chanting the same mantra to viewers: Be afraid; be very afraid.

Spooky fare—whether paranormal or horror-themed—has yielded ratings spikes for traditional linear players like Sci Fi, Lifetime and WE, with A&E hoping to cash in next. And digital upstarts like Comcast's FearNet and NBC Universal's digital channel Chiller have nothing to cheer but fear itself.

They're giving TV audiences more than classic horror movies. The newest breed of reality thrill series mix the filmic look of fright-time classics with digital technology and true-life characters and incidents.

Most emblematic of this new breed of scary TV is A&E's *Paranormal State*, a reality show from *Laguna Beach* producers Go Go Luckey, which focuses on a team of Penn State students who travel around the country trying to help people spooked by spirits. The show launches Dec. 10 and features a blend of horror-film techniques (plentiful point-of-view shots, constant foreground matter) and the use of new cameras like the FLIR, which picks up thermal readings.

"Any show that takes you away from what you're doing and thrills you is good storytelling," says Go Go Luckey Partner and *Paranormal* Executive Producer Gary Auerbach. "When you're dealing with something in the reality space that's scary, that double-intensifies the feeling."

Several reasons explain the surge in this reality fare. Practicality certainly plays a part: The shows draw younger viewers and typically require one-quarter the budget of a scripted program. They also, perhaps surprisingly, often skew slightly more female than male—Sci Fi's *Ghost Hunters* pulls 53% females, says the network.

But there are more profound reasons. Programming execs point to research showing that right after Sept. 11, viewers weren't ready to be scared. More than six years later, viewers are more prepared for TV where the security threat level is higher.

"In a post 9/11 era, [people didn't] want to be emotionally challenged by dramas that tackled horror scenarios," says Sci Fi General Manager Dave Howe. "Years later, there's a resurgence because people are feeling more secure."

Networks have been eager to respond. On Jan. 9, Sci Fi premieres an international spin-off of the spook-chase *Ghost*, and it upped the episode count for chilling investigation show *Destination Truth* for its second season. A live two-hour Halloween special of *Ghost* drew more than 2.8 million viewers, helping lead Sci Fi to its best performance in the 18–49 demo on a Wednesday since 2002.

Lifetime recently completed seasons of *America's Psychic Challenge* and *Lisa Williams*. A reality show about the medium/clairvoyant, *Lisa Williams* grew 33% from first to second season. It also helped launch its lead-in, the competition series *America's Psychic Challenge*, which grew to an average of 1.6 million viewers for its finale.

In the works elsewhere is a slate of original and acquired series and specials on WE, Cablevision's women's network. On the heels of debuting a second season of *John Edward Cross Country*, featuring the famed medium, WE green-lit a slew of similar shows with titles like *Rescue Mediums*, *Extreme Ghost Stories* and *Abducted by UFOs*, in a programming block called "WE Go Supernatural."

FearNet, the video-on-demand/broadband channel Comcast launched on Halloween 2006 with studios Lionsgate and Sony, is notching more viewers than it had banked on. The network, which has grown distribution to include Cox, saw a respectable 10.5 million movie-views on VOD in October on Comcast alone and averaged a lengthy 74 minutes for viewing of an original film online.

NBCU's VOD channel Chiller, the digital home for the company's horror-themed library content, is seeing success with viewer-created content for its Website, drawing some 300 upstart filmmakers to its "Dare to Direct" contest this fall. Chiller seeks to grow TV distribution beyond its 13.5 million homes.

In programming all this paranormal fare, executives are tapping into another familiar appetite among viewers: hunger for the unknown. That's harder to come by in an era of the 24-hour news cycle, with cable networks and the Internet bombarding audiences with competing facts.

"So much of the world is known now; there are few mysteries with Google Maps and CNN and coverage of everything," says Rob Sharenow, A&E's senior VP of non-fiction and alternative programming. "This [programming] is an area that's very mysterious and unknown."

FearNet, which targets the 18-to-34-year-old horror fan, has added to its 1,000 movie titles on VOD with original content such as *Catacombs*, a film by the producers of the "Saw" franchise. It drew nearly 700,000 VOD views in one month. Its live stream online helped FearNet grow 94% month to month in Web traffic. Among many new features and fresh content online, the network is running the original Web series *Buried Alive*, in which one of 40 new episodes debuts every day for two months.

"To be successful in these platforms, you need to be a niche within a niche," says FearNet chief Diane Robina, president of Comcast Emerging Networks. "I don't agree that the millennials have a short attention span."

Certainly not when it comes to this niche, where the engagement of viewers across the board continues to be scary-good.

When Love Is Strange[*]

Romance Continues Its Affair with the Supernatural

By Gwenda Bond
Publishers Weekly, May 25, 2009

Think of a writer known for creating one of the most popular and memorable vampire series in history—one with 17 million copies of her books in print in 35 countries, one whose fans are so devoted that in 2008 the annual convention honoring her sold out in less than three minutes, one who managed six #1 rankings on the *New York Times* bestseller list in just over a year. No, not Stephenie Meyer—this publishing phenomenon is the reigning queen of the wildly successful paranormal scene, Sherrilyn Kenyon.

Over the past decade, Kenyon's Dark-Hunter series has increased in popularity until the latest installment, *Bad Moon Rising*, is virtually assured to land at the top of the lists when it hits the shelves on August 4. Her editor at St. Martin's, Monique Patterson, says, "It's been amazing to watch her grow, literally by leaps and bounds. Dark-Hunter is a brand, a franchise, now. Sherrilyn has a sixth sense for what readers want in their characters, in their stories, and she knows how to speak to their emotions."

Patterson promises that readers won't be disappointed by *Bad Moon Rising*, though they may be surprised. "It's a whole new arc in the story line. I can't say exactly what, but it's big."

That's only one of several Kenyon releases this year. St. Martin's will be reissuing expanded versions of the first three books in her long-out-of-print League series—*Born of Night, Born of Fire and Born of Ice*—in a major back-to-back release beginning in late September. The publisher also launches the Dark-Hunter series into manga in June. While Avon had planned to release *Darkness Within*, the newest in Kenyon's Lords of Avalon series (previously published under the name Kinley MacGregor) in August, that title has been delayed for the moment.

Kenyon is just one example of arguably the most in-demand and prolific authors in America these days. Writers of all kinds of paranormal are experiencing a major surge, and the variety of work being published under the banners of paranormal romance and urban fantasy shows no sign of diminishing anytime soon.

DEGREES OF DIFFERENCE

It's fairly easy to settle on a definition of what makes a book part of the current paranormal trend, because it can be anything with supernatural elements or that departs from reality. But even that broad definition is open to interpretation, says Chris Keesler, senior editor at Dorchester. "I think that booksellers and many romance readers tend to pigeonhole paranormal, defining the books by the most visible and successful of their type: the vampire romance. Werewolves and other monsters are also common."

Often it is the most prominent paranormal element that's used to classify a book or series as part of a certain subgenre. In addition to vampires and shapeshifters, it's not hard to find books featuring witches or demons, psychics or time travel within the romance category and also in science fiction and fantasy.

In fact, the terms urban fantasy and paranormal romance are often used interchangeably. But most of the category's major editors work on books that fall into both categories and caution that while the two frequently cross over among audiences, there is a key distinction. Avon executive editor Erika Tsang explains: "In paranormal romance the relationship between the couple is the focus of the main plot. In urban fantasy, the world that the couple exists in is the focus."

Figuring out the best category can sometimes be hard. Tsang remembers the fan reaction when she chose to publish Jeaniene Frost's *Halfway to the Grave* as romance rather than urban fantasy. "Readers were up in arms because the characters didn't end up together. But the relationship was essential to the story, so it's a romance to me," says Tsang.

Choosing the category can be dangerous ground, says Heather Osborn, romance editor at Tor. She employs a simple standard for making the decision. "My number one consideration is if there's a resolution of the romance at the end of the book. If there's no resolution of the romance, and it's in the romance section, readers will let their anger be known."

Osborn also identifies another factor that must be considered, which is the willingness of the different readerships to leave their home section of the bookstore. "We see romance readers go to the science fiction and fantasy section for the books. Fantasy readers will buy from displays, but not go into the romance section," she says.

There are plenty of authors comfortable in both worlds, though. Marjorie Liu debuted with the paranormal romance series Dirk & Steele, which she describes as being about a "group of psychics and nonhumans (gargoyles, mermen, shapeshifters and so on) who band together to help others under the guise of working for an internationally respected detective agency." The series' ninth installment, *The Fire King*, releases in August from Dorchester. But in 2008, Liu launched Hunter Kiss, a darker urban fantasy series, from Ace, with *The Iron Hunt*. The follow-up, *Darkness Calls*, is due out in late June.

"I think we worry way too much about where books should fit inside genres," says Liu. "In a romance, the hero and heroine are on a journey together, and no matter how awful it gets, by the end of the book they'll be in love, with the probability of a happy ending."

Viewing the trend in a more historical context helps explain its broad appeal to readers who prefer either type of book. Most editors say that *Buffy the Vampire Slayer* marked a turning point toward the new breed of paranormal, but that its roots are far older. "There are romantic tales in mythology and folklore with clear fantasy aspects to them," says St. Martin's Patterson. "But everything is cyclical in terms of popularity. Eight or nine years ago, you couldn't give away paranormal romance."

Dorchester's Keesler says the coinciding rise of the supernatural across the entertainment spectrum has exerted a strong influence, creating a hunger for similar books. "How many people of the last few generations haven't seen *Buffy* or one of its spinoffs? Above all, I think every genre is driven and perpetuated by the talent of its most successful authors, authors who cater to the public, to their day and age's literary zeitgeist."

Timing is everything in publishing, and pop culture's impact on readers is reflected by the age of the audience coming into the romance category. "TV and entertainment media are bringing in people in their 20s and 30s. Romance as a whole skews to an older audience," observes Tor's Osborn. "People talk about the glut of vampire and werewolf romances, but there is always room for more. Romance readers read tons of books a month."

Paranormal romance—like romance in general—is doing extremely well during a period when the economic meltdown has exiled much of publishing to severe doldrums. "What's going on in the world now has an impact. With wars and the economy, romance is fantasy—these books are the ultimate escape," says Tsang from Avon. "Readers are always looking for something new."

THE NEXT BIG MONSTER

The continuing Twilight mania and Alan Ball's adaptation of Charlaine Harris's novels into the HBO series *True Blood* may have injected an even longer life into books about vampires.

"It's clear that vampires have never been hotter in the romance genres," says Claire Zion, editorial director of NAL. She cites the breakout success of J.R. Ward's *Lover Avenged* when it released earlier this month. The seventh Black Dagger Brotherhood novel and the first to be released in hardcover, *Lover* took high slots on several bestseller lists.

The paranormal field is in no danger of a vampire shortage. Other hot releases featuring bloodsuckers include Jeaniene Frost's *Destined for an Early Grave* (Avon, July), Lynsay Sands's *The Renegade Hunter* (Avon, Sept.), and Katie MacAlister's *Crouching Vampire, Hidden Fang* (Signet, May). Berkley plans a back-to-back release of Emma Holly's *Kissing Midnight* (June), *Breaking Midnight* (July) and *Saving Midnight* (Aug.).

There are also plenty of shape-shifters to be found this season. In another back-to-back release, Avon will launch Pamela Palmer's Feral Warriors series, beginning in July with *Desire Untamed*, followed by *Obsession Untamed* and *Passion Untamed*. Tor has high hopes for C. T. Adams and Cathy Clamp's *Cold Moon Rising* (Aug.), blurbed by popular urban fantasy author Jim Butcher. Meanwhile, Kendra Leigh Castle's *Wild Highland Magic* (Sourcebooks, May) continues the MacInnes Werewolves series, and Patricia Briggs fans will no doubt snap up *Hunting Ground* (Ace, August), which follows the developing love story between werewolves Anna and Charles.

Although werewolves and vampires are still tremendously popular, they better look out for the new trendsetters coming behind them. According to Dorchester's Leah Hultenschmidt, "Demons are the new vampires," calling attention to the publisher's *The Dangerous Book for Demon Slayers* by Angie Fox, released this month. "I predict after demons come fallen angels."

It's true that demon and angel-themed series are becoming more prevalent. Kensington has seen Richelle Mead's urban fantasy series featuring shape-shifting demon Georgina Kincaid take off; its fourth book, *Succubus Heat*, comes out in June. And Grand Central was so pleased with last year's reception for newcomer Larissa Ione's *Pleasure Unbound* that it released two follow-up Demonica novels, *Desire Unchained* and *Passion Unleashed*, in March and April. Both landed on various bestseller lists. "It's a sign that readers are still willing to take a chance on new authors," says Amy Pierpont, editorial director of Grand Central's Forever line.

For those fallen angels, try J. R. Ward's hotly anticipated new spinoff series, kicking off with *Covet* (Signet, October). And what about urban fantasy? Readers who want a little less romance and a lot more fantasy world-building can keep an eye out for titles like S.J. Day's *Eve of Darkness* (May), *Eve of Destruction* (June), and *Eve of Chaos* (June) from Tor, debut author Kelly Gay's *The Better Part of Darkness* (Pocket, Nov.) and Caitlin Kittredge's *Street Magic* (St. Martin's, June).

Not to mention Harlequin's first foray into young adult fiction. The new program launches with Rachel Vincent's *My Soul to Take in August*, with *Intertwined* by Gena Showalter to follow in September. "These books promise to have crossover appeal between young and adult women," says Loriana Sacilotto, executive v-p of global editorial for Harlequin.

All this without getting into a number of other developing trends—faeries, immortal protectors and a little bit of anything else you can imagine. Kensington editor-in-chief John Scognamiglio says, "Paranormal romance remains red hot and shows no signs of stopping. Anything paranormal is immediately moved to the top of the submission pile."

Readers may wonder if there's any creature that won't eventually end up in the role of leading man. The answer is yes—there's a strong consensus against zombies. "Zombies are not sexy. Romances don't feature zombies," says Tsang, laughing. "Zombies are rotting dead flesh who eat brains. When you say vampire, you think David Boreanaz. Until David Boreanaz becomes a zombie—no way."

In Search of Today's Ghost Stories[*]

New Technology a Blessing and a Curse for Supernatural Series

By James Hibberd
TelevisionWeek, August 22, 2005

The latest generation of ghostly reality shows claim success at documenting paranormal events, but fans are more skeptical than ever.

Sci Fi's "Ghost Hunters" and "Proof Positive," the Travel Channel series "Most Haunted" and TLC's upcoming investigation show "Dead Tenants" use modern-day forensic techniques to try to prove ghosts exist. The shows use enough high-tech gadgets to fill a RadioShack—including infrared and night-vision cameras, digital voice recorders and electromagnetic field detectors—to provide a scientific backbone while renewing a classic TV genre.

Skeptical fans, however, are up on technology, too. They are accustomed to Hollywood's ability to create and manipulate images, and are themselves armed with the recording power of DVRs, image-enhancing software and the Internet—making possible frame-by-frame analysis of footage and communal message-board debunking.

The new online world of ghost-show discussion is in fact a far cry from squinting at Bigfoot and flying saucer photos while watching "In Search of . . . " and "Ripley's Believe It or Not!"

Of the shows, "Ghost Hunters" has created the biggest online groundswell of fans—and the most ferocious debates. Launched last year, the show follows Jason Hawes and Grant Wilson, two Rhode Island Roto-Rooter plumbers by day, leaders of paranormal investigation team The Atlantic Paranormal Society by night.

Fans say the show's appeal lies in the casting of the squad of blue-collar investigators and the teasing threads of paranormal "evidence" collected each week. As on "The X-Files," each episode of "Ghost Hunters" seems to creep closer to discovering if "the truth is out there."

"Since television has been on there's been ghosts and people 'in search of,'" said executive producer Craig Piligian ("American Chopper"), who created the show after reading a 2003 *New York Times* profile of TAPS. "But the interesting part was that [paranormal investigating] wasn't Grant and Jason's day job. They weren't fanatically saying ghosts are out there. For the most part, they're debunking it. They're smart, they're articulate, they're scientific."

Since the show's 2004 debut amateur groups have sprung up across the country. Companies selling ghost-hunting gear—such as electromagnetic field detectors and infrared cameras—are booming due to the show, according to *BusinessWeek* (May 12, 2005). Mark Stern, Sci Fi's senior VP of original programming, said the success of "Ghost Hunters" and other modern paranormal shows can be attributed to their reality style, in which viewers watch a team seeking answers rather than a narrator presenting information.

"It gives you a great opportunity to deal with paranormal subjects with a great credibility. It gives viewers a chance to feel like they're watching it happen, and then they can judge whether to believe it or not, rather than being told what to believe," he said.

Each "Ghost Hunters" episode takes the TAPS team to a purportedly haunted location, where the TAPS team takes a skeptical look at the claims of paranormal activity, throwing out bogus evidence but occasionally "catching" something—a whisper on a tape recorder (dubbed an "EVP," for electronic voice phenomenon), a moving chair or an inexplicable shadow. The "evidence" is then posted on the TAPS Web site for fans to debate, though TAPS founders claim proof positive of the paranormal is unlikely and unobtainable.

"We will never find that evidence," Mr. Wilson said. "You cannot show a piece of video in this day and age [of digital manipulation] that will convince everybody that ghosts exist."

Added Mr. Hawes: "If you're trying to prove the paranormal, you're in for a hard time. If you're trying to help people with their paranormal experiences, you can have success in every case. We're not trying to battle with the skeptics."

But some skeptics are looking to battle them. Not since Sci Fi's own similarly metaphysical "Crossing Over With John Edward" has a show prompted such intense speculation about the integrity of its production process. A recent episode of "Penn and Teller's Bulls**t" on Showtime took aim at modern-day ghostbusters, criticizing those without scientific training who investigate hauntings with gear never designed to spot ghosts. Though TAPS was not specifically mentioned, the episode was a clear shot at the Sci Fi show.

Professional skeptics say the new wave of ghost shows is just profiteering.

"I've been investigating hauntings for more than 30 years. I've been in more haunted places than Casper, and there's no scientific evidence ghosts exists," said Joe Nickell, a paranormal investigator, an author of 16 books about paranormal claims and a columnist for *Skeptical Inquirer* magazine. "These shows are selling a mystery. It's astonishing to me that this stuff is taking over the airwaves. When they don't have obvious explanation, they say, 'Maybe it's a ghost.' It's arguing from ignorance. You can't draw a conclusion from 'I don't know.'"

The TAPS team claims to be as skeptical of psychics as skeptics are leery of them.

THE NONBELIEVERS

Unlike most paranormal investigation outfits, for example, TAPS has never charged home and business owners for their investigative services, saying it's unethical to take money to investigate a phenomenon that has not been proven to exist.

"We could put up an ad on our Web site saying we want X amount of money for an investigation and we'd get it," Mr. Hawes said. "We won't even accept gas money."

Likewise, the team criticized the upcoming scripted CBS series "Ghost Whisperer," which is based on the experience of medium Mary Ann Winkowski. Ms. Winkowski charged clients hundreds of dollars to help loved ones trapped in an earthbound limbo make it to "the other side," according to news reports.

"Psychics say it's a God-given gift," Mr. Hawes said, disgusted. "God gave you this gift and you're charging people $500?"

For the upcoming "Dead Tenants" on TLC, executive producer Thom Beers said he plans to challenge "Ghost Hunters" for the title of the most-skeptical ghost show.

"We have one nonbeliever on each show to go on camera and tell the world that ghosts don't exist," Mr. Beers said. "Then we watch over the next hour as our psychics, researchers and technicians all pool their findings to create a very compelling case for the haunting. I hope we will be the first to actually catch a real ghost on screen—I believe that it will happen, and on my show."

The biggest online controversy over paranormal show footage occurred after "Ghost Hunters"' second-season premiere July 27. In the show, the team visited Myrtles Plantation in New Orleans. TAPS ruled the location haunted due to among other findings a lamp caught on video moving across a table in the plantation's former "slave shack." Though Mr. Hawes expressed doubt about the footage, after a failed attempt to re-enact the movement, the viewer is left with the impression the lamp was likely moved by spirit activity.

The next day, online fans went into a frenzy. Upon close inspection, fans concluded, the lamp was being pulled by its own cord. Even worse: a night-vision shot appears to show the cord extending from behind the table to Mr. Wilson's hand. And the so-called slave shack, Internet researchers said, was built recently and never housed slaves.

"I don't know what it is," Mr. Piligian said of the lamp footage. "We called Grant and Jason. They didn't even want [the footage] to air. I don't believe they were involved in it. We wouldn't have put it on the air if we felt they were messing with us."

As for the slave shack, Mr. Piligian said, "That's what we were told it was [by the plantation staff]."

Some fans declared the ghostbusters busted. Others insisted TAPS would never stage anything. "I don't think Grant had anything to do with the lamp moving, at least knowingly," one poster said. "TAPS have worked hard to build up their credibility. I doubt that Grant and Jason really want to destroy that credibility by doing something stupid."

Another poster mused: "None of us know what pressures have been placed on them to make things happen to get the ratings up."

Though Sci Fi benefits from being held to a quasi-fictional standard, Mr. Stern said the network wants and expects "Ghost Hunters" to be taken seriously.

"It's definitely important to us that this show is not manufacturing anything, and our assurance comes from those doing that show, because it's even more important to them—Jason and Grant's reputations are riding on this more than anybody's," he said. "I believe the show is real and I'm the biggest skeptic out there."

Mr. Nickell said he refuses to view footage posted by a television show. "We're supposed to disprove these people's claims, and it dignifies their work," he said. "What people should say is: 'Why should anybody take you seriously?' Not go to science and ask them to investigate amateur videos."

As for Mr. Piligian, he said he doesn't believe in the paranormal but does believe in the integrity of his team.

"We have to play it straight," Mr. Piligian said. "It's what the show is all about. We tell it like it is—ghost or no ghost."

'Ghost Hunters' Redefines Reality TV[*]

By Aaron Sagers
Examiner.com, March 17, 2009

About halfway through the fifth season premier of the Sci-Fi Channel's "Ghost Hunters" at Philadelphia's Betsy Ross house, paranormal investigator Grant Wilson began the oft-heard sentence, E.V.P. stands for electronic voice phenomenon.

And as Wilson read off the definition on camera, me and a few friends watching the show from my living room, finished the line with him, following the cadence and rhythm as closely as we might if a red ball had been bouncing across words on the screen.

That's when it struck me that I was witnessing something pretty rare, like the pink albino dolphin or a coherent Britney Spears. Wilson and partner Jason Hawes—along with their team, The Atlantic Paranormal Society (T.A.P.S.) featuring Kris, Steve, and Tango—have become more than just stars on a popular show that draws about 2.8 million viewers a week. It doesn't matter if you believe in ghosts or not because the stars of the four-year-old show are pop-culture prodigies.

Since the 2004 premiere, "Ghost Hunters" has re-invented the reality-TV genre by focusing on a topic outside most of our realities. It's not about contests on an island, weird foods, big families, lousy roomies, bachelor's harems and hot tubs, racing, singing, dancing, or working for, and being eliminated by, a perpetually angry boss. But it is about a group of friends that started a hobby with the intent to help people as well as get answers about the afterlife.

Whether by design or mistake, the show is also unique among its reality-TV brethren for observing the basic formulas present in the best of pop fiction.

The heroes are believably human. From Peter Parker to Homer Simpson, most memorable heroes are flawed but likeable with an everyman attitude. Unlike the cocky, overconfident nitwits who populate reality-TV and lack the potential for introspection, Wilson and Hawes (and especially Tango and Steve) achieve this and do it without seeming to take themselves too seriously.

"Ghost Hunters" has also implanted its mythology into our consciousness. I have known about T.A.P.S. since a 2002 *New York Times* article and have interviewed the stars on a few occasions, but most of us can recite a version of the Wilson, Hawes, and Co. story from the show alone. After about 80 episodes, even if the names are fuzzy, they're well-known as the Roto-Rooter plumbers with the working-class appeal from Rhode Island who investigate the paranormal. Since the group began in 1990, when a door opens on its own in an old house, they try to find out why; when there is a loud crash in the dark, they give chase instead of running away (except for the one catchphrase-making "Dude, run" incident). And when something truly startling happens, audiences are likely to hear "What the frig"? instead of a scream.

But along with a familiar mythology, "Ghost Hunters" honors a code we love to see in our pop-culture. There are three rules to owning a Mogwai: charge the power ring every 24 hours, observe the Prime Directive, you must reach 88 miles per hour to generate 1.21 gig watts of power needed for time travel, and always try to debunk ghostly reports before calling it haunted. Audiences may enjoy surprises, but we also like a framework of rules and expect our heroes to follow them.

In the case of the so-called T.A.P.S. method of debunking before believing, the show has also redefined what audiences are used to seeing in reality-TV, and haunted house shows in particular. As opposed to the Travel Channel's "Most Haunted" (featuring shaky cams, dramatic phsychics and jumpy Brits) or MTV's deceased show "Fear" (featuring head-mounted cameras and a lot of screaming), "Ghost Hunters" places emphasis on the process of investigating instead of trying to deliver scares.

By giving off a CSI: Paranormal vibe, the show allows a sometimes anti-climactic climax. This reduces the audience expectation of a spectral money shot; if there is one, and there isn't always, they get ever more traction from it.

Although the T.A.P.S. team sometimes catches spooky disembodied EVPs on digital recorders, or amorphous forms on a heat-sensitive thermal camera, or electro-magnetic field anomalies on a gadget called the K-2, much of their show is about something we all relate to: waiting and talking. They talk to scared homeowners, they wait around reviewing hours of evidence, they wait around in the dark while talking. It's compelling television, but it's not always very exciting.

Of course, anytime something new is created and becomes a fixture in popular culture, there will be followers and imitators, as well as detractors and naysayers. That's to be expected as much as the "Ghost Hunters" spin-offs and T-shirts, and the eventual T.A.P.S. breakfast cereal, action figures and video games. Most of the imitators won't last long, and the controversies won't prove to be true, I suspect, but they don't matter anyhow.

Frankly, whether ghosts do exist or don't doesn't matter either. Even if the truth isn't out there, as Mulder believed, "Ghost Hunters" is a very real game changer on the reality-TV scene and has secured a spot in pop-culture history.

Bibliography

Books

Bennet, Jeffrey. *Beyond UFOs: The Search for Extraterrestrial Life and Its Astonishing Implications for Our Future*. Princeton, N.J.: Princeton University Press, 2008.

Birnes, William J. *The UFO Magazine UFO Encyclopedia*. New York: Pocket, 2004.

Broderick, Damien. *Outside the Gates of Science: Why It's Time for the Paranormal to Come in from the Cold*. New York: Thunder's Mouth Press, 2007.

Carey, Thomas J., and Donald R. Schmitt. *Witness to Roswell: Unmasking the Government's Biggest Cover-up*. Franklin Lakes, N.J.: Career Press, 2009.

Coleman, Loren. *Cryptozoology A To Z: The Encyclopedia of Loch Monsters, Sasquatch, Chupacabras, and Other Authentic Mysteries of Nature*. New York: Fireside, 1999.

Danelek, J. Allan. *UFOs: The Great Debate: An Objective Look at Extraterrestrials, Government Cover-ups, and the Prospect of First Contact*. Woodbury, Minn.: Llewellyn Publications, 2008.

Friedman, Stanton T. *Flying Saucers and Science: A Scientist Investigates the Mysteries of UFOs*. Franklin Lakes, N.J.: Career Press, 2008.

Hawes, Jason, and Grant Wilson, with Michael Jan Friedman. *Ghost Hunting: True Stories of Unexplained Phenomena from the Atlantic Paranormal Society*. New York: Pocket, 2007.

Hines, Terence. *Pseudoscience and the Paranormal*. Amherst, N.Y.: Prometheus, 2003.

Horn, Stacy. *Unbelievable: Investigations into Ghosts, Poltergeists, Telepathy, and Other Unseen Phenomena, from the Duke Parapsychology Laboratory*. New York: Ecco, 2009.

Irwin, Harvey J. and Caroline Watt. *An Introduction to Parapsychology*, 5th ed. Jefferson, N.C.: McFarland, 2007.

Jones, Marie D. *PSIence: How New Discoveries in Quantum Physics and New Science May Explain the Existence of Paranormal Phenomena*. Franklin Lakes, N.J.: Career Press, 2007.

Kachuba, John B. *Ghosthunters: On the Trail of Mediums, Dowsers, Spirit Seekers and Other Investigators of America's Paranormal World*. Franklin Lakes, N.J.: Career Press, 2007.

Kelly, Lynne. *The Skeptic's Guide to the Paranormal*. New York: Avalon Publishing Group, 2004.

McLeod, Michael. *Anatomy of a Beast: Obsession and Myth on the Trail of Bigfoot*. Berkeley, Calif.: University of California Press, 2009.

Meldrum, Jeff. *Sasquatch: Legend Meets Science*. New York: Forge Books, 2006.

Morris, Mark: *The Ghost Next Door: True Stories of Paranormal Encounters from Everyday People*. Lincoln, Neb.: iUniverse, 2004.

Newton, Michael. *Encyclopedia of Cryptozoology: A Global Guide to Hidden Animals and Their Pursuers*. Jefferson, N.C.: McFarland & Company, 2005.

Radin, Dean. *The Conscious Universe: The Scientific Truth of Psychic Phenomena*, Reprint edition. New York: HarperCollins, 2009.

Schoch, Robert M. and Logan Yonavjak. *The Parapsychology Revolution*. New York: Tarcher, 2008.

Tart, Charles T. *The End of Materialism: How Evidence of the Paranormal Is Bringing Science and Spirit Together*. Oakland, Calif.: New Harbinger Publications, Inc., 2009.

Telep, Trisha, ed. *The Mammoth Book of Paranormal Romance*. Philadelphia: Running Press, 2009.

Web Sites

Readers seeking additional information pertaining to the paranormal may wish to consult the following Web sites, all of which were operational as of this printing.

The Atlantic Paranormal Society

www.the-atlantic-paranormal-society.com

Promising to bring "professionalism, personality, and confidentiality" to the field of paranormal investigation, the Atlantic Paranormal Society (TAPS) uses high-tech gadgetry to determine the validity of ghost sightings and other such phenomena. TAPS founders Jason Hawes and Grant Wilson—Roto-Rooter plumbers by day—are stars of the cable program *Ghost Hunters*, which premiered on the Sci-Fi Channel in 2004. The TAPS Web site features articles on the paranormal, a glossary of related terms, information on ghost-hunting devices, and guidelines for membership. The organization is currently accepting applications from investigation teams around the country.

Cryptozoology.com

www.cryptozoology.com

Neither founded by nor aimed at professional cryptozoologists, this Web site nevertheless offers a wealth of information on various "cryptids," or creatures whose existence science has yet to verify. The Web site contains news articles, accounts of cryptid sightings, a glossary, photo gallery, and member forum.

The Mutual UFO Network (MUFON)

www.mufon.com

Dedicated to studying UFOs "for the benefit of humanity," the nonprofit corporation MUFON has its roots in the Midwest UFO Network, a regional organization founded in 1969. Now an international agency with thousands of members, MUFON aims to investigate sightings, advocate for scientific research on UFOs, and educate the public. The group's Web site contains information on recent cases, photographic and video evidence, and a form that allows visitors to report their own sightings. In addition to publishing a monthly journal, MUFON hosts a yearly symposium on UFO research.

Paranormal Research Blog

www.paranormalromanceblog.com

Run by publisher Harlequin Enterprises, the Paranormal Research Blog is a resource for fans of "paranormal romance," a literary genre that focuses on the love lives of vampires, werewolves, demons, and other such fanciful creatures. The blog's operators encourage readers to post comments and share their thoughts on a wide range of novels, not just those printed by Harlequin. The site also features news, contests, and information on other paranormal-related pop culture.

The Parapsychology Foundation

www.parapsychology.org

For more than 50 years, the nonprofit Parapsychology Foundation has endeavored to support research of psychic phenomena, or psi. The group publishes a range of journals, books, and pamphlets; maintains an extensive library, located in Greenport, New York, of parapsychology-related reading materials; makes grants for research projects; organizes conferences and lecture series; and conducts public outreach. The foundation's Web site features a number of articles, a glossary of psi terms, and links to other useful sites. There is also information on applying for grants and an online store, which sells many of the books, pamphlets, CDs, and DVDs the foundation has produced.

The Skeptic's Dictionary

www.skepdic.com

Started by atheist, former philosophy professor, and all-around champion of science Robert T. Carrol in 1994, the Skeptic's Dictionary seeks to debunk all manner of paranormal phenomena—everything from UFO sightings to Bigfoot. The site contains more than 500 entries, all espousing skepticism as an antidote to the blind faith and conjecture Carrol insists lead people to believe in things that cannot be proven. Carrol also provides book reviews, links to critical-thinking essays, and other resources for skeptics.

Additional Periodical Articles with Abstracts

More information about the paranormal and related subjects can be found in the following articles. Readers interested in additional articles may consult the *Readers' Guide to Periodical Literature* and other H.W. Wilson publications.

Orbs, Blobs, and Glows: Astronauts, UFOs, and Photography. Jane D. Marsching. *Art Journal* pp56–69 Fall 2003.

In this article, part of a special section on photography and the paranormal, the writer reflects on UFO photography, particularly those images taken by astronauts. Asserting that these images reveal a hunger for the other, for a world inhabited by more than clear science, she considers the possibilities offered by a psychological and scientific perspective on our desire to see something in nothing. She contends that astronomical UFO imagery reveals our desire for belief, for a faith that holds us trembling on the brink between fact and myth, between technology and experience, between the known and the unknown.

Searching for Truth in Strange Places. Thomas K. Grose. *ASEE Prism* p18 March 2006.

The author provides information on the Society for Scientific Exploration. With a membership that includes serious scientists and engineers from leading research schools, this society examines issues rarely addressed by traditional science, including paranormal phenomena, strange creatures, and unidentified flying objects.

Alien Planet. Bob Berman. *Astronomy* pp90–91 March 2001.

Berman discusses how the planet Venus is often mistaken for an unidentified flying object (UFO). He points out that, in his experience, the best case against UFOs is the fact that very few knowledgeable amateur astronomers ever see such things. Advice on observing Venus is provided, especially during the period from about March 24 to 29, when the planet can be easily viewed as both a morning and evening star on the same day.

Belief in the Paranormal and Suggestion in the Séance Room. Richard Wiseman, Emma Greening, and Matthew Smith. *British Journal of Psychology* pp285–297 August 2003.

The authors of this paper describe a series of experiments. In the first, participants took part in a fake séance. An actor suggested that a table was levitating when, in fact, it remained stationary. After the séance, approximately one third of participants incorrectly reported that the table had moved. Results also showed a significant relationship between the reported movement of the table and belief in the paranormal, with a greater percentage of believers than disbelievers reporting that the table had moved. Experiment 2 varied whether the suggestion was consistent, or inconsistent, with participants' belief in the paranormal. Results again showed that believers were more susceptible to suggestion than disbelievers, but only when the suggestion was consistent with their belief in the paranormal. Approximately one-fifth of participants believed that the fake séances contained genuine paranormal phenomena.

"It's Still Bending": Verbal Suggestion and Alleged Psychokinetic Ability. Richard Wiseman and Emma Greening. *British Journal of Psychology* pp115–127 February 2005.

Some alleged psychics appear to be able to deform metallic objects, such as keys and cutlery, by thought alone. The authors of this paper describe two studies that examined whether one aspect of these demonstrations could be created by verbal suggestion. In the first study, participants were shown a videotape in which a fake psychic placed a bent key on a table. Participants in one condition heard the fake psychic suggest that the key was continuing to bend, whilst those in the other condition did not. Participants in the suggestion condition were significantly more likely to report that the key continued to bend. These findings were replicated in the second study. In addition, participants who reported that the key continued to bend displayed a significantly higher level of confidence in their testimony than others, and were significantly less likely to recall that the fake psychic had suggested the continued bending of the key. Neither experiment revealed any differences between participants who expressed a prior belief in the paranormal compared with those who did not. The paper discusses the implications of these results for the psychology of suggestion and the assessment of eyewitness testimony for anomalous events.

Battling Pseudoscience. *The Futurist* p12 November-December 2000.

The students of Henri Broch in France are using science to shatter paranormal beliefs, the author reports. The director of the Center for the Study of Paranormal Phenomena at the University of Nice-Sophia Antipolis has been investigating whether applying scientific techniques to paranormal phenomena will arrest the declining status of reason in society. Broch notes that belief in the paranormal is becoming more widespread. He blames the increased speed at which electronic media can disseminate information and educators who perpetuate old ideas.

Sermons in the Sky: Apparitions in Early Modern Europe. Alexandra Walsham. *History Today* pp56–63 April 2001.

According to Walsham, the apparitions widely reported across early modern Europe provide historians with a glimpse of the deepest fears and anxieties of the people of the time. Mysterious heavenly sights were very common in 16th- and 17th-century England and early modern Europe and generated interest among all classes of society. According to lay and clerical commentators, the bizarre and eerie images people saw projected in the air were "heralds" alerting mankind to the punishments that God would shortly be inflicting upon it. Sinister visions of violence and bloodshed seen in early modern England and Europe proliferated significantly in contexts of political and religious instability. Despite growing awareness that these apparitions could be explained in terms of natural causes, both the rich and poor continued to see them as disturbing signs of divine indignation. Historians may see them as symptoms of profound political, ecclesiastical, and social disequilibrium.

The Science of Magic: A Parapsychological Model of Psychic Ability in the Context of Magical Will. David Luke. *Journal for Academic Study of Magic* pp90–119 2007.

The parapsychological model of psychic ability known as psi-mediated instrumental response (PMIR) attempts to explain the unconscious use of precognition, telepathy, clairvoyance, psychokinesis, or other "psi" faculties as a means of serving the needs and desires of the organism, Luke notes. The model draws on the principles and research of cognitive and behavioral psychology, as well as parapsychology. However, by extending the inferences of the model and by making minor changes in order to reorient it to a magical perspective, it could possibly be a useful tool for explaining the psychology of magical operation, or at least one part of it, in a truly scientific manner. Indeed, while PMIR may be limited in its conception of conditions favorable to psi, it is a particularly useful model for explaining the factors necessary for psi.

Psi and Associational Processes. Stuart Wilson, Robert L. Morris, and Niko Tiliopoulos. *Journal of Parapsychology* pp129–155 Spring 2004.

One way by which psi might manifest itself is by influencing ongoing cognitive processes. Word association has previously been suggested as a possible vehicle for psi. In this paper, the authors describe two experiments that look at the influence of psi on interpretation of homophones (words which are acoustically identical, but can have different meanings). In Experiment 1, no overall psi was evident, although results indicate a potential "experimenter effect" and an apparent "response-bias" effect, in which less-favored responses tend to elicit more psi-hitting. A potential "stacking-effect" artefact is also considered. Experiment 2 was a replication and extension of Experiment 1, with "true" randomization techniques. No psi-effects were found, although a marginally significant gender effect was observed. Results are discussed along with potential implications of this approach.

Psychedelic Substances and Paranormal Phenomena: A Review of the Research. David P. Luke. *Journal of Parapsychology* pp77–107 Spring/Fall 2008.

In this paper, the writer reviews the research on psychedelic substances in relation to so-called paranormal phenomena, such as telepathy, clairvoyance, and precognition (i.e., ESP), as well as out-of-body experiences (OBEs) and near-death experiences (NDEs). Reference is made to the age-old shamanic use of these substances to specifically induce such experiences, and to contemporary reports from within academia and psychotherapy bearing witness to such phenomena. However, Luke focuses primarily on describing and critically evaluating the contribution of controlled experiments that have attempted to induce ESP using psychedelics, and of surveys, which have either directly or indirectly investigated the belief in, and experience of, the paranormal in relation to the use of such substances. Furthermore, Luke offers a methodological critique of the experimental research alongside some recommendations for further research in this field.

Tarot Cards: A Literature Review and Evaluation of Psychic versus Psychological Explanations. Itai Ivtzan. *Journal of Parapsychology* pp139–149 Spring/Fall 2007.

Tarot cards, considered by some a tool to predict the future and understand one's inner issues, originated in ancient Egypt and remain popular in our day, Ivtzan reports. The clash between the paranormal and the nonparanormal explanations revolves around people's claims that the cards accurately reflect their own individual issues. The paranormal explanation claims that the cards portray opportunities, hidden motives, and potentials, therefore allowing clarity concerning the individual's questions and conflicts. The cards, according to the paranormal explanation, provide a reflection of the client's inner processes. The nonparanormal explanation, on the other hand, is based upon two psychological explanations: the Barnum effect and "cold reading." The Barnum effect refers to our tendency to interpret general statements as applying specifically and accurately to one's own unique circumstances, whereas "cold reading" refers to a set of deceptive psychological techniques that are being used in the psychic reading to create the impression that the reader has paranormal ability. In this review, the author juxtaposes these two perspectives while reporting studies that involve tarot cards.

Anomalous Experiences in North Carolina: A Survey. William J. Dewan. *Journal of Popular Culture* pp29–43 February 2006.

Over the past 60 years, thousands of articles and books have been written on the subject of UFOs, the writer observers. Combine this with the vast literature, both sympathetic and skeptical, devoted to the subject of parapsychology, and it becomes readily apparent that the pursuit of the unknown, whether in the guise of extraterrestrials or restless souls of the dead, has enjoyed a unique resurgence in the 20th century. Depending largely on your scholar or researcher of choice, experience and belief in supernatural phenomena can be explained as a result of a series or combination of delusions, hoaxes, misidentifications, religious desires, or genuine contact with an unseen world. Such works generally focus on answering what is seen as the ultimate question, i.e., are these experiences "real," in the sense that they are actual interactions with ghosts and/or aliens, or are they essentially misunderstood, mundane phenomena? This article focuses on one facet of supernatural experience widely reported in North Carolina and in the United States in general—the sightings of anomalous lights, including so-called "ghost lights," orbs, UFOs, and other labels attached to the observance of unexplained lights or aerial phenomena. The central problem addressed here is relatively straightforward. What drives the pursuit and interest in anomalous lights? Conversely, how frequently do such perceived experiences occur in the general population?

Believe It or Not: Religious and Other Paranormal Beliefs in the United States. Tom W. Rice. *Journal for the Scientific Study of Religion* pp95–106 March 2003.

Paranormal beliefs are often divided between those that are central to traditional Christian doctrine, such as the belief in heaven and hell, and those that are commonly associated with the supernatural or occult, such as the belief in ESP and psychic healing. This study employs data from a recent nationwide random sample general population survey to catalog the social correlates of paranormal beliefs and to examine the relationships between religious and other paranormal beliefs. The results indicate that standard social background factors do a poor job of accounting for who believes in paranormal phenomena and that the importance of specific background factors changes dramatically from phenomenon to phenomenon. The results also show that the correlations between belief in religious phenomena and other paranormal phenomena are largely insignificant. These findings call into question many prevailing theories about paranormal beliefs.

Raising a Monster. John Branigin. *Indianapolis Monthly* pp50–55 March 2009.

Sixty years ago, reports of an elusive giant freshwater turtle roaming a small Indiana lake captured the imagination of farmer Gale Harris, who used a variety of elaborate methods in his indefatigable search for the beast. The writer, whose precocious son became interested in the story of the so-called Beast of Busco, describes their journey to the small farm lake in Whitley County in search of the allegedly large freshwater turtle sighted there in the 1940s.

The Search for Monsters of Mystery. Amy Nathan. *National Geographic World* pp25–28 March 1999.

For many years, in various countries throughout the world, people have claimed to see mysterious animals in water, jungles, or mountains. Psychologist Stuart Vyse believes that people's persistence in searching for these creatures stems from a fascination with the magical. The writer describes six of the most famous mythical animals, from the Loch Ness Monster in Scotland to the Abominable Snowman in Nepal.

On the Edge of the Known World. *New Scientist* pp32–33 March 13, 2004.

Part of a special feature on parapsychology, this article discusses how replicability is one of the most controversial issues in the debate surrounding the possible existence of psychic phenomena. Many skeptics argue that conclusive proof of the paranormal can only be provided by replication on demand, whereas parapsychologists argue that statistical replication, whereby the effect should be replicable more often than would be expected by chance, is sufficient. Some parapsychologists even claim that the failure to replicate results is a positive result that confirms that paranormal phenomena are inherently elusive and cannot be pinned down in a lab.

The Power of Belief. John McCrone. *New Scientist* pp34–37 March 13, 2004.

This article, part of a special feature on parapsychology, looks at the experimenter effect, which is being drawn back into the debate about the existence of paranormal powers. The experimenter effect is a phenomenon whereby the outcome of an experiment depends on the beliefs of the person running it: Believers tend to get positive results, whereas skeptics do not. About 20 years ago, parapsychology researchers accepted that the effect was undermining their work and agreed to stop invoking it. Now, however, some parapsychologists are claiming that the effect arises because experimenters use extrasensory powers to pick the right moment to sample fluctuating processes and catch fluky but natural departures from randomness. Skeptics argue that the return of the experimenter effect proves that parapsychology has been unable to produce any convincing data.

Close Encounters of the Fourth Kind. Ziauddin Sardar. *New Statesman* p21 September 3, 2007.

UFO sightings in the U.S. have almost stopped being reported, Sardar contends. Kevin Fitzpatrick, a philosopher-cum-psychologist from Cardiff University in Great Britain, suggests that aliens acted as a projection of people's inner irrationalities, anxieties, and fears, and that UFOs were a cultural device for making sense of things that were otherwise incomprehensible to ordinary people. Fitzpatrick suggests that instant global communications have changed people's cultural reference points and that the Internet offers a new, all-encompassing tool for the projection of people's fears.

Unlocking Minds. Jerry Adler. *Newsweek* p50 March 19, 2007.

The writer discusses the research the late clinical psychologist Elizabeth Lloyd Mayer conducted for the book *Extraordinary Knowing: Science, Skepticism and the Inexplicable Powers of the Human Mind*. He concludes that it is a human instinct to pursue wonder in the world and to pursue communion with a higher power that connects everyone and everything.

Weird Science: An Expert on the Paranormal Explains Why Society Is So Smitten with Supernatural Phenomena. Nancy K. Dess. *Psychology Today* p34 September/October 2001.

In an interview, Ray Hyman, professor emeritus of psychology at the University of Oregon and an expert on the paranormal, discusses such topics as the paranormal phenomenon that most interests him and the coverage of the paranormal in the media.

Deconstructing the Dead. Michael Shermer. *Scientific American* p29 August 2001.

Spiritual mediums, Shermer argues in this piece, are unethical and dangerous. According to the author, a variety of tricks and techniques were observed being used by the popular spirit medium and former ballroom-dance instructor John Edward while he presented his New York cable television series *Crossing Over*. Such people, Shermer says, should be exposed for the frauds that they are, because they tend to prey on the emotions of the grieving at a particularly vulnerable time. Shermer sees it as an insult to the humanity and intelligence of the living to pretend that the dead are gathering in a New York studio to talk with a former ballroom-dance instructor.

Great American Skeptics. Daniel Loxton and James Loxton. *Skeptic* v. 14 pp81–89 2008.

A number of famous Americans have helped debunk the paranormal through the years. The authors of this article cover Benjamin Franklin and his investigations into mesmerism, Harry Houdini and his attacks on spiritualism, Mark Twain and his dealings with hypnotism and phrenology, and Johnny Carson, who exposed the psychic Uri Geller and the faith healer Peter Popoff.

Meeting the Man with the Camera Brain: The Curious Case of Ted Serios. Calvin Campbell. *Skeptic* v. 12 pp40–43 2006.

The writer recounts his meeting with Ted Serios, a man who claimed to have the ability to imprint his thoughts onto Polaroid film using only the powers of his mind. In the 30 or so years since Serios made his claim, no one has successfully debunked it. However, skeptics have long since discounted Serios as a very talented con artist who used an optical device to produce the images that appeared on the film.

Million Dollar Excuses. James Randi. *Skeptic* v. 12 pp6–7 2006.

The writer discusses a proposed generalized reason why all applicants for the $1 million James Randi Educational Foundation (JREF) prize have failed. French veterinarian Andre Wassen, a self-described fan of what he calls bio energy fields and a practitioner of acupressure for treating animals, has suggested that dowsers who undertake the JREF challenge fail because they are doing it for the prize money, rather than as a selfless act for a higher good. This suggestion provides a perfect escape clause because it allows an applicant who fails the challenge to blame the influence of the prize money or a desire to show off, whereas an applicant who succeeds can claim that he was able to suppress his ego and showmanship or that he ignored the prize.

Psychic for a Day. Michael Shermer. *Skeptic* v. 10 pp48–55 2003.

The writer discusses how he managed to learn to successfully perform psychic readings in just one day. To prove that an inexperienced person could learn the allegedly spiritually granted gift of mediumship, he practiced Tarot card reading, palm reading, astrology, and psychic mediumship 24 hours before reading five different women who believed he was a genuine psychic. The entire process was filmed for Bill Nye's PBS science series *Eyes of Nye*. All five people were successfully convinced that he possessed special psychic powers. The fact that it took only one day of preparation to give this impression indicates how susceptible vulnerable people are to these very effective nostrums.

Round Trip to Hell in a Flying Saucer: The Relationship Between Conventional Christian and Paranormal Beliefs in the United States. Carson F. Menchen, Christopher D. Bader, and Ye Jung Kim. *Sociology of Religion* pp65–85 2009.

The authors of this paper examine the relationship between conventional Christian and paranormal beliefs. Conventional Christian beliefs are those such as belief in Heaven, Hell, and the existence of God. Paranormal beliefs include belief in UFOs, astrology, haunting, communication with the dead, and Bigfoot. The authors test three hypotheses about the relationship between these two belief types with factor analysis and regression analysis. The data they use are from the Baylor Religion Survey, a national random sample collected by the Gallup Organization in fall 2005. The factor analysis results show that there are two well-defined spheres of supernatural beliefs, one conventional Christian and one paranormal. The authors find a net positive relationship between these two belief clusters. However, a test of the compatibility hypothesis shows that church attendance and religious tradition moderate the effects of conventional Christian beliefs on paranormal beliefs. The authors conclude with a discussion of the implications for theory and research.

Schooled Not to Be Fooled. Kim Clark. *U.S. News & World Report* pp76–77 August 26–September 2, 2002.

In this selection, part of a special section on hoaxes, the writer discusses the career of James Randi, perhaps the world's most important hoax-buster.

Index